oranje and blue

oranje and blue

The Arthur Numan Story

Arthur Numan
with Mark Guidi

BLACK & WHITE PUBLISHING

First Published 2006
by Black & White Publishing Ltd
99 Giles Street, Edinburgh EH6 6BZ

ISBN 13: 978 1 84502 112 2
ISBN 10: 1 84502 112 6

A CIP catalogue record for this book is
available from the British Library.

Typeset by RefineCatch Limited, Bungay, Suffolk.
Printed and bound by Creative Print and Design Group Ltd.

ACKNOWLEDGEMENTS

Thanks to Mark Guidi for helping me to write this book.

To Brian McSweeney for his tireless efforts behind the scenes helping to bring it all together. Darrell King, Bob Chambers and David McKie – your input is appreciated. Thanks also to the *Sunday Mail* for their help at all different levels.

I'd like to thank the people who've helped me during my career and moulded me into the person I am.

Thanks to Joop my agent for being with me every step of the way.

Thanks also to Mum, Dad and Jeroen and to the three special ladies in my life – Marjon and our daughters, Britt and Maud.

All my royalties from the sale of *Oranje and Blue* will be divided between the following four charities: the Yorkhill Children's Foundation, the Scottish Motor Neuron Disease Association, St Andrew's Hospice and the Rangers Charity Foundation.

PICTURE CREDITS

Thanks to Lynn Cameron at Rangers Football Club, Rangers Football Club, *Sunday Mail*, Jeff Holmes at SNS, Eric McCowat and www.fotoleovogelzan.nl.

CONTENTS

FOREWORD

BY DICK ADVOCAAT

When I agreed with David Murray to become the manager of Glasgow Rangers in the early part of 1998, one of the first things that came into my mind was to go for Arthur Numan. It was vital to get him to come with me from PSV Eindhoven. If I could get Arthur to sign then I knew other top-quality players would follow his example.

I'd known Arthur since he was seventeen when he worked under me for the Holland under-18 side and in club football at FC Haarlem. From the first few training sessions and games he played in, I could see Arthur had a determination to succeed. Such was his desire, he would have trained five times a day to improve himself and there were occasions I had to tell him just to take it a little easier.

He was always going to go to the top in football because he had talent and he had a competitive streak. From that raw teenager, I followed his career to see him develop into a fine football player. When I moved to PSV in 1995 it was great for me to already have Arthur there.

He was a left-sided midfielder at that point and he was an accomplished performer in that area of the pitch. But I felt if he was to become a regular in the Holland team, it would benefit him to move to left-back.

I knew Arthur would be excellent in that position because he had the ability to read the game, he was clever enough to cope with attacking wide players and he was excellent going forward to pressurise the opposition.

It pleased me that he listened to my advice and took on the challenge of playing at left-back with enthusiasm and a determination to do well. He went on to become one of the finest full-backs Holland has ever produced and has set the standard for other players in that position to live up to. He also set excellent standards on and off the pitch at Rangers. I knew my chances of being a success in Scotland would be enhanced if I had Arthur at Ibrox.

I didn't think it would be a problem getting him to work for me, but it was going to take a bit of persuading to get him to play his football in Scotland. When I asked Arthur to move with me he wasn't too sure and I had to open up on my plans for Rangers. I told him we were intent on bringing in top players to make the club one that was respected once again on the continent.

With some excellent results in Europe, I think we achieved that aim, but I wish we had progressed further in the Champions League.

When Arthur agreed to sign for Rangers I asked him to become the captain. I wanted him right beside me. But he refused and told me it would be better if a Scotsman was appointed. At that time, the problem was that there wasn't an outstanding Scottish candidate. Yes, Barry Ferguson was there, but he had played only a few first team games under Walter Smith and was still to assert himself.

I made Lorenzo Amoruso our skipper and I have to say, in all fairness, he was a good leader for most of the time. We didn't always see eye to eye and I know he criticised me in his own book, when he said I treated him like a child. I don't think that criticism is accurate but I expected that kind of thing from him in his autobiography.

Lorenzo's problem was that he thought he was a world-class player, but he wasn't. He was a very good defender but not as good as he thought he was. When results weren't going our way Lorenzo always thought it was the fault of other players and he was blameless. Again, he wasn't.

It wasn't just me who had problems with Lorenzo. Some of the other players did as well and they lost confidence in him. That's why I had to replace him in my third season and appointed Barry Ferguson the captain.

I've sometimes played back in my mind the situations I found myself in with Lorenzo and thought that it would have been much better to have Arthur as captain. As a manager, especially at a club as big as Rangers, it is important to know your captain is there, standing shoulder to shoulder beside you, in good times and bad. Having Arthur as captain would have given that extra stability, but I respected and understood his decision not to accept my offer.

One thing he didn't have a choice on was to room with Barry Ferguson. I watched Barry on the videotapes that were sent over to me before I arrived at Rangers and I could see with the way he touched the ball that he had it in him to become a great player. But Barry was quite insecure about his future at Rangers when I joined in the summer of 1998 and he didn't know whether to stay or go. I wanted him to sign a long-term contract and we managed to persuade him to do so towards the end of the pre-season.

That was just the start of the plan for Barry. Arthur played a major part in the next stage of his development. Barry needed to have more confidence in his own ability and I know that during the times sharing a room, Arthur would say positive things to Barry to boost him. Barry listened to Arthur because he respected him as a footballer and as a person.

The first two seasons we had together at Rangers were very successful. We won the treble and then the League and Scottish Cup Double. The third season was my poorest as Martin O'Neill came in and brought good times to Celtic. I loved the competition with Celtic; it was a pleasure to be at the heart of such a rivalry. However, I feel the Old Firm must move to England to really reach the next level – a level they deserve.

I stood down halfway through my fourth season and it is one of my regrets in football that I didn't stay on to see out the final months, go all the way to the last game and then wave goodbye in the summer. We were still in the UEFA Cup with a game against Feyenoord to look forward to after staying in Europe beyond Christmas, and we still had a chance of winning the two cups, as Alex McLeish managed to come in and do.

David Murray was taking a back seat and I felt it was right for me to go with him. David asked me to stay on as Director of Football because we didn't know for sure if Alex would be able to do the job as manager of Rangers. That kind of role just wasn't for me. I had to sit in the stand watching games, powerless to do anything. I didn't enjoy that side of it – it was a really difficult period, particularly not being in charge for the Feyenoord games.

Having to stop working on a day-to-day basis with players the calibre of Arthur was another reason I was sad to stand down in November 2001. Arthur played a major part in the success I had as manager of Rangers and PSV Eindhoven. I'm not the type to get personally involved with any of my players, but it's a little bit different with Arthur. I regard him as a friend, despite there being more than twenty years of an age gap. We keep in touch and I'm glad to see him enjoying his retirement from football, taking advantage of the freedom. He is making the most of his life with his family and that's a good way to do it. Of course, he would receive offers to get into coaching if he made it known that was his wish.

Knowing his father, Hans, as I do, I can see where he gets his manners and professionalism from. His parents are right to be proud of his achievements in life.

On a lighter note, I also met Arthur's brother, Jeroen, on a couple of occasions. When I was manager of PSV Eindhoven and Arthur was there, Jeroen was a sort of 'travelling salesman' and would sometimes drive into the training ground with a van full of stuff, anything from bikes to cutlery sets. I bought a bike from Jeroen and was happy with it. Well, at least I was for the first couple of weeks until it started to fall apart! I still have it in the garage and I laugh when I see it, thinking about it. Thankfully, Arthur was much more reliable. Really, you couldn't get any better.

1

AN OFFER I COULDN'T REFUSE

Moving house is often regarded as one of the most stressful things you do in life. But moving football clubs is also fraught with pressure and worry. I've only been transferred three times in my career – from Haarlem to Twente Enschede in 1990, to PSV in 1992 and, from there, to Rangers in 1998.

All my moves weren't without incident and all I can say is I'm glad I didn't play at as many clubs as my friend Pierre van Hooijdonk! I joined PSV in 1992 from Twente Enschede. There was interest from Manchester City and I almost signed for them. It was a worrying time as I had four weeks not knowing where I was going to play. I was either moving to PSV or City, or staying with Twente. Eventually I had to go to a tribunal to sort it out and I was one of the first players in Europe to go to court to have a footballing matter resolved.

Thankfully, the transfer to Rangers was much more straight-forward, but it did have one or two complications along the way.

The interest from Glasgow started in April 1998. A month or two earlier, my manager at PSV, Dick Advocaat, told me in confidence he had an agreement to join Glasgow Rangers as successor to Walter Smith at Ibrox. At that point he sounded me out about joining him in Glasgow and being part of the new regime. I can't deny I was flattered and was also very interested, but it was a difficult situation because I had been with PSV for six years and was the club captain. Also, in December 1996 I'd signed a new contract extension to stay at PSV until the summer of 2002, by which time I would have been thirty-two. I was happy to agree that deal and the club were delighted I'd pledged my future to them because there was interest from clubs in Italy, Spain and England.

After signing my new deal, naturally, I felt I was going to finish my career in Eindhoven. I enjoyed it at the club. It was a great team to play for and I had a nice lifestyle, living in an apartment in the city just five minutes from the stadium and ten minutes from our training ground. Not only did I relish playing for them but I enjoyed being in a team with some wonderful players. In seasons 1996 and 1997 we had a good period – no surprise, considering we had Jaap Stam, Luc Nilis, Wim Jonk, Ronald Waterreus, Phillip Cocu and Bolo Zenden. There was an excellent mixture of youth and experience and having these guys around me gave me the perfect platform to pursue my international career.

After Euro 96 in England, I became a regular starter for Holland. I worked hard to make the left-back position my own. Naturally PSV were happy to have the national team left-back captaining them and pledging his future to the club, but they couldn't stop sides showing an interest in me. It's part and parcel of football.

AS Roma were keeping tabs on me in November 1996 and I decided to talk to the Italians. I drove with my agent, Joop Korevaar, to a hotel in Amsterdam to meet agent Mino Raiola and a Roma club director. The director made it clear as soon as we sat down that he wanted me to sign. He even brought over a Roma jersey with my name on the back. He'd made a real effort to try to impress me.

I told the Roma representative I was interested but would prefer him to sort out a transfer fee with PSV before we became too deep in negotiations about my personal terms. I also requested he put his interest in writing on official club notepaper. However, I sensed there was a reluctance on his part about what I was asking him to do. I'm not sure why, but I was wary of dealing with

Italian clubs. Nothing ever seemed to be straightforward, there always seemed to be something lurking in the background, something they were not prepared to tell you about.

I had met with officials from Napoli a couple of years before when I was with Twente and had the same feeling about them. The move came about due to Raiola, who had an association with my old club, FC Haarlem. He is well connected and has been involved in deals to bring Zlatan Ibrahimovic and Pavel Nedved to Serie A. Napoli wanted to sign me, but at the time there was a five-foreigner rule in the European game, so the Italians wanted me to move there, and then they would put me out on loan. I flew to Italy to spend two or three days in Naples and got to see the stadium and a bit of the city. Again I sensed some kind of hidden agenda and never felt entirely at ease when dealing with them. The move never materialised.

After I met Roma I informed PSV that talks had taken place but they weren't happy and sent an urgent fax to Roma President Francesco Sezzi claiming they were tapping me up and were acting illegally.

During the meeting in Amsterdam, I wasn't sure they were going to go the whole distance to get me. Yes, they praised me highly and told me I would be an important part of the team, but when the subject of how much money I was going to earn came up and how long the length of contract was going to be, it was strange. They asked me to name a price for my salary but I said it was up to them to make me an offer. Is that not how it works? We were going on and on and eventually started talking figures and came close to verbally agreeing terms. They even got their president on the line to try to persuade me to sign. He wanted to hear me say to him I wanted to move. He spoke Italian and for all I know he could have been reciting his mama's spaghetti Bolognese recipe!

We left the meeting and arranged to speak on the phone the next day to arrange another discussion for the following week. In the meantime, they would contact PSV and start negotiating a transfer fee. As I drove back to Eindhoven, I expressed some misgivings I had to Joop. I told him I had my doubts about the Italian league – it was too defensive for me. Also, Wim Jonk and Dennis Bergkamp had told me they enjoyed their time with Inter Milan but their experience was spoiled by a league that constantly played with sides containing five defenders and three defensive midfielders. At the most, there would be one attacker and one attacking midfielder. It wasn't really for me.

There was something gnawing away inside me that left me feeling a move to Serie A wasn't the best way to progress my career. PSV wanted to keep me and I had a very good meeting with the chairman, Harry van Raay, and an excellent offer was put on the table. He was open and honest about the situation and made it clear he didn't want me to leave. He wanted to bring in quality players to challenge again in Holland and set his sights on us re-establishing the club in Europe again. I was excited and didn't feel it would be right to walk out on them. So, I decided to stay at PSV and signed a deal committing me to the club until 2002.

Joop was pleased with my decision. I asked for his advice. I've been with him since I was sixteen and trust him, and we are open with each other. I always knew he had my best interests at heart and would never try to make money off me behind my back. Joop used to work for the players' union and their role was always to put the player's interest first.

Everything seemed fine and my future looked resolved. However, we had another situation to deal with when Dick told he wanted me to join him in Glasgow.

It was awkward for Dick. It was February or March 1998 and we were on the training ground and Dick said to me, 'Arthur, it is not public knowledge but I am talking to Glasgow Rangers about becoming their trainer and I will probably join them in the summer. Do you want to come with me? I know you want to leave and I'm telling you this in confidence.'

4

Despite the fact I'd always vowed never to play in Scotland – with only ten or twelve teams playing each other at least four times a season, I thought the standard of football wouldn't be high enough – or Turkey, I told Dick I was interested. We both had to be careful about this. We still had games to play and had a chance of winning the Dutch Cup. We decided to wait and see if another team was interested and then that would allow Dick to make his move to take me to Glasgow, because he didn't want to be seen trying to unsettle me.

But make no mistake, the bottom line was I was tapped up, as Advocaact approached me before the clubs agreed a fee. It's not legal but it's part of the game and happens at clubs throughout the world.

At the time I was playing well and there had been talk for a few weeks that Atletico Madrid were keen to sign me. Our chairman, van Raay, wasn't happy. He was trying to build a team for the future and the last thing he wanted was his captain walking out. A few teams in Europe were looking for an attacking left-back.

However, it was known I had just signed the new contract that contained a clause allowing me to leave in the summer of 1999 for 7 million guilders (around £2.5 million) but there was no get-out fee until that period.

So any side interested in me would have to start from scratch with PSV over a fee. Van Raay wasn't happy when I told him I wanted to leave. To be honest, I surprised myself that I felt it was time to move on. I remember speaking to my partner, Marjon, about a year prior to that and told her I was really settled at PSV and couldn't envisage ever playing abroad.

However, when the interest came from Rangers and Atletico, I was twenty-eight and knew it was a good time to start a fresh chapter in my career. I told myself it was now or never to make the break and go for a new challenge, in a new country. I thought a new experience, a new adventure, was right for me. Whenever we gathered to play for the national team, the guys who played abroad were always positive and on many occasions I felt a little envious and wanted to try it for myself. So I decided to take the plunge and go for it. It was just a case of a club agreeing a fee with PSV.

In March 1998, Atletico asked for permission to speak to me. Van Raay was disappointed and his mood wasn't helped by the fact that, at the time, Stam was being linked with every top club in Europe. Manchester United were the favourites, Atletico were also interested. I was very close to Jaap and he was keen on a switch to Old Trafford. So van Raay told me if he gave me permission to speak to clubs it would open the floodgates for other clubs to pick off our players one by one, as we were doing well at the time. Phillip Cocu was leaving on a free transfer at the end of the season to Barcelona and Zenden and Luc Nilis were attracting scouts and interest from across the continent.

Van Raay was distraught and could see his master plan breaking up in front of him. Advocaat was leaving and there was a danger five or six of his top players could also be walking out. I felt for him, I really did. Initially, he was stubborn and refused to let me speak to other clubs. However, I had always been loyal to the club – stuck with them through the difficult years when we were not making a challenge at home or abroad. I think my loyalty persuaded him to change his mind but he made it clear I would only be leaving PSV for a good price, much more than the amount in my get-out clause that was due to kick in twelve months later.

When Atletico were granted permission, it allowed Advocaat to make his move to take me with him to Rangers. It moved on pretty quickly after that. Indeed, before I had time to draw breath, the arrangements were made for me, Marjon, my agent and Dick to fly from Rotterdam to Edinburgh airport in Rangers' owner David Murray's private jet. It was a great touch from Murray and that kind of thing must give him an advantage when trying to attract players to his club. It's much better than flying with a scheduled airline. I felt like a superstar.

The flight was leaving on a Sunday morning and we were late. Roadworks on our way to Rotterdam held us up. Advocaat was not happy. He is strict about time-keeping and he was on the phone, shouting at me telling me to get a move on. We got there about twenty minutes late and Advocaat's face was like thunder.

Murray's Learjet was luxurious, really impressive. From memory, I think it was an eight-seater. I think Murray later sold it to the Grand Prix driver David Coulthard but tragically the plane crashed in 2000 and two people lost their lives.

However, what I remember very clearly about our journey to Edinburgh was Advocaat serving me tea, coffee and sandwiches. There was no air steward on board so Advocaat took on the role of trolley dolly! It really was funny to see. A few times I kept hitting the little button above my head to get his attention, to ask for more coffee. I thought I'd never be in a situation like that with him again and that I should make the most of it! Of course, Advocaat assured me he would get his own back in training the next day.

Despite the private jet, I still had negative thoughts about Rangers. I didn't know much about the Scottish Premier League. At that time I couldn't even name three or four of the Rangers players, but I knew the supporters were passionate. My only connection to the game in Scotland was watching brief highlights on Dutch television of games involving Rangers and Celtic. We got that because the likes of Pierre van Hooijdonk, Peter van Vossen and Pieter Huistra had played for the Old Firm. In contrast, Advocaat was positive and really tried to sell the club to me on the flight over. He had gathered lots of information about Rangers, was well informed about their history and was determined to re-establish them on the European stage. He had also been promised serious money from Murray to spend on quality players.

John Greig was waiting as the plane landed to pick us up. John was friendly, open and doing his bit to sell Rangers to me. He drove us from the airport into Edinburgh and on the way into Murray's office we had a look at the city and Marjon seemed suitably impressed.

Now, it is here I have a confession to make. That day, I had no idea who John Greig was. I thought he was just another employee of Rangers and his job was to pick up potential signings and give them some background on the club. Of course, John is officially the Greatest Ever Ranger and it wasn't until after I had signed with Rangers that I found out exactly who he was. He is a legend and a really nice man.

We all headed for Murray's office in Edinburgh. He gave me a warm handshake and I could tell he was a confident man. He also knew everything about me as a footballer. I was impressed he'd researched my career. He made it clear he wanted to sign me. I was the first player to be approached in the new era at Rangers and to be honest it felt like, if I agreed to sign, I was taking a gamble. I knew great Rangers players such as Ally McCoist and Ian Durrant were leaving and that the club had recently sold Paul Gascoigne. But I wanted to know the players Advocaat and Murray were interested in signing. I wanted assurances they were going to be good players, players capable of taking Rangers to a higher level in Europe. At that time, Advocaat assured me he had excellent signings in mind. He had a list of about twenty and Andrei Kanchelskis was one of the targets on it. I also found out that Sergio Porrini, Lorenzo Amoruso and Jorg Albertz were at the club and they were all good players.

After I had asked Murray a few questions, he just came right out with it and said, 'OK, Arthur, you know why you're here. I rate you and we want to sign you and I have an offer of a four-year contract for you to look at. The offer is a good one and reflects on your status as an international player.'

The offer was made less than ten minutes after meeting him in his office. He put the written proposal down in front of me and my agent. Well, you should have seen my face. Honestly, I couldn't believe it, it was more than double my wages from PSV.

Usually, the opening terms are a little bit on the low side, sometimes a little bit cheeky. But this was a very good offer. I was delighted but trying not to give anything away, despite the fact I was tapping Joop's foot under the table with excitement. I don't know how I managed to keep a straight face when I looked at it and then said to Murray, 'I'll think about this offer. Can Joop and I leave the room for five minutes to discuss it?'

So we left and as soon as the door closed behind us I said to Joop, 'OK, there is not a lot to think about. Can I have your pen?' We went back into the room, asked for a little bit more here and there, as is normal, and that was it sorted out. I agreed a deal for a basic wage of £500,000 net per year with other bonuses and incentives. It was great to have my personal terms sorted out quickly as sometimes it can drag on for weeks and weeks, making it a difficult time.

The only thing that now needed to be resolved was the transfer fee between Rangers and PSV. Murray asked me and I told him it would take a figure in the region of £5 million for PSV to sell.

Yes, the money was good, but I was still taking a big gamble going to Rangers. I had established myself as the left-back for Holland and part of me felt I was jeopardising my international career. Other Dutch players were leaving PSV that summer but, with all due respect to the Scottish League, Cocu and Zenden were going to Barcelona, and Stam was joining Manchester United. Playing in those environments would ensure their continued involvement at national level.

From Murray's office, we drove to his house in Edinburgh and settled down to watch Rangers play Celtic in the Scottish Cup semi-final at Parkhead. Hampden was being renovated at that time and that's why the game wasn't played there. Rangers won the game 2–1 and made it through to the final. Overall, it was a satisfying day for the Ibrox chairman.

I was pleased for him that day. He impressed me. The story he has to tell is an amazing one, from losing his legs in a horrific car

9

accident to going on to become one of Scotland's most successful businessmen and owner of Rangers. You have to admire
the way he has made such a success of his life under such
difficult and trying circumstances.

As we flew back from Edinburgh that night I knew, unless
there was a late bid by a big club, that it was down to a straight
choice between Rangers and Atletico. I had been to Madrid for
talks a few weeks before I was in Edinburgh to meet Murray. It
was near Easter time and Marjon and myself expected the
weather to be nice and we would mix business with a little bit
of pleasure around the city. However, it was freezing in Madrid
and there was snow falling.

Somehow, an agent from Belgium got involved in the deal to
take me to Madrid. I had never met him in my life before but
he tried to muscle his way in when we arrived in Madrid with
Joop. He told me what kind of money he could get me and we
listened to him and thanked him, but informed him he was not
getting involved in things from our end. I had no need for him.
I had Joop. But this little man kept popping up and wouldn't
leave us alone. He was only there to try to fill his own pockets.
In the end he became a real pain in the ass and we told him in
no uncertain terms to leave us alone.

Whereas I had complete trust in Joop, I knew there were
dodgy agents out there always touting for business. One example I remember is when a Dutch agent phoned me before I had
signed for Rangers and asked me if I would be interested
in going to Spain as he had a club there interested in me. I presumed it would be Atletico, as I knew about their interest, and
told the agent to contact Joop to discuss any deal. I heard nothing more about it until three years later at Frank de Boer's wedding when Louis van Gaal tapped me on the shoulder and said
to me, 'Arthur, I was really disappointed you didn't want to join
me at Barcelona in 1998.' I wondered what he was on about but,
after a little bit more conversation, I realised it was connected to
that phone call I'd received from the agent. Van Gaal had

instructed this intermediary to go and get me, but because I wasn't willing to do the deal without Joop's involvement, the agent decided not to pursue the deal. That made me angry because the Nou Camp would have been a very attractive option – playing for one of the most revered clubs in the world was denied to me because of the selfishness and greed of one agent.

Thankfully it was a straightforward discussion with Atletico who were treating us well. They put us up in a swanky hotel and took us to a private room in a top restaurant for dinner. Miguel Gill, son of Jesus, was leading the talks and doing everything to persuade me to move to the club. He told me he wanted Atletico to get back to the top of Spanish football and challenge Real Madrid, Barcelona and Valencia. However, there was a reluctance to make me a concrete offer and it was the usual stuff of not getting down to the nitty-gritty.

We started to talk terms and the deal they made was very generous. They offered me a three-year contract with a one-year option. Also, as a signing-on fee, they threw in an apartment in Marbella that was bought and paid for and was mine to keep for life. I could do what I wanted with it – keep it or sell it – it was mine. So, as was the case with Rangers, I asked Atletico to put the offer in writing, on club headed notepaper with a signature from the president or a director.

Both offers arrived and I had to make my mind up. It was a tough call. When I have a major decision to make, I like to go through the details thoroughly so, one night, I sat down with a pen and paper and wrote down the plus and minus points of both clubs. I had ten categories – manager, tactics, preparation, climate, culture, media, living, city, contract and wages.

Rangers had the edge with the manager because I was going to be working with Dick, someone I knew very well. It was the same with the tactics. Preparation was also in favour of Rangers, as Spain is such a big country that I could have been spending two or three nights a week in a hotel for games and that's too much. The climate was something that didn't bother me and that was 50:50 – although the weather is better in Madrid, I was going to play football as my job, I wasn't going for a holiday. Anyway, Scotland has a similar climate to Holland. Madrid got a plus point on the living part of things as I quite like sitting outside in a café, relaxing, having a coffee. That appealed to me.

Again, it was a 'draw' when I considered both cities. When considering the contract situation it was a plus point for Rangers because they offered me a four-year deal. Madrid were ahead with the wage packet as better money and the apartment in Marbella was on offer.

Rangers had more going for them and I have to admit one of the biggest factors in signing for Rangers was Advocaat. He lives for football twenty-four hours a day, eats, sleeps and drinks the game. Because of my relationship with Dick, and the fact I felt I was taking a gamble moving to Scotland, I insisted on a get-out clause in my contract. The clause I had inserted was that if Dick left before his two-year deal was up then I could go too. Murray was not happy about the clause but he reluctantly agreed to it.

As it was, Dick signed an extension to his deal at the end of his first season and my clause then became void. I was contracted to Rangers until the summer of 2002. Rangers and PSV eventually agreed a fee in the region of £4.5 million and I was preparing to play in the final league game of the season at PSV's stadium knowing it was almost certain I was leaving to go to Glasgow.

At that time it was confirmed that Advocaat, Cocu, Stam and Zenden were all leaving to move to new clubs and they had the good fortune of being able to say a proper 'goodbye' to the fans. They were presented with flowers and stood on the back of a jeep for a lap of honour on the trackside. I had tears in my eyes. I knew it was also going to be the end for me, the end after six great years with the club. I was really upset I didn't get the chance to say my farewells in the same manner as the rest of the players.

This was a really unsettling time for the club and fans because they realised their team was breaking up. During one game towards the end of the season, against Volendam, the hardcore fans didn't enter the ground until ten minutes after the start as a form of protest against the sale of the best players. They didn't sing and didn't clap in the first half, but at full-time they were happy as we won the game 10–0.

There was chat that I was going to leave but, deep down, the fans still hoped I'd stay. I felt terrible – it was heartbreaking. I wanted to jump on the back of the jeep with the rest of them and get it out in the open. You know, tell the fans I was moving on and thank them in public for the support they'd given me.

We also had the Dutch Cup final to prepare for against Ajax in Rotterdam. The game was on a Sunday but, five days before that, I was told Rangers and PSV had agreed a fee. I told Marjon that it was all settled and we were going to be starting a new life in Scotland. But I couldn't believe her reaction. She started to cry and told me she was not leaving Holland. I think she might also have thought that no club would have paid £4.5 million to get me. She underestimated my qualities! It hit her that she was leaving her life in her own country to start afresh. She found it difficult to leave her friends and family.

We had a great social life in Holland and loved it in Eindhoven. Sometimes we would socialise with Stam and his wife, Cocu, Jonk, Faber, Waterreus and Palphatz. A couple of times Stam never turned up as we'd planned and I later realised it was because he was away speaking to Manchester United about a move. All the time he'd kept it to himself.

Marjon realised she was giving all of this up.

My father also expressed his doubts about me leaving PSV to move to Glasgow. He told me he was not sure about my decision. He said, 'Why are you leaving a great club? Everything is fine at PSV – you should not go. This could be a bad move for you personally and for your career. You are the captain of the team. You are respected by every person at the club. I'm really not convinced about this move.' I told him it was time for me to try something different, the beginning of a new chapter in my life, and I would regret it if I didn't take this opportunity.

I was a little bit disappointed with my father. I felt that because I was so happy they should have shared my enjoyment, not dampen it. However, as we started to talk more about it, the truth behind my father's reservations came out. The only reason he didn't want me to leave was because of his fear of flying. He was thinking that if I moved away then he would not be able to go over to Scotland to see me in action for Rangers.

When I was a kid we would never fly anywhere on holiday. Our destination was always reached by car. We would normally drive to Belgium for time away in the summer. In the end we had a laugh about it. And the good news was that my father did fly over to Scotland to see me playing for Rangers, in my second season. But initially my parents travelled to Scotland separately. My mum flew in from Holland, but my dad took a boat on the Thursday morning and arrived in Scotland more than thirty hours later on the Friday night!

I played my last game for PSV in the Dutch Cup final against Ajax. It was still not public knowledge that I was leaving PSV; somehow it had stayed under wraps. We had had problems for a while at the club, with Advocaat leaving and other players moving abroad. It was hard to keep it all together. There was upheaval at the club. I felt strange before the game because I knew this was my last game for PSV and it was the perfect chance to leave on a high.

The game wasn't a sell-out; the fans were afraid to travel to the game at De Kuip stadium in Rotterdam, home of Feyenoord. A lot of Feyenoord fans came to the stadium to cause trouble. The weather was lovely and it was a great occasion. It should have been safe for parents and children in the main stand but it wasn't. Trouble started, and as the players lined up just before kick-off, we could see people running for cover, looking for safety. Thankfully, with the help of the stewards and the police, the trouble seemed to pass off. The referee thought about delaying the game to let the rumpus ease off but he decided to get on with it and we started really well. However, we didn't take our chances. Of course, we paid the price.

Normally, this fixture was a close one but we were losing at half-time. It wasn't to be our day. The heads were down during the interval and Advocaat tried to motivate us. It was just too much to ask. Ajax destroyed us in the second half. Our legs were gone – we had no energy to compete with them. Ajax won the game 5–0.

Our fans were so disappointed and it meant we finished the season without any silverware. The game was being shown on a big screen in Eindhoven's main square and if we'd won we would have gone back there to join in the celebrations. That was running through my mind as I sat in the dressing room after the game. I sat there for twenty minutes on my own. My head was down. I was sad at leaving PSV – sad at not having the chance to go out on a high, to say some kind of decent goodbye to the fans.

Then my thoughts turned to Rangers. I knew I had to go to Glasgow the next day for my press conference at Ibrox. Before that, there was a party to attend at the chairman's house after the Cup final. It was a farewell do for the guys who were leaving. I dropped my car off back at PSV's stadium, got dressed in the changing rooms and then got the team bus to van Raay's house. It was like going to a funeral.

The evening didn't actually turn out that bad and live singers were there to entertain us. Van Raay made a speech and thanked Advocaat and the players for their service over the years. He also wished us all good luck for our new adventures. Van Raay spoke to me later that night and said the door would always be open for me to return to PSV. I felt really sorry for van Raay. He wanted the team to stay together. It was a sad evening – but it was time to move on.

The bus headed back to the stadium, but we stayed for a few more drinks. I got back to the stadium near enough at one in the morning and was one of the last to pick up my car. The place was deserted. Marjon sat in the car and I headed towards the main reception to pick up my bag and boots from the dressing room.

Walking close to the kerb, I was about 200 metres from the main door. Then, out of nowhere, three guys appeared on bikes. Then, without any warning, I felt something hit my face. For ten seconds I was shaking. I had been punched in the face by a full fist. I felt like I had been hit by a truck. One guy was particularly wound up and really giving me verbal abuse – he had probably been drinking all day, taking pills and tablets. I could see the anger and hatred spilling out of him as he shouted and bawled insults at me.

Then I noticed blood pouring from a cut just above my eye. I had a white shirt on and it was covered in blood. The guy kept up his tirade and shouted, 'You are the captain of the team. Why are you leaving to join a club like Rangers? Rangers are not as big as PSV. You are just going there for the money.' I was expecting the guy to attack me again, so it was going through my mind that I should get in there first and punch or kick him.

Then I was thinking it was three guys against me and the odds were not in my favour. Also, I was worried I could end up seriously injured in all of this and it could jeopardise my place in the World Cup squad. I also had my press conference with Rangers the next day to announce my signing and didn't want that to be called off because I was in hospital.

The guy was pulled away by his two friends and then Marjon came running over. She was shouting at them. She was really upset. I just told her to be relieved all I had was a cut eye and that it could have been worse. I could have had a broken

16

nose or been beaten black and blue. I was scared I could have missed the World Cup finals because of one idiot.

We collected my things and went home. The bleeding stopped and I only needed a plaster above my eye. I didn't call the police, didn't want them involved. Some people phoned the newspapers and the incident made the press on the Tuesday morning. When the journalists called to ask about the story, I thought about lying and telling them a team-mate injured me in training. In the end, I told the truth.

I received phone-calls from PSV supporters to tell me they knew the identity of the culprit and that they would 'sort him out' if I wanted them to. But I insisted the attacker was to be left alone. The guy eventually turned himself in to the police but I didn't want anything to happen to him. A Dutch journalist criticised me for not taking legal action against the person. He reckoned I should have made a stand on behalf of all footballers by getting the police involved to bring the person to justice. I discussed the possibility with the PSV lawyers but thought a court case would have been too distracting with the World Cup on the horizon.

Anyway, the morning after the attack, I flew to Glasgow to sign for Rangers. I arrived at Ibrox for the first time and looked around the place and the truth is I wasn't too impressed. The dressing rooms were nothing special. At PSV we had a Jacuzzi in the dressing room. There wasn't anything like that at Rangers.

So I thought, 'Hmm, not very modern.'

The treatment room was also old-fashioned but I knew it was the people who worked inside the room that mattered.

However, what did catch my attention in a positive way was the history of the club. Honestly, between the wooden panels on the walls and the marble staircase, you could sense the aura of a successful tradition, a great history. But, most importantly, when I walked out and stood at the mouth of the tunnel I began to get a feel for what this club was all about. I took a deep breath, looked round the empty stadium and imagined what it would be like running out in front of 50,000 passionate fans. I started to feel good about the move and couldn't wait to run out on the pitch and start a new chapter of my career in Scotland.

Also, the people were proud to work there. Peter, the front-door man, was very proud, always immaculately dressed in his club blazer and tie. The staff were all friendly.

I tried to delay my signing conference for a while but Rangers insisted it took place on that Monday morning. I'd wanted a couple of days to myself to relax, pack my bags and prepare for the World Cup. Rangers, though, insisted I turn up on the Monday.

The club had just missed out on ten-in-a-row and wanted something positive to report. Rangers felt the fact they were parading me made a statement about their ambition for the future, not only to win the title back, but to become a genuine force in Europe. I expected only about five or six journalists to be there but the media room inside Ibrox was packed. It was full of people from the newspapers, radio and television. It really hit me then just how big a club I was joining. I knew that everyone in the Scottish media wanted to know everything about Rangers.

Because my English wasn't too good, I was nervous at the press conference. Advocaat and Murray were at the table beside me and were a great help as I tried to answer questions diplomatically. I stayed in Glasgow for a few hours and then flew back to Amsterdam. I was meeting up with the Holland squad on the Wednesday morning and had to go home to get everything ready for an event that turned out to be one of the most exciting and heartbreaking few weeks of my life – the 1998 World Cup finals.

2

THE WORLD CUP 1998

We went into the 1998 World Cup finals in France with Guus Hiddink in charge and high expectations.

Our preparation for the tournament had been first class and we headed to Switzerland for a week's training which was perfect for the players after a long, hard domestic season with our respective clubs. I was really excited about the whole thing; the thought of facing the best players in the game, on the biggest stage in the world really appealed to me.

I was in the squad in the Euro 96 finals in England but didn't get a game in a tournament I'd rather forget about. That was not a good tournament for us. Edgar Davids was sent home in disgrace after our second game against Switzerland. Davids played in our first game against Scotland but was picked out for criticism by our skipper, Danny Blind, and Ronald de Boer after the 0–0 draw. Davids criticised Hiddink in public and accused the manager of having his head stuck up the de Boer twins' asses.

That was just one of several problems we had that summer. Some of the Ajax players in the squad were not getting along with each other and it was no surprise that we only qualified for the knockout stages of the tournament by a single goal.

Sadly, the club problems at Ajax crept their way into the national squad. Patrick Kluivert, Clarence Seedorf, Edgar Davids, Winston Bogarde and Michael Reiziger all felt they were not being treated the same and felt they were being underpaid by Ajax and wanted the same money as the de Boer twins and Danny Blind. The tension between all of them made it a really negative atmosphere for the rest of the squad and management.

After one training session, a meeting was called for the entire squad. Reiziger kicked it off and tried to find an explanation for the tension inside the camp. Some of the players like Reiziger and Seedorf were also not happy with the way Blind conducted himself as the skipper for Holland. Seedorf tried to get the backing of Dennis Bergkamp, a former Ajax player who by that time had moved to Arsenal, asking him, 'Dennis, what about you? What do you think about the whole situation?'

Dennis was very diplomatic and quite rightly chose not to get too involved.

Nothing was resolved at the meeting because it was more a club matter and had not a lot to do with Holland. We just had to make the best of the situation. The Ajax boys – Patrick, Edgar, Clarence, Winston and Michael – were so tight together that they called themselves 'The Cable' because they were so connected and nothing could pull them apart; for them this term wasn't derogatory – it indicated their friendship and closeness. But Danny was particularly annoyed by Seedorf's behaviour and at times they'd be arguing and yelling at each other.

In our final group game of Euro 96 we were losing 4–0 to England at Wembley and were down and out. England were going to win the group and Scotland were on course to finish second, as they were beating Switzerland 1–0. However, Kluivert saved our skins when he scored late on and we scraped through on goal difference. We eventually lost on penalties to France and I was glad it was over. It was a relief to get home. I got little enjoyment out of the tournament.

Hiddink was again in charge in 1998 and he knew things had to be different from the painful events of two years earlier. I reckon the squad we had in 1998 was much stronger. We were a very good team, with a combination of skill and strength. Every training session was competitive – there was no holding back. And every player was desperate to do well after the débâcle of Euro 96.

We were all desperate to start our first game. Despite the fact I had just signed for Rangers and had a new career in Glasgow to look forward to after the World Cup, I didn't let it interfere with my concentration on doing my job for Holland.

We had a fantastic base just outside Monaco for as long as we were going to be in the tournament. The hotel sat on top of a cliff, with a wonderful sea view, only ten minutes away from the centre of the city. At night, there was a fantastic view of the principality, all lit up. A perfect setting. Our accommodation had been arranged months in advance and it was close to our training complex. Pierre van Hooijdonk was my room-mate and I was happy with that arrangement. I'd known Pierre for many years. We were in the 1992 Holland Olympic squad in Barcelona along with Marc Overmars and Frank de Boer. We were now in the full squad for this World Cup and it gave us all a lot of satisfaction.

When you are away for four or five weeks it is important to have the right room-mate because if you don't you'll end up wanting to kill one another! There's nothing worse than being confined to a hotel room with a person who irritates you. You must like each other, feel comfortable in one another's company. Pierre and I had that. We enjoyed, and still enjoy, a good rapport. Hiddink did not consult me on the room-mate arrangements but I'm sure he was aware of our relationship and put us together deliberately.

Pierre is a fantastic lad. Yet, he has a bit of a reputation of being a troublemaker, mainly down to the way he left clubs such as Celtic, Nottingham Forest and Fenerbahce. In my opinion, he is a great character, a really happy person.

During his time in the Dutch national team he was never assured of starting games – most of the time he was on the bench – because guys such as Patrick Kluivert, Dennis

Bergkamp, Ronald de Boer and Ruud van Nistelrooy were always ahead of him. But he never once complained. He accepted he was more or less there to come off the bench and make an impact, whereas other players would have moaned about being a sub and would have bitched about the situation. I remember Pierre coming off the bench quite a few times and scoring important goals for us.

Off the pitch, he acted as a peacemaker on a few occasions when some things threatened to get out of control between players in the squad. As soon as Holland qualified for the Euro 2004 finals in Portugal, Dick Advocaat, the then national boss, stated that van Hooijdonk would be the first name on his squad list. He knew Pierre would do well on the pitch but, more importantly, was a fine man to have about the squad and in the hotel because of his ability to keep things together with players in the squad.

The other reason I enjoyed having Pierre as my room-mate was because he was able to fill me in on life in Glasgow as an Old Firm player – on and off the park. I knew next to nothing about the city and wanted to know as much as possible. Pierre told me I had signed for a fantastic team and a massive club. He informed me that there was a great atmosphere inside Ibrox, with the team in front of a 50,000 sell-out every week. I was also glad to hear that the city was vibrant with good shops, restaurants and nightlife. I knew I'd have no problem adapting to my new 'home' as it all sounded similar to Holland.

There's a downside to most things in life and Pierre said that one of the few things that got to him was that he was playing the same sides at least four times a year. Depending on cup draws, it could be up to six times in a season. His words came back to me during my second year at Rangers when we played St Johnstone a total of eleven times in two seasons.

Another interesting thing during that time was that Advocaat wanted van Hooijdonk to sign for Rangers and was using me as a go-between. Now and again, from the hotel in

Monaco, I would speak to Advocaat to see what was happening at Rangers. He was telling me about players he was trying to sign and also that Giovanni van Bronckhorst had agreed to join. But he was desperate to get Pierre. He said to me, 'Arthur, we need Pierre at Rangers. I want him and you have to do everything to get him to come.'

Pierre was aware of the interest. I started to turn up the heat and we had a long and deep conversation about it one night in the room. I said to him, 'Pierre, why don't you come?'

His reply was straight to the point and he said, 'Arthur, you've no idea what the rivalry is like. It is impossible for me to go back. I have played for Celtic and when you do that you can't go to the other side. The rivalry is worse than anything that exists between PSV, Ajax and Feyenoord. There will be no hiding place and I will not put myself or my family through that kind of thing.'

I kept at him – I felt a duty to Rangers and Advocaat to get Pierre to change his mind. From a selfish point of view, I also wanted someone I knew to be with me in Glasgow. I said to him, 'Pierre, come on, you can do it.'

Again he said no but was more forceful in his reply. He told me, 'Arthur, the only way I could do it would be to live in Edinburgh and travel to work every day in a tank with four bodyguards. Trust me, it's the way it would have to be. And, I don't want to go back and score a goal against Celtic, a club that gave me a big opportunity. I could never betray their fans.'

Advocaat also spoke to Pierre a few times on the phone and tried his best to persuade him. Despite Pierre's reasons, my opinion is that he was tempted to come to Rangers, he really was. However, after living in the west of Scotland for two or three months, I knew exactly what he meant about the Old Firm rivalry and fully understood and respected the explanation he gave me for why he wouldn't join Rangers.

Even though I was in France, playing in the World Cup finals with Holland, I was learning more and more about Rangers every day. The Scottish media were always asking to interview me, trying to find out bits about me to inform the Rangers supporters back in Scotland.

On the pitch, I was aware the Ibrox fans would be watching the Holland games to see if Rangers had invested the £4.5 million transfer fee wisely. In the build-up to the opening game I felt 100 per cent, physically and mentally. I was flying in training and was as fit as a fiddle. I was expecting to be named in Hiddink's starting line-up at left-back because I'd played almost every game in the qualifiers and build-up. I felt tense and nervous in the few hours leading up to the game against Belgium in the Stade de France. I wanted to perform, I wanted to play well, I wanted to make sure I'd impress Hiddink to keep my place in the second group game. I didn't want to give Hiddink any excuses to leave me out of his team, so I always kept things simple but effective.

We were disappointing against Belgium. Kluivert was sent off for an elbow on Belgian defender Lorenzo Staelens and we had to settle for a point as we struggled in a 0–0 draw. Kluivert was provoked by the Belgian, who probably taunted the striker about some incident in his private life. In our next game when we faced Yugoslavia in Marseille, we flew to the match by helicopter. It was a great feeling, although my hands were sweaty through nerves. We were only told after breakfast on the day of the game that we were travelling by chopper and we felt like superstars. Just five players at a time travelled and I enjoyed the experience. Again, it was something that helped to break up the usual routine. It was different.

The other thing we enjoyed was that our hotel had a private beach and it was used by the 'high society' of Monaco. Princess Stephanie was a regular, who always enjoyed some time on the sand. The other guests didn't pay any attention to us – quite rightly, they preferred to look at her!

Hiddink was always aware of the boredom factor and was good at giving us time to ourselves. Wim Jonk, Jaap Stam, Marc

Overmars, Pierre and I enjoyed being together; we had the same sense of humour and were on the same wavelength about most things. After the trouble he had faced with members of the Euro 96 squad, Hiddink knew a real effort had to be made to make sure we were all in this together and there were no frictions or cliques in the group.

Davids was back in the squad and everything was fine. I suppose it made a change to have a group of players in the Dutch squad that were getting on. On the day we left for the USA for the 94 finals, Ruud Gullit said he didn't want to go there to play because he had a difference of opinion with Advocaat on tactics. There's always so many negatives.

We missed out on 2002 in Japan and South Korea when Louis van Gaal was in charge. It's just typical of our country to have so much talent but never put it to proper use. The Dutch are always opinionated – it's always 'Yes, but . . .'! We have an entire population of experts on management.

One thing I did find harder in Scotland was adjusting to the Scottish press. The press in Scotland are harder than in Holland. I found the stuff in the Scottish newspapers could be personal. It's always about getting a headline, sensationalising everything.

I remember after Rangers played Monaco in a Champions League group game and we conceded a late goal to finish the game level. The result prevented us from progressing to the next stage of the tournament. We were all bitterly disappointed and Lorenzo Amoruso was blamed by certain people for making a mistake at the decisive goal. I spoke to the press about thirty minutes after the final whistle and tried to be as honest as possible, but I would normally never criticise a team-mate or a member of the management in public. However, the next day there was a headline in one of the tabloids, 'Numan Blames Amo'. I was furious. I'd never mentioned Lorenzo's name once during the interview.

For the next couple of days, Lorenzo showed his anger towards me and I knew it couldn't go on. We would have ended up fighting if nothing was said, so it was best for him to get it off his chest. Two days later I approached him in our hotel, in Aberdeen, the night before we played at Pittodrie. I should have gone to him sooner, I know that.

We were in his room and I tried to explain to him that the interview was taken out of context but Amo was screaming and shouting. I stayed calm. I knew it couldn't have been nice for him to read. It was my mistake but I had nothing to hide from him as I was also a victim in the whole thing. Eventually, after I'd explained the situation, we sorted it out that night and it was put behind us.

In Holland, the one and only time I approached a journalist was to ask him why he was always favouring other players for my position. In the build-up to Euro 2000 the broadcaster, Frits Barend, kept highlighting the positives of Winston Bogarde and some other players who were my rivals for the left-back slot. I wasn't fully fit when I joined up with the squad and he seemed to want me out before the final squad list was named and sent to UEFA for the tournament (two or three players had to drop out). I was worried about my fitness and this was putting extra stress on me. Thankfully, despite his comments, I made it into the final squad.

Normally, I wouldn't bother what people say about me, I think it is just a waste of energy. But it wasn't nice for my mum and dad and Marjon to be listening to it. Eventually, I'd had enough and decided to confront Barend. He was surprised I spoke to him because he was unaware I'd taken offence at his remarks. He never felt he was saying anything wrong.

Pierre had prepared me for life in Scotland and constantly being under the microscope. When we roomed together during the World Cup, he'd get the British papers delivered every day to our room. He'd always look at the back page first and it was good to see them and keep up to date with what was happening at Rangers. He also warned me to be careful about what I said in Scotland because every paper has fifteen or sixteen pages of football to fill every day. I didn't really believe him when he said that I'd only need to speak to the press for two minutes and they would get two pages out of it.

The media is huge business now and I accept that. It's not just about newspapers – there's the glossy magazines for men and they all want some juicy football stories in them. If you are a top footballer, it is impossible to escape the limelight, although I suspect some of the top players absolutely love it.

Anyway, I was in the spotlight for the wrong reasons during our World Cup game against Mexico. I was booked for taking a throw-in at the wrong place. I felt the referee got it wrong. I was then substituted when we were 2–0 up and I was angry at Hiddink's decision. I'd already been booked and maybe Hiddink didn't want to run the risk of seeing us go down to ten men. Mexico fought back to get a 2–2 draw. In our next game we beat South Korea 4–0 and I was subbed again.

I don't know why Hiddink replaced me – I was playing well. I always felt that under him I had to perform at the top of my game for every minute and that one mistake would give him an easy excuse to take me off. I remember in our first World Cup qualifier, against Wales, I had to get things off my chest and decided to confront him after he left me on the bench for Bogarde.

Bogarde wasn't totally fit that week and only trained with the squad the night before the game. I was playing really well for PSV at the time and expected to start. I stayed on the bench for that Welsh game but played every time after that, so having our little chat didn't do my international career any harm.

We beat Yugoslavia 2–1 in our final game, Davids scoring the winner and that was enough for us to qualify for the last eight. Hiddink gave us a day off after that and a few of us – Jaap Stam, Overmars, van Hooijdonk and myself – decided to have what we thought would be a relaxing day at the beach.

We were like little kids, totally hyperactive, and ignored Hiddink's advice to relax and take it easy. Yes, there we were, three days before a World Cup quarter-final tie against Argentina, and we decided to go out on the jet skis. We were all on individual ones and we were, at best, like crazy holiday-makers, and, at worst, like kamikaze pilots. We tried to go directly for one another at 50 mph to see who would chicken out first.

Overmars fell off and we were all circling around him, making waves so it was near-impossible for him to get back on his jet ski. He wasn't happy. And no wonder! It was ridiculous behaviour. To think Hiddink assumed we were relaxing, being sensible, taking it easy by the pool.

Also during that trip, when we had a day off, Hiddink allowed us to go out at night. The usual bunch and I ended up in Jimmy's discotheque in Monaco. Now, this is THE place to be seen. If you have money to spend, or want to give out the impression you have money to spend, you head to Jimmy's. We were very apprehensive about going out to a bar so late at night. We thought it was a silly thing to do and could land us in a lot of trouble. Then we thought, 'What the hell, we've got to go for it' – we needed a release.

When we arrived, we walked in to find most of our team-mates already there! We had a few drinks and midway through our time in there we spotted a few guys coming in. They had the look of bouncers about them and that's exactly what they were. Walking in the middle of them, completely dwarfed by the height and physique of the bodyguards, was superstar diva Whitney Houston.

The way they looked just made me scared. Her bodyguards were guys that you would not attempt to take the piss out of. Kluivert had other ideas. He was not intimidated in the slightest. Kluivert ended up on the dance-floor, throwing a few moves about the place. Whitney is small and has a petite build. She was full of energy and was up for a right good laugh with the lads. Patrick has all the technique on the dance-floor and she seemed to be quite impressed with him. Me? Well, I didn't

get a second glance. I think she must have thought I was dancing with my clogs on!

The next day, we got rid of the alcohol and the hangovers by
doing some running in training. Hiddink knew the players had
been drinking the previous night. He'd have to have had no
sense of smell if he didn't! But he turned a blind eye as he knew
the players needed to let off some steam. It was good management on his part.

Our next game was the quarter-final tie against Argentina. It
was an afternoon start. After lunch we spoke about our line-up
and their team. We went over things such as how we would
play when we had the ball and how we would adjust when
Argentina were in possession.

I like later kick-offs but I don't enjoy the waiting around in
the hours leading up to kick-off. After the pre-match meal I got
dressed. I put on my national suit and I felt on top of the world.
We got on the coach and headed to the stadium in Marseille –
the impressive Stade Vélodrome.

I'm always really nervous on the day of a game but once I get
to the stadium I'm totally fine. I'd always play my best for club
and country in the big games – I enjoy the pressure and hype
that surround them. I became more relaxed as we approached
the arena. Travelling through the crowds is always an exciting
time and a humbling experience. I could just see thousands
upon thousands of oranje scarves and oranje jerseys.

The Holland fans are very well behaved and only want to
party and enjoy the football. It is the same with the Scotland
support when they travel to Hampden or go abroad – they put
on their kilts and play their bagpipes and have fun. I think
there is a different atmosphere with the nationals compared to
the club games. When fans travel abroad to watch their club
team, sometimes there can be trouble.

Hundreds of thousands packed Amsterdam to watch the
game. The whole country is turned upside down during a
World Cup finals. Yet, the players are detached from it all. We

don't get a true feeling of exactly what is going on back home and we have to rely on media coverage and phone calls to Holland to get some sort of understanding.

My only thoughts now were to entertain the Holland fans in this game. Play good, attractive football and try to get the victory. With Bergkamp, Overmars, Kluivert, Jonk and the de Boer twins in the team, I had a genuine feeling we were going to beat Argentina and go all the way to the final in Paris. I was twenty-eight and I was psyching myself up. 'It's now or never,' I remember telling myself.

We went for a walk on the pitch before kick-off and I felt the tension easing out of my body. I got back into the dressing room and started to loosen up my muscles and put my bandages on. This was a big game for me and I wanted to show I deserved to be the left-back for the national team. No middle ground. Arthur Numan is the best in the country. In 1994 and 1996 I had just been a squad player; 1998 was different. It was my big chance.

Playing Argentina had me really excited. I'd always regarded them, along with Brazil, as a top, top nation. I remember watching the 1978 World Cup final when they beat Holland 3–1 with a mixture of good football and brute force. However, I'm sad to say my opinion changed about them after this game.

That day, shamefully, Argentina had talent in their team but the talent was sadly overshadowed by their ridiculous diving and cheating. After about fifteen minutes Davids rolled a pass towards me. It wasn't too accurate and Ariel Ortega was trying to nick it. I had to slide in and I timed my tackle well to get the ball. I did not hit Ortega. But he rolled about and I was booked by the Mexican referee, Arturo Carter.

We knew what to expect from them after the way they had over-reacted to David Beckham's tackle for England against Diego Simeone earlier in the tournament. Of course contact was made by Beckham but there was no need for Simeone to roll about.

So I was on a booking and knew I had to be very careful. One mistimed challenge and the opposition players were going to make a meal of it. I put it out of my mind and felt I was playing well. I was finding space in the second half and overlapping to good effect. I was putting my heart and soul into this game, every ounce of energy I had. Then I got cramp in my left calf. I was on the other side of the park from the technical area and was waving over to the bench for assistance. The technical area thought I was waving over because I needed a new pair of boots and hadn't realised the agony I was in. Our kit man offered me a different pair of boots but I was short with him, saying, 'No, no, tell Hiddink I have cramp.' It was 1–1 at the time. Bolo Zenden warmed up at the side and was standing on the touchline, ready to come on for me. Unfortunately for me, we just couldn't get him on quickly enough.

We were attacking but lost possession. The ball was in the middle of the park and I was sprinting to get there. Simeone nipped in ahead of me and I caught him. I kicked him three metres in the air and knew I was going to be sent off. Simeone rolled around as if he'd been hit by a sniper. I approached the ref to make a case for myself but there was no way I was not going to see the red card waved in my face. And it was.

For a few seconds I felt like the loneliest guy in the world. It seemed like an eternity as I trudged off the pitch. I kept thinking, 'Why me, why me?' and I just wanted to wind the clock back. It was terrible. I kicked the water bottles over at the side of the pitch. I wasn't allowed to go to the bench and had to head straight to the dressing room.

I sat there and prayed we wouldn't lose the match. The main reason was that I wanted to see us go through and to deprive the cheating Argentinians of progressing. The other was purely for selfish reasons, as I was worried I would be made the scapegoat if we lost. Beckham was absolutely slaughtered by the English media and fans for his sending off and I feared the same when I got back to Holland. Beckham was shown no mercy and I thought that might happen to me because I was sent off, leaving the team with a mountain to climb.

I watched the last fifteen minutes of the game in a security guards' room.

Soon afterwards, Ortega was sent off for head-butting Edwin van der Sar. It was a big relief to see the game now evenly balanced at ten against ten. Then we scored a beautiful goal with only a minute left. A goal that typifies everything football should be about. It was a work of art.

Frank de Boer hit a fifty-yard ball upfield towards Dennis Bergkamp. Dennis brought it down with the inside of his right foot and then just put it into the net with the greatest of ease. Few, if any, players would be capable of producing such a piece of sublime individual brilliance in the last minute of a game of that importance. It was a great moment to be a footballer, a great moment to be Dutch, although I think every football fan all over the world would have stood up to applaud that goal. I sprinted out of the room and headed up the tunnel to get to hug Frank de Boer. But I wasn't allowed to.

We won the game and there was a great feeling afterwards. It was also a great relief for me because, apart from the media, I knew that if any player wanted to blame someone in the dressing room for losing to Argentina, I would have been the number-one target.

I was suspended for the semi-final game against Brazil. Winston Bogarde was to step in and take my place but he broke down in training the next day. It meant we had lost three left-sided players – myself, Overmars and Bogarde – in the space of twenty-four hours. Cocu played left-back and we all knew he would be comfortable there even though it wasn't his best position. I was looking forward to the game but it's not the same when you are not directly involved with events on the pitch. There was nothing I could do to influence the outcome of the game. I just had to hope we won to give me a chance of playing in the World Cup final.

Brazil were favourites to lift the trophy and rightly so. But we knew we could get at them. Hiddink had us believing we were going to win this game.

The match found us back at the Vélodrome again and we went a goal down. Ronaldo, my former team-mate at PSV, scored it. But we fought back and got the equaliser through Kluivert with only three minutes left. The game went to a penalty shoot-out and there was a look of 'Oh no, here we go again'.

We have a terrible record at sudden-death situations. We lost to Denmark in the semi-finals of Euro 92 when Marco van Basten missed a penalty. We lost in Euro 96 to France when Seedorf crashed his over the crossbar. We lost in Euro 2000 to Italy when Frank de Boer and Kluivert missed penalties during the ninety minutes and we missed another three in the shoot-out.

So we faced yet another traumatic fifteen-minute spell as we awaited the outcome of this latest test. Players will always volunteer to take kicks and it is a horrible situation to be put in. The guy who misses will always be remembered; the keeper can be the hero.

Well, this time, it was the turn of Ronald de Boer to miss. He took a careless penalty and his brother Frank absolutely slaughtered him, right on the pitch in front of everyone, as we went out 4–2 in the cruellest of circumstances. The Dutch have a reputation of telling the truth to one another. But these two? My goodness, they're on a different planet when it comes to letting each other know exactly where they stand. They go right in where it hurts and to hell with the consequences or the other person's feelings.

So our tournament was over, a golden opportunity gone. Brazil were through to the final and we had to stay on for the third-place play-off against Croatia. This was a game none of us wanted to play in. We wanted to pack our bags, get out of France and go home to family and friends. There was just an empty feeling and the thought of waiting four more days to play a game certainly wasn't hitting the spot.

After the Brazil match we went back to the hotel, had a few drinks and talked about what had happened out on the pitch. As usual, the conversation was full of ifs, buts and maybes. In the build-up to the Croatia game, the training was relaxed. Really, we were going through the motions. On the day of the game, however, we thought that we'd be as well going home with a medal for finishing third than with nothing.

I was in the line-up and wanted to play. Some other guys in the team were deflated and down after missing out on the final because they had come to France determined to win the World Cup. In the end we lost 2–1. As I watched the Croatia players with the medals around their necks, they were very proud. They were happy and ready for a celebration. We had messed up. We should have put more into the game and left France with something to show for our hard work over the period of five weeks or so.

The only thing I did leave France with was a few extra tops for my collection. My favourite jersey of all is from the 1994 World Cup finals in the USA. I got Romário's top from that tournament when we met Brazil in the quarter-final in Dallas. I was in the Dutch squad but didn't play in this one.

We were team-mates at PSV and I asked their kit man if I could go into the Brazil dressing room. While guys like Jan Wouters and Ronald Koeman were distraught with their head in their hands after defeat, all I wanted was Romário's jersey. When I entered their dressing room Romário, who is normally very reserved, was dancing around the dressing room with Bebeto, celebrating their victory. I approached him and the Brazil players must have been looking at me saying, 'What the f*** is he doing in here?' Romário broke off his celebrations, came over and asked me in Dutch, 'Hey boy, how are you doing?' We chatted for a couple of minutes and he gave me his jersey.

I was so proud of this, so happy. I was acting like a little schoolboy. I asked him if he wanted mine but he just looked at me and smiled. With his unmistakable lisp, he said, 'Arthur, it's fine. You keep it. Give it to one of your friends or to a charity organisation for fundraising.' He was laughing a little as he said it. But it was in a nice way, not in a way that was intended to belittle me. We both knew exactly what he meant.

From the party in the Brazil dressing room, I headed back to the quiet of the Holland dressing room. But I had my jersey. It meant so much to me because Romário had played a big part in getting me to PSV from Twente Enschede. We played against PSV and he was impressed with me. He said in a magazine interview that PSV should sign the impressive left-footed player, Arthur Numan. At that time he was influential at the club. When Romário spoke, people took notice. I'm glad they did.

The 1994 and 1998 World Cups were to be my only ones. I was fortunate to be involved in two such glamorous and memorable occasions.

When we got back to Amsterdam airport after our involvement in France 98 ended, we were well received by the Dutch people. We felt we could have gone all the way to the final and this was a wasted opportunity for such a talented squad. However, that chapter of my career was over and now a new one was ready to begin – playing for Glasgow Rangers.

3

BATTLING BROTHERS

Maybe my motto when I was growing in Beverwijk should have been 'I see dead people'. Every day I'd walk past them on my way to school. No, I'm not psychic and I wasn't like the wee boy Cole in *Sixth Sense*; it's just that the house I grew up in overlooked a graveyard.

It didn't particularly bother me that our small, two-bedroomed flat stood beside a cemetery because, overall, I had a really happy upbringing. I say overall because the one aspect that was sometimes annoying for me – and my parents – was the constant fights and rammies I had with my wee brother, Jeroen.

We were a close family and still are. My dad, Hans, is a bookkeeper and my mum, Marjan, stayed at home to look after the kids. Our apartment had a tiny kitchen, a compact living room and two bedrooms. I shared a room with Jeroen and we slept on bunk beds – I was on top and my brother below. There wasn't much space and I suppose that was part of the reason why we always fought. Some of the fights were ferocious – you would have thought we were real enemies – and I used to feel like Inspector Jacques Clouseau when I got home wondering when my brother (aka Cato) would pounce on me!

I was born on 14 December 1969 in Heemskerk Hospital and grew up in Beverwijk, a village about twenty minutes from Amsterdam. From a young age, all I wanted to do was play football. We lived in a quiet street and there were loads of kids around to play with. We'd play football on the pavements or down at the playground of my primary school, which was just a thirty-second walk from our house. We also liked to dress up and play cowboys and Indians in the street.

It was a dream for any kid – fall out of bed and walk straight into the school playground! Thankfully there was no need to get up hours before class, no running to catch a bus to take us to school.

Things changed a little when I was six, not long after my grandfather died. My grandmother was alone and someone tried to break into her house. The experience really unsettled her and she didn't feel at ease in her own house, so we decided to swap homes with her. Gran had a nice, spacious house with three bedrooms and a back garden. It was better for her to be in an apartment-type environment and we had more space to live in, so the arrangement was perfect for all of us. I now had my own bedroom, but that didn't stop Jeroen and me from fighting.

Every day, though, I popped into my grandmother's on my way to school to bring her the morning paper and she used to send me away with chocolate bars and crisps. It was great! I continued to play football and my first club was Beverwijk; although most of the kids played for DEM, I was happy at my local team. My dad and uncles played for them and it was natural to follow in their bootsteps. I was about eight at the time and remember being more into playing football than supporting any particular team. I had an affinity for AZ Alkmaar but rarely went to see them. Like most kids around the mid 1970s who were into football, I adored our greatest player, Johan Cruijff, and I remember I had a scarf of his on my bedroom wall.

Beverwijk trained for an hour on a Wednesday afternoon but for the rest of the week I was 'training' on my own as a ball was never far from my feet. We were in school from 8.45 in the morning until 12.15, then I'd go back home for a lunch prepared by my mum. We couldn't eat our lunch quickly enough to get back to the playground for more football, before we started the afternoon session.

My dad was my biggest influence as a youngster and throughout my career. He put a lot of time and energy into developing my game and moulding my career. He was into sport and I remember the weekends I spent with him and my brother were brilliant. My love of football and my burgeoning talent were in the genes as my dad was also a player, a left-winger, but he sadly broke his leg in his twenties and was never the same after his injury. He was renowned for his speed and his nickname was 'The Hare'. Maybe his injury, and the fact his career was curtailed, helped my dad to get the best out of me.

I couldn't wait for a Saturday morning when the games came around and I had my boots polished and my bag packed on a Friday night. I could hardly get to sleep, I was so excited.

I remember my first pair of black Rucanor boots were at least one size too big for me so they'd last me a while – although I could almost use them as skis, they were so large! I had to wear a pair of thick, knitted, woolly socks under my normal socks so the boots fitted me better and I'd get at least a couple of years out of them. I was really proud of my first football outfit and used to strut around the house, in front of the mirror, thinking I was the top man.

In Holland, 5 December is a favourite day for kids because we celebrate Sinterklaas. The children's story goes like this . . . Sinterklaas sails from Spain and when he arrives his horse is waiting for him on the shore to go round the houses and deliver the gifts and put them beside an open shoe which kids have left in front of the fire.

Sinterklaas is a special time in Holland but not quite on the same scale as Christmas is celebrated in Scotland. We don't really have the culture where every workplace goes out for a Christmas night out! I reckon it just might be an excuse for people to get drunk. Not that I'd ever complain about that – indeed it's one Scottish tradition I've gladly embraced since I arrived on these shores!

On a Sunday morning we'd get up quite early and my dad, Jeroen and I would go to the forest for a run and, of course, we'd play some football. My dad relished spending time like that with his sons and in the afternoon my mum would join us and we'd go to watch the Beverwijk first team play. On the way home we'd enjoy a Chinese carry-out and this was my favourite meal of the week – chicken satay with rice. We had to be back in the house by seven o'clock so we could settle down to eat then watch the football highlights programme on television.

When I watched the games on telly on a Sunday night I knew I wanted to be a footballer. There was a determination inside me and I set myself the goal of one day starring on that TV myself!

But I was up against it as I was small for my age and very slightly built. In an attempt to build myself up, I joined a judo class when I was about twelve or thirteen. I was determined to get stronger and speed up my movement. I enjoyed the judo and managed to reach brown belt and as the weeks wore on I began to feel stronger. As well as the martial arts, I also started skipping to strengthen my legs and improve my footwork and co-ordination.

My mum also used to feed me porridge to build me up but I must admit I wasn't a huge fan. I was growing. However, when I was about sixteen I had a problem with my right nipple. Fluid was seeping out of it and I had no idea what the problem was and thought it may have something to do with the friction from my judo outfit. I was afraid it was serious and when something like that happens my natural instinct is simply to pretend it's not happening and hope it will go away. I know that may sound childish and naïve but I don't like facing up to something and knowing what the potential dangers are.

Eventually, though, even I knew I'd have to confront this problem and I showed it to my mum and she almost slapped me. 'Why did you wait so long to tell me?' she screamed. I went to the doctor and after he had a look I was admitted to hospital the next day. They diagnosed some kind of small cyst below my nipple and they decided to remove the cyst and the nipple rather than risk any more problems in the future.

Apart from niggly football injuries, that was the only serious health problem I'd experienced in my life. But that relatively clean bill of health was suddenly shattered in February 2005, when I had a serious scare because I genuinely feared I had testicular cancer.

I'd noticed a bit of swelling in my groin and my muscles were sore in that area but I thought nothing much of it; maybe I was reverting to type and simply hoping it would go away. I'd first noticed the swelling just before Christmas and I phoned Dr Ian McGuinness at Rangers to see if he could have a look. He's a good mate of mine and someone I knew I could turn to in a time of crisis. I hoped a couple of anti-inflammatory pills would sort it.

Sadly I couldn't meet Doc McGuinness, as he had gone to hospital to check on an injured player and I had to return to Holland to sort out some business. In many ways I was secretly pleased the appointment was cancelled, as it helped shut out the problem, helped me pretend there was nothing wrong with me. And if there was an issue this would simply delay me hearing the truth. I stupidly kid myself into thinking that if you ignore a dilemma it will disappear and everything will be fine.

But the problem wasn't disappearing and the pain started to intensify during January. I told Marjon about it and she urged me to get it checked. So I phoned the Doc again and went to see him at Murray Park. He checked my groin area and told me I had a swelling in my testicle and recommended we go straight to hospital for a scan. He tried to reassure me it didn't look cancerous but that didn't allay my growing fears.

He drove me to hospital and I must have lost three of four kilos of sweat during that journey. The sweat was lashing out of my body. He was angry with me for cancelling our appointment before Christmas and he apologised for not being available earlier.

I was examined and the hospital specialist confirmed there was a lump on my testicle. At that point, all sorts of scenarios were going through my head. But the over-riding feeling was fear. Health is the most important thing in life and I genuinely feared the worst. For some reason, and I can't quite work out why, I've always had a worry most of my life that I'd be struck down by a serious illness at some point. It's something I've had gnawing away at the back of mind for years and I've never been able to shake it off. Now, maybe I'd come to the point in my life where I was about to confront my greatest fear.

An appointment was made to see the specialist a couple of days later and I was sick with worry. Some people might ignorantly believe that because you've been a football player 'bad things' don't happen. But that's stupid, we're ordinary people who are just as susceptible to illness and bad health as anyone else.

Ex-Celtic player Alan Stubbs had testicular cancer and I was thinking about his predicament and how he coped with his illness during those traumatic few days. Also a guy I used to coach with in Holland when I was younger died from cancer when he was twenty-eight. He had so much to live for and it made me realise life can be so cruel and fragile.

I successfully came through the operation to remove the lump and was assured there were no complications and the infection wasn't malignant. It was exactly what I was hoping to hear. I was knocked out for the operation and once the anaesthetic started to wear off I started singing and entertaining the nurses.

I was reluctant to tell my parents because I didn't want to worry them unnecessarily but I eventually broke the news to them and their initial reaction was sheer relief when I told them everything was fine. I have had a motto throughout my life that 'your health is your wealth' and it certainly struck home more than ever during that period.

Jeroen found out about my health scare just before an Old Firm game, as he was meant to come over the following weekend and I phoned him to cancel. He wasn't happy and I was reluctant to tell him the real reason, but he kept going on about it so he fully understood when I told him why.

Jeroen has been a big part of my life and, although we fought like cat and dog until I was about sixteen, we calmed down after that and we learned to deal with each other like two grown-ups! Whether it was football or a game of Ludo, I've always been competitive and hate losing. Even though Jeroen was a couple of years younger, I never let him win at anything. He was also a decent footballer but found it frustrating that he could rarely get past me. It used to put him off playing with me and I had to bribe him or offer him an incentive to play. If we had a kick-around in the back garden we'd use the garage as the goal and I would tell Jeroen I'd give him a sweet for every save he made.

On a Sunday morning we would be up about 6.30 and used to play football in the living room with a tennis ball. We would get carried away and get too competitive and inevitably it would turn into another battle between the Numan brothers. Not a great start to a quiet Sunday morning for my parents and they'd start banging on the floor, shouting at us to keep quiet as they tried to grab a couple of extra hours' kip at the weekend. Sometimes it would get too much for our parents and when we heard the footsteps coming downstairs we knew we had to take cover!

One day the arguing between me and Jeroen got out of hand. It was bedlam, like an explosion had happened, so my dad took us upstairs and handed us a boxing glove each. He threw us in the bedroom, closed the door and told us to sort it out once and for all. Even then, despite my father's harsh words, my competitive instincts came to the fore and I made sure I got the right-handed glove because that was the stronger of the two. Too strong in hindsight, as I walloped Jeroen in the face and burst his lip open!

Another time, we were in the house on our own and Jeroen was chasing me around the living room after another of our arguments. I ran out of the house, he locked the door and I was stuck in the back garden. It started to pour with rain but Jeroen was teasing me from behind the door and refused to let me in, so I took a broom from the garden and told him he had to let me in or else I'd put it through the window. Jeroen called my bluff and then started to cry when the broom smashed through the door. He was hysterical. We made up a story to our parents that we were playing football in the garden and the ball smashed the window.

Looking back, we were really hard work for our parents as we couldn't sit still for five seconds. We were hyperactive and a complete pain in the ass to them much of the time. But I suppose they wouldn't have changed a minute of it!

Thankfully Jeroen has now calmed down and is doing well in his job as a broker in the Amsterdam Exchange Market, although it was a long and varied road before he got there as he'd been a jack of all trades. He sold bikes, cutlery, watches, pots and pans. But his pride and joy was his carpet business. Then, after he became a stockbroker, he turned the carpet showroom into a bar.

Our behaviour was especially tough on my mum because she looked after us all the time – my parents thought it was a better option than having a child-minder. My dad left the company he worked for to set up his own business doing accountancy work on a freelance basis and he converted our garden shed into a nice office. It meant his hours were quite flexible, which was good for me with my football as he sometimes took me to games involving the under-16s.

My dad would often get involved in the arguments between Jeroen and me, whereas my mum would act as the peacemaker.

She is also a sporty person and still keeps herself fit by going to the gym and doing a bit of light jogging. My mum has such a lovely nature, it's impossible to argue with her or not like her. She is a loving person and most people lucky enough to meet her find her charming. I reckon the only time I felt hostility towards her was when Jeroen and I were sent to summer camp for two weeks.

It was from Monday to Friday and lasted from nine in the morning until five in the evening. I hated it and didn't want to go and I remember being on the bus for the camp and not looking her in the eye. I was shouting and crying, trying to make her feel bad for packing us off there. To be honest, we were sent to summer camp to give her a break during the school holidays. Having me and Jeroen about the house full-time for five or six weeks was more than any person could stand.

I preferred going to the beach during the holidays; there is a lovely one at Beverwijk which is always busy during the summer. When the weather is good it's like being in Spain or Portugal, the sandy beach packed with people enjoying the sunshine or sitting in a bar or café overlooking the sea. Absolutely beautiful. Outsiders don't normally associate Holland with having a beach culture but I'm positive any person who came to visit would enjoy it and want to come back. I have great memories of going there when I was a kid to play with my cousin Nancy and friends. I still go there when I'm back in Beverwijk and I'll jump on the bike with my elder daughter Britt in front, since it's just a fifteen-minute cycle away.

Overall, I can't complain about any aspect of my childhood. It was full of love and full of fun. Oh, and the odd fight here and there!

4

THE FUTURE'S BRIGHT . . .

'I like you as a football player. You have ability and you have potential. But to get to the top level you need to stand out more. You need to demand the ball more and stop being shy. Players with big mouths that couldn't lace your boots will get noticed before you because they are loud on the pitch. You need to become more domineering. If you do, you will go all the way.'

These words were said to me by Wim van Hanegem – a fantastic footballer in his day with Feyenoord. A legend in Holland. He's been there, seen it and done it. He was assistant manager to Dick Advocaat during his second stint in charge of the national team when they qualified for the 2004 European Championships in Portugal.

Van Hanegem was given his own television programme in Holland and his show was all about identifying promising footballers, trailing their play over a few weeks and then interviewing them. I was nineteen, playing for FC Haarlem and chosen to be one of van Hanegen's 'subjects'. Face to face, he gave me that assessment and it was an honest appraisal. Plenty of compliments but plenty of concerns. He was afraid I would waste my potential and his assessment was totally accurate.

I was approached to see if I'd like to be a part of one of his shows and I agreed. I met him after one of my games with Haarlem and greeted him by saying, 'Hello Mr van Hanegem.' He started to laugh, 'Call me Wim.'

I replied, 'OK, it's just that I was taught by my parents to show respect towards my elders.'

He seemed a nice guy and for some bizarre reason we went to a small zoo to do the interview. It went really well apart from when one of the goats started to chew at my leather jacket and I had to tug it to get away! Overall, my introduction to van Hanegem came at a perfect time.

When you meet someone like him you listen and take his points on board. It worked, because my game definitely improved after meeting him. It was a pivotal moment in my career but the person I have to thank more than most for moulding my career is my dad. My father was my biggest influence but also my harshest critic. I remember getting into his car after youth games, feeling quite pleased with my performance; my dad, however, would analyse my display then give his honest verdict – good or bad. If something needed to be said, he never shirked from saying it. It might not necessarily have been what I wanted to hear but he said it with my best interests at heart.

One of the many things he told me that I have never forgotten was, 'If you want to be better than the rest you have to do more.'

Dad watched my career develop with interest and pride. I attracted the attention of FC Haarlem when I was thirteen and playing for Beverwijk. Their scout, Henk van Dorp, was impressed and asked me to join them but my dad thought it would be better for me to stay put and if they really wanted me they would come the following season. Thankfully, they did make me a second offer and this time there was no holding me back. Haarlem made a very good impression on me. The first-team coach, Hans van Doorneveld, came to my house and persuaded me to move. Beverwijk were unhappy with my decision but I think they may have been a little jealous because I was bettering myself.

My dad was pleased but told me I would have to travel on my own to training, which was three times a week. I think it was his way of making me more independent and trying to get me to stand on my own two feet. Fortunately another player from Beverwijk, Edwin Blomvliet, had also joined and his dad was able to take us to training a lot of the time. It took twenty minutes by car to get there but sometimes we had to take the bus and that doubled the journey time.

The standard at Haarlem was at a higher level than I was used to. Training sessions were competitive and I enjoyed working with the better players and the coach, Gerard Garrelts.

When I turned sixteen my life became busier and more complicated. I left Mavo secondary school to start at the PE college, CIOS. I wanted to be a footballer but also had to be sensible and have another career ready to pursue if my number one ambition didn't materialise. There was high demand to get into CIOS and places were limited, so I had to sit tests on various sports such as gymnastics, judo, tennis, swimming, basketball and football. Thankfully I was accepted, although I was one of the youngest in the class, with some of my classmates aged twenty-six or twenty-seven.

I now had to get up at six o'clock. to be on the bus to college in Overveen for the ninety-minute journey to make sure I was there on time for the eight o'clock start. My classmates were a big help to me as they could see I was sometimes quite nervous when, for example, I had to give solo presentations in front of twenty-five classmates and the lecturer. I was shaking when I made my debut presentation but my classmates were there for me and helped calm my nerves. They made every effort to help me settle and give me a bit of guidance.

One friend in particular was a source of comfort and help. His name was Ruud Man and we became great pals at college and still are to this day. I knew Ruud from the football, as he played for Haarlem's under-21 reserves. He lived near me so we would travel together every day to college. We quickly developed a close friendship and this helped us motivate each other to do well. Ruud joined the college the year before me, although unfortunately he had to repeat the first year. But that was a blessing in disguise for me because it meant I had a companion for the long journey into college.

Days at college were hectic. We began in the pool, followed by a couple of hours in the gym, then four hours of theory in the classroom followed by two hours of judo.

Once a week, as part of the course, we'd take dance and movement classes. Our teacher was female and the boys were forced to wear tight blue leggings and white ballet shoes and dance around in front of a mirror to music like Madonna. The only thing missing from the outfits was a tutu! We were prancing around this hall like big elephants and the tight leggings didn't leave a lot to the imagination – especially if you weren't wearing any underwear. The only consolation for the lads would be if they were dancing or exercising behind a pretty girl!

Gymnastics was also fraught with worry for some of the guys, especially with the exercises on the ring. You'd be hanging up there, holding on for dear life, then told to dismount; but some of the boys were dead scared to do a somersault before they landed and they'd be frozen rigid, unable to move.

When we finished college at four o'clock, I'd go off to training with Haarlem and I wouldn't be back in the house until ten o'clock. My mum would always have my dinner ready, then I'd crash out and *Groundhog Day* would start again the next morning.

I was lucky to be in the top sports class at college and we had some great individual talents studying there. We had the world karate champion and a female Dutch international volleyball player. If I or any of the others had to attend a sporting event, the college was very accommodating at giving us time off.

But there was no leeway given when it came to passing exams. The tests were in December and May but the studying had to start in August. Some students, thinking there was plenty of time, neglected their studies and would cram at the last minute. To pass the exams you had to be disciplined and not squeeze everything into the last few weeks. We had to learn about body parts, the joints and the muscles and some of the terms were in Latin. We also had to do massage as part of the course but my biggest weakness was swimming. I hated swimming and it came as no surprise I failed that part of the exam.

My course was three years of hard work and studying but, despite the graft and the hours and hours of having my nose in a book, I really enjoyed it.

Football was still my first love, though, and I looked forward to my game with Haarlem on a Saturday. But when I got home that night I had no energy left because I was knackered. I'd collapse on the couch and watch some television. Saturday night and I was lying zonked on the couch, while other boys my age were out partying and enjoying their teenage years. I had no social life – my life was dedicated to college and football. During my second and third years at college I made football my priority subject and received my coaching badges to enable me to train youth teams and be an assistant coach at any level of football in Holland. I was one of the youngest ever coaches to qualify.

College was going well in combination with the football but I felt I was not as physically strong as I'd like to be. Henny de Reght, the Haarlem under-18 coach, convinced me that I was good enough – and strong enough – to move up a level and play for his team. It was good advice as I quickly made some decent progress, coping comfortably with the step up. During one of the selection games for the under-18s my dad overheard a conversation between two scouts about me. They said I was a good player but was too small to reach the top of the game. Basically, they'd written me off and reckoned I'd never make it.

I was about 20 cm smaller than the average height for my age, but I didn't let the criticisms get me down and I worked away at my game. Eventually, I received a call-up in 1987 to the Dutch under-18 team where we played a tournament in Scotland involving the hosts plus Italy and Belgium. All the matches were played at Rugby Park, Kilmarnock. Later in the year we also played in a tournament in Portugal and won it after beating teams like Spain.

One of our first games for qualifying for the European Championships was in Albania, along with Hungary and Bulgaria. Former Celtic player Rudi Vata played for the Albanians and what I remember most about that trip was the poverty and destitution in Albania – it was quite an experience to witness that kind of Spartan communist existence at first hand. There were soldiers everywhere and the standard of facilities in the country looked more like the 1930s rather than 1980s. It showed the gaping gulf in the standard of living between Eastern and Western Europe.

At Haarlem we hosted an under-21 tournament involving PSV, Nottingham Forest and Sporting Lisbon. We reached the final but lost on penalties to Forest after I ballooned my spot-kick out of the stadium! It would not be the last time I'd endure the misery of penalties in my career! Roy Keane scored the winning penalty for Forest but there was some consolation for me as I was voted the Most Valuable Player of the event.

My dad was still a major motivation in my career and part of his advice was always to be one step ahead of my opponent, never stand still and know my next move before I've received the ball. He and my mum enjoyed coming to see me play at this stage of my career and I always knew he was there for me – watching my every move, good or bad. He would always find a spot to stand on the touchline. Then, when I started my warm-up, he'd give me his trademark whistle so I knew where he was.

I don't know if it was because he wanted to find the perfect spot to watch the games from, but he always insisted on leaving for all my matches HOURS earlier than we should have. Any time I moaned about it he'd always say, 'It's better to be early than to be late' and I knew he was right. We'd sometimes arrive at grounds FOUR hours before kick-off. We'd find the ground, park the car, then go to a café for a game of pool and a drink of juice to kill the time before kick-off.

During my second season at under-18 level there were no doubts that I had an excellent chance of making the top grade. To protect their own interests, Haarlem gave me a contract and paid me £2,500 per year. It meant if any team wanted to buy me they had to pay at least ten times my wages as compensation.

I made my professional debut for Haarlem first team in March 1988, when they sold Wim Balm to Twente and I took his place. Funnily enough, when Balm left Twente I also went there as his replacement! At Haarlem I came on for the last twenty minutes and I don't mind admitting I was terrible, probably because I tried too hard, put too much pressure on myself. My next game was away at PSV and I was more relaxed. Advocaat told to me to imagine I was playing for the under-18 side and just be as calm as possible when in possession.

I was still at college in my third year but the schedule wasn't as hectic and Monday was my most important day as that's when I was receiving my coaching badge classes. Part of that process was to shadow Gerard van der Lem – the under-21s trainer – for a year but he was great to me and allowed me to have a night off in the winter to give me some rest for the game on the Saturday. I was training in the afternoons, had a shower, then was straight back out again. The schedule allowed me to train with Haarlem at 3.45 in the afternoon as we were part-time but trying to survive in the Premier League.

I graduated at the end of my third year and having my results behind me gave me the security of knowing I had something to fall back on but I desperately wanted to be a footballer and move to a full-time club. I had to join the army when I was nineteen, as back then it was compulsory, although there's no conscription nowadays in Holland. I wasn't keen to go. I felt it might jeopardise my football career just as it was starting to take off.

I was based full-time in Den Bosch for two months and Haarlem agreed I could train with the under-21s from the town's team.

I found the army tough going. The running, the marching, the shooting practice, the discipline, the attention to detail and the insistence on a tidy room. I was given a rifle and it was a bizarre feeling having to hold it, load it then fire it. One of our exercises involved going to a mock gas chamber and as soon as it was filled with gas, putting your mask on and getting out. It was an ordeal. Some privates couldn't get the mask on quickly enough and were vomiting when they managed to escape. One guy, I recall, waited deliberately until the sergeant was in front of him and was sick over his boots.

The army instilled certain qualities and behavioural patterns in me and one thing I definitely took from it was being organised. I think that's why, to this day, I hate a disorganised house! I detest mess but I don't have to worry about it round my house as Marjon always keeps the place spick and span, even with two young kids to look after.

The chairman of Haarlem, Henk Hut, had a contact in the army and he arranged for me to be moved from Den Bosch and based in Haarlem barracks. But the drawback was this – the only way I'd be guaranteed a place in Haarlem was if I became a waiter to the army staff.

I could have become a sports instructor because of my qualifications as a PE teacher but that would not have guaranteed me a place in Haarlem – and I could have ended up elsewhere in the country. Moving away from Haarlem could have jeopardised my playing career. I could have been sent to Germany or somewhere as far as that so it was really decent of the chairman to arrange my place in Haarlem.

Being a waiter meant an early start, in the dining room for 6.30 a.m. to make sure the tables were set, the cutlery was sparkling and the breakfast was ready. After breakfast, I'd work until lunchtime and leave at 2.30 to be at training four days a week. I stayed in the Haarlem base for about a year and my fourteen-month stint in the army seemed to fly along.

My football career was going well and I was given a three-year professional contract by Haarlem. It took a while to negotiate as Joop, my agent, insisted there was a clause inserted allowing me to leave for a maximum transfer fee of £225,000. FC Utrecht and Willem II were interested in me and I had agreed personal terms with both but they couldn't afford the fee. They offered around £150,000 plus one of their players, but Haarlem wanted straight cash. I also heard later on that Leo Beenhakker was interested in taking me to Ajax but they had financial problems at that time and couldn't afford the fee either.

Only a couple of months after pledging my future to Haarlem, following Advocaat's advice, I couldn't believe it when the manager resigned. The next year we were relegated to the first division and I thought my career was also on a downward spiral. But dropping down a league helped my development. It toughened me up, improved my battling qualities, and Twente must have noticed because they came in for me. The manager, Theo Vonk, called me at home to see if I would join them and asked about the get-out clause in my contract. He told me he was going to make a move for me and assured me he would get to work on it. I presumed any move would happen at the end of the season but a couple of days later I met Twente officials and the deal was agreed.

Twente paid the £225,000 and I signed for them on 14 December 1990 – my twenty-first birthday. It was the highest fee paid by a Premier League club to sign a player from the first division.

5

PERFECT MATCH

I've been lucky to enjoy the privileges of having a successful football career. But despite the security and wealth the game has given me throughout my adult life, they pale into nothing compared to the joy and happiness my family has given me. I have a wonderful partner, Marjon, and together we have two beautiful daughters, Britt and Maud.

Marjon has been an important part of my life since I was twenty-one and has been by my side throughout my career – through the good and bad times. She was brought up in a small town called Heemskerk, close to Beverwijk. We started dating in the summer of 1991 – I had bumped into her a few times before that, but there was never anything more than a polite 'hello' exchanged between us.

Marjon loved sport and was a fine athlete who enjoyed high jump and hurdles and she used to train at the athletics track in Beverwijk, only a few hundred metres from my parents' home. Her elder sister, Mieke, was a former Dutch champion at the long jump and sometimes, if there was a good meeting on at the track, I would walk round to catch it. Her younger brother, Joost, played football and was in the same age group as my brother Jeroen, so we used to bump into each other watching their games. It was at one of those matches that I first met Marjon properly. I was about sixteen or seventeen and I immediately thought, 'Oh yes, who is that?'

She has beautiful features and a lovely smile and she was also well-mannered and friendly, both qualities I like. I fancied her but how could I tell her how I felt about her? When it came to girls I was really shy and used to crumble in front of them and lose my power of coherent speech. On the rare occasion I went out I remember going home on a Saturday night and kicking myself for not approaching a girl I might have fancied in the disco. I didn't start to drink alcohol until I was twenty-one, so I never even had the benefit of a few beers to pluck up some 'Dutch courage'. It usually took me an hour to ask a girl a question as I was afraid of rejection. Thankfully, Marjon never gave me the old custard pie and I remember the day we first started to fall for each other.

I was on my summer break in 1990 and spent a day down at the Wijk Aan Zee beach. I was on my own, enjoying the nice weather, topping up my tan. I could see Marjon in the distance and was delighted, but taken aback, when she came over and asked if she could sit beside me.

Not wanting to refuse the company of a beautiful girl, I told her it was no problem and, for once, I wasn't too nervous in a girl's company and we spent some time chatting together. Some of the local guys came over to speak to me about the football, to ask how things were going, and that interrupted the flow I had with Marjon. Marjon doesn't like football and couldn't get into the conversation with the guys. After a while she got up and told me she was away to join some boys from her neighbourhood who had just arrived at the beach. I was jealous and I remember admitting this to her when our relationship developed; but she explained she just felt totally out of any conversations about football.

It wasn't until the following summer that we chatted again. Funnily enough, it was at the beach again and she told me she was going out with some friends that night. I wasn't sure what my plans were, so I didn't commit myself to anything. I ended up going out with Michel Doesburg and another friend and our plan was to drive into Amsterdam to spend the evening there, but one of the boys had to get up early for work the following morning and didn't want to venture too far. So we went to a local disco – and Marjon was there sitting with a guy, but smiling over at me.

After about half an hour she came over and we spent the rest of the night chatting. Marjon asked why I didn't come over to speak to her when we first spotted each other and I explained I didn't want to come across as being too forward. And anyway, the guy she was with was quite a big lad. I didn't fancy my chances!

We were inseparable for the rest of the evening and I asked Marjon if I could walk her home. Well, help her ride her bike home! I had my car but asked one of my friends to take it and I took the bike. It was almost a forty-five-minute journey, but that was fine because it meant Marjon held her hands around my waist tightly for nearly an hour! She invited me into the house for a drink and we spent an hour on the couch chatting in her parents' living room. When I was leaving, I asked if I could take her bike to get back home but it was really just an excuse to come back the next day to see her again. I plucked up the courage to ask her for a kiss as I left and I think a planted a beauty on her MOUTH!

I went back round the next day and was introduced to her mum. It turned out she knew my mum, which helped break the ice and made me feel a little more settled. I had a coffee and told them I was heading to the beach for the day but I didn't have the courage to ask her to join me. Thankfully, Marjon took the initiative and asked if she could come with me. From there it progressed pretty quickly and soon Marjon became my first fully fledged girlfriend.

Marjon came to my parents' house for dinner on a few occasions and at times must have wondered what she had let herself in for, as my dad and brother are very loud. I knew it would be a bit of a culture shock for her because her own family are tame and quiet by comparison. Marjon would be polite and say she was full up and didn't want anything, but my dad would wind her up and say, 'It's OK. If you don't like my wife's cooking, you just have to say!'

The following week I had to leave to go back to Enschede for pre-season training. It wasn't ideal because I wanted the relationship with Marjon to develop.

Enschede was two hours away but we used to keep in touch by phone and the lines between us must have been buzzing because we were constantly chatting on the phone. Marjon agreed to come and visit me in Enschede but the flat I had bought wasn't ready yet as the furniture had still to arrive. Honest! So I booked a hotel for Marjon's arrival and told her I had reserved two rooms and that it was her decision if she wanted me to share so I could keep her company. Of course, I had only booked one room. My shyness must have disappeared a little bit . . .

That was three weeks after we met and for the two days she was there I couldn't finish training quickly enough!

Three months after we met I asked Marjon to move to Enschede so we could be together, have a proper relationship. It was something I wanted as I felt very close to her, comfortable in her company, and had tremendous feelings for her. From there we moved to Eindhoven after my transfer to PSV in the summer of 1992 and Marjon had no problems uprooting. It was something we spoke about and she realised that being a footballer's partner would inevitably mean never being settled in one place for too long. She understood and accepted it and said she would always follow me.

However, when the time came for us to move to Scotland, Marjon had serious doubts and it looked as though she wasn't going to make the journey with me. For a scary few days I thought moving to Rangers was going to cause the break-up of our relationship.

It all started when we came back from holiday in France and went to Eindhoven to pick up our clothes and belongings from our apartment. It was a Saturday and I was going to Glasgow on the Monday morning to prepare for the second leg of the UEFA Cup tie against Shelbourne, which would be my competitive debut for Rangers. Marjon was due to fly over on the Thursday. During the car journey from Eindhoven to her parents' house, we started to argue. We were yelling and shouting at each other, the most heated exchange of words we'd ever had.

In the car Marjon made it clear she did not want to move to Glasgow. It had really just hit her that she was leaving Holland to start a new life and there were no guarantees that it was going to work out, or that things would be enjoyable for her in Glasgow.

I told her she should have voiced her doubts before I had signed the deal and that she was out of order to pile this pressure on me when I was just about to leave. At one point during the argument, she screamed at me, 'I'd rather be with someone with a normal job.' Marjon isn't interested in status or social importance. She treats everyone the same way and takes them on their merits – whether she finds herself in the company of royalty or someone in the supermarket.

We were still squabbling when we arrived at Marjon's parents and they were surprised by her reaction. After we argued, I was fed up and stormed out the house and said to her, 'OK, I'm leaving. Good luck with the rest of your life.'

I was still angry and phoned my brother and Michel and we went out and got pissed until five o'clock the next morning. Marjon called me several times on the Sunday morning but I'd switched off my phone. In the afternoon, I got myself together, gathered my thoughts and decided I needed to speak to Marjon. I went round there and we spoke at length and gradually started to appreciate the points of view from both sides. There was still a little bit of tension between us but we knew we'd sort it out.

Marjon's mother was obviously concerned about the situation and she seemed a little nervous and apprehensive that day.

We shortly found out why she was feeling uneasy. Both our families had organised a surprise leaving party for us that night. I was unaware of this when my brother asked us to his apartment for a barbeque. I wanted to go to the beach as it was a scorching day and told him he was crazy to have a BBQ on his small balcony. But he insisted and the beach was put on hold.

A few people were there and I thought some of them seemed quite restless. Suddenly I heard the skirl of bagpipes and the sound of horses approaching. I looked down from the balcony and then the penny dropped. The horse and carriage waited outside for us and they'd arranged for me to wear a full Highland outfit. I thought a ride through Beverwijk had been organised and I was a bit embarrassed as we rode through town together in a horse and carriage. Then, I noticed up ahead, towards the Notaris bar, it looked really busy for a Sunday. Again, it all fitted into place when we got to the entrance as the bar owner, Marcel van der Wijst, was wearing tartan. Ironically, the bar used to be called the Scottish Piper Club.

The surprise party was in full swing and there were more than a hundred people inside. Marjon and I were speechless. It turned out to be a brilliant night and, despite the awkward start, we all had a fantastic time. A lot of hard and effort had gone into the preparation and it was a lovely farewell gesture from our families.

Michel was there, but he was a little bit on edge as he was waiting for news on his proposed transfer from AZ Alkmaar to Motherwell. Eventually the news came through at nine that night that it was all signed and sealed and, incredibly, he was also on his way to Scotland. It was strange that my best friend was also heading to the same country and we opened some champagne to celebrate. But Michel didn't look entirely happy and told me he had doubts about the move. I told him he had to make the move, at least give it a try. It was also comforting for us both to know that we'd be working not too far from each other and could help if there were times of unrest and homesickness.

The first two or three months in Scotland were not the easiest of times for us. Marjon and I were staying in a hotel. That's never ideal for such a length of time and it was a real test of our relationship, but we came through it all and now love living in Hamilton. We arrived as a loving, young couple but now have two lovely daughters, both born in Glasgow's Southern General Hospital. Britt arrived on 26 July 2003 and Maud was born on 11 October 2005.

Marjon and I may not be married but we are completely committed to one another. The reason we have never tied the knot is down to me as I've just never fancied it. A wedding day, for me, is more like having a party for other people to enjoy and not necessarily the two most important people there. Putting pen to paper, what exactly does that mean? As far as I'm concerned, having kids is the biggest thing any couple can do. That bonds two people forever. I know it's special for a woman to wear a wedding dress and the glamour and attention that comes with it, but it's just not for me. Maybe we will in the future and I've said to Marjon that one day we may just go to Las Vegas and do it. We'll see what happens.

6

DOWN UNDER TO THE DOCK

I was the captain of the Holland Olympic team as we tried to gain qualification for the Games in Barcelona in the summer of 1992. At the start of our bid to get there the Dutch media never paid us much attention but there was a belief in the squad we could do well and our coach, Nol de Ruiter, was always very positive.

Most of the players were eighteen or nineteen, on the first step of the ladder in professional football. Some of the players from that squad, such as Ronald de Boer, Marc Overmars and Pierre van Hooijdonk, went on to have excellent careers at the top level. Frank de Boer also played for the team at the start of our campaign.

We all took our bid to reach Barcelona really seriously. At the time none of us knew what lay ahead in our careers, so this was the chance to play in a major event – in my opinion, the next big thing after the World Cup and European Championship finals. We wanted to be successful and win a medal for our country and give ourselves unforgettable memories. It was all about innocent success, money was irrelevant and financial rewards of any kind were never mentioned.

The Dutch press were quite negative about our involvement at the start. Our qualification section saw us up against Portugal, Malta and Finland. The Portuguese had an excellent side and had a fine history of success at under-age levels. They'd won the World Cup at under-16 level and had also lifted top prize at the under-19 European Championships.

The winner of the group played the winner of another group over two legs to qualify for Barcelona. We won our group and had to play Sweden. The Swedes had Thomas Brolin in their side. He was big news at the time as he'd already secured a transfer to Italy and was playing regularly for Parma in Serie A.

I felt honoured to be captain of my country as I was playing for Twente Enschede at that time and quite a lot of the players in the squad were attached to Ajax, PSV and Feyenoord. I played in central midfield as we beat Sweden 2–1 at home but lost 1–0 over there a week later to crash out on the away goal.

The Olympic rules, at that time, still allowed us to qualify as we had to play Australia for the final place. Again, it was over two legs and gave us all the chance to travel to the other side of the world. We headed out to Manly Beach, on the outskirts of Sydney. We had to take a ferry to get to the mainland from our hotel. It was a beautiful spot and I enjoyed getting up in the morning, having breakfast and then going for a nice stroll on the beach. It was winter in Australia but the climate was still warm enough to give you the impression you were on a summer holiday.

For the first three or four days we had easy training sessions so we could recover from the jet lag. We stepped up the pace after that and got in a few harder sessions to prepare for the game. We were also given some time during our stay to do the 'tourist' stuff and it was great to see some parts of the city. Sydney is one of the nicest places I've ever been to and I would love to go back. We were also allowed a night out by de Ruiter and went out to celebrate Ronald de Boer's birthday. His father-in-law, who travelled over with us from Holland, hired a private boat for the party and we enjoyed a few hours on the water with a barbecue. We had a great time and it was the perfect preparation for our big game.

The match itself turned out to be a good ninety minutes for us and we weren't disappointed to come away with a 1–1 draw. The only negative aspect of the game was Michel van der Gaag suffering a cruciate ligament injury. Australia had a good team, with the likes of Paul Okon, Ned Zelic and my old Ibrox team-mate Tony Vidmar in their line-up.

We travelled straight back to Holland after the game and I was absolutely knackered after a marathon twenty-four-hour journey. We all got plenty of rest to make sure we were ready for the return game in Utrecht a week later. I was confident – all the players were – going into the match in front of our own supporters and had no doubts we would get the result we needed to take us to Barcelona. However, we were shocked when the Aussies took the lead and knew we had to score or else we were out. I remember feeling nervous at that point, as I feared we could go out and we'd be letting down the 14,000 Dutch fans who'd came to cheer us on. The backing we received that afternoon was incredible and that was probably helped by the fact that the press were now starting to take a long-overdue interest in our campaign. They were right behind us, although it would have been better to have received that backing and positive publicity from the outset.

The crowd spurred us to force the game back on level terms when Ronald equalised after I set him up with a header. The match went into extra-time and we were, once again, confident of doing the business in front of our fans.

Our pressure and confidence paid off when I made it 2–1 to put us in the driving seat. I also missed a chance to double our advantage and van Hooijdonk and Overmars also squandered decent chances. It was the second period of extra-time and Australia had to go for it to keep alive their Olympic dream. They took a few gambles, hardly left any players at the back. It paid off for them. As they pushed forward, the inevitable happened when they made it 2–2 with a fluke goal in the last minute of extra-time. No, make that a freak of a goal. One of their players tried to cross it into the box and our keeper came off his line in anticipation of cutting out the cross. But the player managed to sneak the ball inside the gap left between the keeper and his near post. It was an impossible angle. Or so we thought!

The champagne was no longer on ice and the flowers were being thrown away. We were out. I was gutted. Distraught. Inconsolable. I lay on the ground for ten minutes and could not believe what had happened to us. It was too much to take in. I was numb. It may seem strange to say after all I've been through on the game but I think that afternoon was the worst I've felt after *any* football game.

The Olympic team had been together for three years, been through a lot of things and we thought our hard work was paying off. To be robbed in the final seconds was cruel. It felt like the three years had been a waste of time, all for nothing. Our coach felt as bad as any of the players and supporters. De Ruiter broke down making a speech after the game and started to cry. He handed me a CD of the song 'Barcelona' he had on him, as he was hoping to play it at the party to get us in the mood for our trip to Spain.

I was down for a few days after that nightmare draw. However, what I didn't know at the time was that that night was to have a dramatic impact on the development of my career. Scouts from all over Europe attended our Olympic qualification games and that game in Utrecht was packed with spies and coaches from clubs all over Europe.

Peter Reid, manager of Manchester City at the time, was at the game to watch one of our players, Max Huibers. Max didn't play too well but I caught Reid's eye and he made a move to sign me. I was keen to go to Manchester City, really excited at the prospect of going to play in English football for an attractive club. I had a few conversations with Reid and he explained he wanted me to play in central midfield, to be his link man between defence and attack. I thought the transfer fee might be a problem but City were willing to pay Enschede about £1.6 million to get me – a very fair price, I thought. Before the club lodged an official bid, Reid wanted me in Manchester for three days' training but I refused. I said there was no way I was going on 'trial'.

I said to him, 'Peter, with all respect, you either want me or you don't.'

He assured me he did want to sign me but his chairman wouldn't sanction a bid of that level on the evidence of a game or two. He wanted Reid to look at me in training to make sure I was the right player for City and worth the money. Reid told me had made his own mind up about me and I was definitely what he wanted. He wasn't bothered how I performed in training; even if I had a nightmare or just stood on the sideline watching, it was irrelevant. It was all about coming over so that he could tell his chairman he had watched me for three days and had no doubts.

Eventually I agreed to Reid's request and went over for a few days' training. The next week City were due to fly to Ireland for a pre-season camp and had games lined up with Rangers and Celtic. The training went well and was relatively easy. I liked Reid and I also had a lot of time for Steve McMahon. He was one of the senior players and went out of his way to make sure I was made to feel welcome. He was a really good help – the type of person every young player is happy to see when they arrive at a new club.

My uncle Jos, my dad's brother, also went over with me to make sure I was OK. Of course, my dad would have made the journey but his fear of flying held him back. But he was keen to know I was safe and being looked after and that uncle Jos would give him the low-down on Manchester and let him know it was a decent place to develop my career.

Reid took me out for a meal to a good restaurant in Manchester to talk about what he expected of me as a player. At that time I was represented by Joop and Rob Jansen of the Dutch PFA. They were also at the meeting, along with my former Twente manager, Theo Vonk, the English agent Mike Morris and two officials from City. I was very comfortable in the restaurant, although I did find it strange that Vonk was there as he'd left Twente and signed for Spanish side Burgos.

Jansen left the dining table for a while, then came back later that night with a written contract offer for me from City. I was delighted with the wages on offer, it was four or five times what I was earning at Twente. At that time, it was unbelievable money for me. Only three years earlier I had been earning around £20,000 a year with FC Haarlem. So no arguments came from my side of the table. Only nodding and smiling!

When I returned to Enschede the local press asked me about Manchester City and I told them the deal was about 99 per cent done. Then, out of nowhere, Joop phoned me to say PSV had registered an interest.

For months there had been speculation linking me with PSV but nothing concrete came from it. PSV had just appointed a new manager, Hans Westerhof, and he really wanted me. To be honest, my mind was made up on Manchester City and I didn't expect a call from PSV. They were a massive cub in Holland and massive in Europe. They had won the European Cup in 1988 and had more international players than City.

I drove to Eindhoven to speak to Westerhof about tactics and what he had in mind for me. He showed me the line-up he wanted to play in the new season and had me pencilled in at left midfield. He must have sensed a little bit of concern on my part about joining such a huge club, but he reassured me it was the right move for me at that stage of my career. He was great with me and told me I would be under no pressure to 'deliver' immediately. Even if I didn't play well in the first three or four games, he assured me I'd be given the time I needed to bed in and that I would be given a run of games in the starting line-up from the first game of the season. From that moment and after that initial meeting I had a real good feeling about moving to PSV and working with Westerhof.

I wasn't going to earn as much money with them – in fact it was about three times less – but this was not about money. This was only about football. About doing what was right for my career. The financial rewards would come later if I turned out to be a success at PSV. I had every confidence I'd be a positive signing and it was the right move for me to reach my goal of playing regularly at the top level for a club and being involved with the full national squad.

However, PSV wouldn't offer more than £800,000 for me and City were tabling a bid of double that amount – which was reported in the Dutch papers as a record fee for the transfer of a non-Englishman. Naturally, that turned out to be a major stumbling block. I had no control over the fee PSV were offering.

Twente tried to put their foot down and told me I was either joining City or staying put. I told them the move to Manchester was not going to happen and I was joining PSV, even if we had to go to a tribunal to resolve the dispute.

I was worried that if the tribunal set a fee of around £1.3 million, PSV would pull out and I'd be totally screwed. I couldn't take the gamble and Joop, my agent, approached Kees Ploegsma, Director of Football at PSV. I told him my concerns and he understood where I was coming from. I made it clear I wasn't comfortable being treated like a piece of meat going to the market to find a buyer. I was a footballer, not a cow. It was never made public but PSV gave me their word they would pay whatever fee was set by the tribunal. Nobody knew this, so there was still speculation and people still thought PSV would abandon any move for me if they thought I was being overpriced.

I felt strange going to a tribunal, but I was comfortable because I knew PSV would pay whatever fee was set by the panel. I think the last case before mine was Johan Neeskens when he moved from Ajax to Barcelona about twenty years earlier.

The hearing was held in Zeist and was presided over by four panellists. I had to answer questions and told them my desire to join PSV was all about what was right for my career as a footballer and to make it as an international player and to win prizes. At the time, any move was NOT about money. During the hearing, which was chaired by Professor Giltay Veth, one of the Twente lawyers said the club wanted to offer me a new deal and hand me a drastically improved salary. I thought it was foolish of him to say that at that time.

One of the lawyers on the tribunal was former player Manfred Nan and that was an advantage to me. Veth and Nan both knew exactly where I was coming from. The tribunal lasted almost two weeks and all the while the media were speculating that PSV would probably pull out of a move if a decision was made to set a high transfer fee. The story became a media frenzy and made the headlines in the papers for days and days.

When the verdict came I looked across at the PSV people and they looked pale and apprehensive. Well, to be frank, they were crapping themselves. Thankfully for them, the fee wasn't exorbitant and the panel's decision was that my transfer fee would be set at £900,000.

So, after weeks of negotiations, talks, newspaper columns and a lengthy tribunal, the fee was only £100,000 more than PSV had originally offered. Of course, even if it had been set at £2 million, I believed PSV would have honoured their agreement with me to pay it.

Peter Reid also attended the tribunal and that was a great gesture. He wanted to assure me he was still interested and if there was a chance PSV pulled out at the tribunal, he was on hand to make another move to get me. He was great about the whole scenario and understood my decision to pursue my desire to move to PSV. He didn't blame me but felt Rob Jansen was to blame for the transfer breaking down. When I was over at City for my three days' training stint, they gave me a strip and I still have it.

I was delighted for so many different reasons that the whole saga had come to an end. Pre-season had started during the tribunal and I had to train on my own, with the help of Toon Gerrits – one of my former youth coaches at Beverwijk. I had sympathy for the powerbrokers at Twente, as they missed out on around £700,000 for me with my decision to go to PSV and not City. But that wasn't the only twist in what was a hectic few months.

The Euro 92 championships were on that summer in Sweden and Holland had qualified. Just before the tribunal there was an injury not long after the Olympic game against Australia and a place became available in our squad.

My name appeared in the papers linking me with a call-up to the squad. It never crossed my mind for a second that I'd have a chance of getting the call but to my astonishment I heard on television I had been asked to join the full squad. I knew nothing about this – it was news to me, as I'd had no contact from the Dutch FA.

The next day it all became clearer when Rob Witschge was selected by Rinus Michels and made his way to join up with the rest of the squad. I've not had this confirmed, but I believe I did have a chance of getting into the squad and Michels and his number two, Dick Advovaat, were keen to pick me. My suspicions, however, are that a few of the senior Dutch players in the squad approached Michels and told him they'd rather have the more experienced figure of Witschge ahead of me.

Not for a second did I think I would make it into the party for Sweden, but I knew my time with the national team would come and playing consistently well for PSV would earn me promotion to the Holland set-up. Despite missing the first three weeks of pre-season at PSV, I managed to start quite well with them. However, the Twente fans still hadn't accepted I had left their club and were trying to make life difficult for me. They would phone my hotel in Eindhoven and threaten to come round and beat me up.

The threats didn't bother me but Marjon was upset and I told reception to vet my calls and not to give my room number out to anyone. I found it quite pathetic behaviour, to be honest. The worst moment came when PSV had to play Twente in Enschede just a couple of weeks into the new season. The circumstances surrounding my move to PSV were obviously still fresh in the minds of the Twente fans and they were not going to let this game pass without trying to cause a major incident.

The PSV team bus made its way to the game and the police stopped us a few miles from the stadium. They spoke to the driver and Westerhof. I was at the back of the bus but advised to come forward by the police. I was informed that the Twente fans were waiting at the front door of the stadium and were going to make life unpleasant for me when I got off the bus. At best it was going to be eggs and tomatoes thrown at me. At worst they feared a fan might try to attack me. So after some consultation it was decided the best course of action was for me to be smuggled into the stadium in the back seat of a police car. The PSV players, as you would expect, gave me pelters, teasing me with the fact I'd only been with the club a few weeks and was already demanding superstar treatment! I wanted to stay on the bus and told the police this but they refused to let me. I was under orders to go to their car.

So, there I was, in my PSV tracksuit, lying down in the back of a cop car for this ten-minute journey with two police coats covering my face and body. The fans were waiting for me and were bitterly disappointed when I didn't emerge from the team bus. I managed to sneak in by a side door that took me through the offices and into the changing-room corridor. The players were already inside and the teasing from them about my red-carpet treatment continued.

During the game, every time I touched the ball I was booed. Yes, it was a messy departure from Twente but the club didn't help the situation after the tribunal when they criticised me in the local newspaper about their disappointment at missing out on a huge transfer fee.

We won the game and I played the ninety minutes. However, the run of play in the match is very vague. I can recall very little about what happened on the pitch, but plenty of what was happening off it! There was also a banner in the crowd, held up by the Twente fans for the entire game with the words 'Philips eindelijk winst na aankoop Numan!' inscribed across it. Translated, it meant, 'Philips finally profit after buying Numan!' – a quip at the expense of the giant electronics company that has a huge stake in PSV.

I was getting really pissed off with the whole situation. Twente really didn't give a toss about me. They only cared about the money. The way they treated me when I left also still sticks in my throat. Some of the club officials said I would never make it at PSV and would be better staying put so I could get a game every week. They reckoned I had no chance of becoming a regular in Eindhoven because I was surrounded by big-name, proven internationals. Their negative comments were all about trying to put doubts in my mind, in the hope I wouldn't leave. I didn't listen to them; I knew I had the quality to succeed.

At the end of the day Twente paid £225,000 to get me from FC Haarlem – which was a record fee at the time paid for a first-division player – and they sold me for around three times that amount. I owed them nothing. Despite their moaning, I had made them a lot of money. The fee I moved to PSV for was also the highest transfer fee between two Dutch clubs.

I was grateful to Twente for allowing me to develop my quality even further at their club but they were always going to be a stepping stone. I always wanted to climb the football ladder and PSV was as high as I could go in Holland.

I had good memories from my time on the pitch at Twente, although I got off to the worst possible start. I signed for them in December 1990 and made my debut, ironically, against PSV – it was the final match before the winter break.

Now, the Twente fans didn't want me at the club; they wanted Mario Been, a former Feyenoord player, to be signed. He was a bigger name and the fans were not in the slightest bit amused at the arrival of Numan from a lower-division club. They let the board know they were unhappy at me being signed instead of Been. His name was chanted all through the game. I played the full ninety minutes and we lost 2–0. It was not a good evening for me. Making your debut is supposed to be a nice experience. Sure, you might not win the game but you expect to be given a civilised reception from your own supporters! But I was a figure of hate and it wasn't my fault. It was so bad that Gerald Vanenburg, who played for PSV that night, came over to me and said, 'Don't worry, you will be a good player for them. Relax, give it time and things will be different in a few weeks.' I appreciated his concern and kind words.

The negative feelings even persisted after the game when around two hundred fans demonstrated – they were not happy with the results and performances. They tried to force their way in through the main door to get to the board members and ask for the head of the manager. The riot police were there and we all had to stay inside for well over an hour until it all calmed down. It was a crazy situation and I wondered what the hell I'd let myself in for!

Twente celebrated their fortieth anniversary in 2006 and got in touch to ask me to select some of my highlights from being at the club. They produced a commemorative book that season showcasing the forty best players in Twente's history and I was proud to be one of them. For highlights, I chose the night I made my debut and the day I had to get off the bus when going back there with PSV. I also chose the game where the fans had a huge banner with the words, 'Binmen, don't forget to take these eleven bags of rubbish away'. Ronald de Boer played that day and he summed it up with a typical Ronald understatement,

'Arthur, I don't think they're too happy with us!' Of course, he was right.

Another highlight was a game against RKC Waalwijk. We were 3–0 ahead at half-time, but drew 6–6. It was the last day of the season and the manager was raging as there was an end-of-season party. He wanted to finish on a high.

Yes, I believe football is a jungle and it's a matter of doing what you can to survive.

Twente was a good experience but instead of leaving the club with happy memories I departed with feelings of resentment and anger. Still, that is football and we must try to overcome the hurdles put in our way. I had to get over a few at Twente and there needn't have been so many put in front of me by them or their supporters. The way quite a lot of them behaved was totally out of order.

7

PSV: PROGRESS, STRUGGLE, VICTORIOUS

If Sir Bobby Robson had had his way I'd have been a PSV Eindhoven player long before my eventual arrival in the summer of 1992.

When I was with Twente Enschede Robson was impressed and told the PSV scouts they must have been sleeping by allowing me to move from FC Haarlem to Twente. The former England boss was also surprised I wasn't playing for one of the big three Dutch clubs – Ajax, Feyenoord or PSV. Nice words from such a great football man who achieved so much success with England and at club level in countries like Holland, Spain and Portugal.

Even though I was only twenty-two, my move to PSV attracted a lot of headlines. It wasn't just because of the tribunal; at that time I was earning myself a good reputation within the game in Holland. But I was conscious of the fact I had to go to PSV and prove I was worthy of being there. I knew I wasn't going to be handed a starting jersey every week just for the sake of it. I wanted to make an immediate impact with my new team-mates and that meant putting in a solid first training session.

PSV's sessions were always open to the public and it was really busy during the summer as the schoolkids were off and a few hundred would be there every day. The squad then went to a training camp in Portugal and that was just what I needed as it gave me the chance to bond with the players and get to know my new team-mates. I knew the day I signed I would have to work hard to get into the side, but seeing players such as Gerald Vanenburg, Erwin Koeman, Gheorge Popescu, Wim Kieft, Hans van Breukelen and Romário, I knew this was a very experienced team.

I roomed with Berry van Aarle. The PSV manager, Hans Westerhof, put me with him on purpose, as his experience and knowledge of the club would be invaluable to me, a young player trying to make his way to the top level at PSV.

I took part in a friendly at the training camp and although I played the full ninety minutes I didn't feel I did myself justice. After winning my first prize with PSV at the curtain-raiser to the season – the Super Cup – I picked up a niggly injury that ruled me out for two weeks. In many ways, that slight knock was a blessing in disguise as it gave me the chance to calm down, relax, gather my thoughts and take a step back to see the workings of the club and the players.

One thing that became apparent early on was that some of the older players wanted to shoot me down. Arie van Tiggelen, in particular, was always on at me, picking on me. I thought he had an agenda. Off the pitch, at lunch and in the dressing room he'd always have something to say. It went on for about three or four weeks and I spoke to my father about it. We agreed it was best not to take the bait, never answer him back. I vowed to keep my head down and prove I was worthy of being a PSV player. His criticism made me more determined to be a success.

Three weeks into the season van Tiggelen gave an in-depth interview to *Voetball* magazine about his career. It was interesting stuff. He also spoke about his disappointment in the attitude of some young footballers in Holland but said the only one he didn't include in that bracket was me. He reckoned my attitude was spot-on and said I had a good future in the game. It was then I realised van Tiggelen was testing me in those first few weeks at my new club. When I arrived he knew I had the ability on the pitch to be a footballer, but did I have the mentality to go with it? By my not reacting to him and working as hard as possible, he could see I had the quality on both fronts.

Another teething problem that may not have helped my settling-in process at PSV was a headline from an interview I gave. I spoke about my delight at joining PSV and my ambitions for my career. The headline screamed, 'Today PSV – Tomorrow National Team.' I was simply answering questions put to me by the magazine and I was well and truly stitched up. The press in Holland are not as sensationalist as the Scottish media and don't exaggerate everything a player says or comments on. But I never meant my answers to come across that way in that early interview I gave at PSV. Some of the older players were not happy about the comments and it was not the kind of start I wanted in my first week!

But I knew I had the quality to be a success. Throughout my career I worked hard to make progress in the game and climb my way up the ladder from my local club, Beverwijk, to Haarlem and then on to Twente and finally PSV. Each time I made the decision for football reasons – to win trophies and improve my game. It was never about wages. I knew the money would come eventually.

Unfortunately, there are not enough players who share that outlook in the game. Players want the riches that come with success and they want it yesterday. Big money comes too easily to young footballers nowadays and they have the fancy car and the penthouse apartment before they have played ten first-team games. Young players believe they have made it and don't keep working at their game. Too many of them all over the world don't live up to their early potential and struggle to crack it at big clubs like the Old Firm.

I had no social life until I was twenty-one – it was only football for me. Nothing else mattered and that's part of the reason I enjoyed a successful career in the game for fifteen years. I always gave my all and my managers appreciated that. When I was at Twente I was the key man in the centre of midfield – everything went through me, the link between defence and attack. It was different at PSV and I had to get used to taking a bit more of a back seat. Van Breukelen was a help to me and always encouraged me, had positive things to say. He was excellent with the young players and invited me to a BBQ round at his house not long after I arrived. It was a nice gesture. He was a real professional, a dedicated football man and an educated man. He was a teacher before turning to full-time football.

But it wasn't always an entirely happy dressing room and there were a few frictions between players at PSV when I first arrived. I remember the team photo was printed in *Panorama* magazine and bizarrely it contained red lines zigzagging from one player to another to show if they were enemies and yellow lines to indicate if they were friends. I was the only guy in the pic without a line attached to me and I wanted it to stay that way. I'd just arrived and didn't want to get involved in trying to be pals with this one or that one, I just wanted to establish myself in the team.

The turning point for me arrived in our fourth game of the season at the Olympic Stadium in Amsterdam, when we played Ajax in front of 52,000. We beat them 2–1 and I scored the winner. Kieft flicked a diagonal ball on with his head and I anticipated it to get there ahead of Ajax's Vink. I struck a left-foot shot low past Stanley Menzo.

It was a tremendous feeling to score such an important goal at such a great venue, against a top club. Also, my parents, brother and Marjon were all in the stand. It was a big day for me, a significant moment in my PSV career. I felt from that day on I became accepted by the dressing room and the club.

We didn't have a good Champions League campaign that season. Our section grouped us with IFK Gothenburg, AC Milan and Porto. From six games we took one point – a 2–2 draw in Porto in our opening match. I scored a goal against Gothenburg to put us 1–0 ahead, but we eventually went down 3–1. In our away game a Jocky Bjorklund tackle from behind tore my ligaments. It ruined the momentum I'd managed to reach.

The atmosphere at the club wasn't good from October onwards and that didn't help us as we tried to win the title. We topped the league for almost the entire campaign but, with only a handful of games to go, we dropped crucial points and Feyenoord pipped us at the post. Ultimately the failure to lift the league title cost Westerhof his job. I thought he deserved one more season because he'd inherited a difficult dressing room. Aad de Mos took over in the summer and embarked on a major rebuilding programme. He allowed a lot of the old guard to move on, the likes of Romário moving to Barcelona and others being told to find new clubs.

The players de Mos brought in were not of the same standard of those who left – whom PSV had been used to in their great days of winning the European Cup in 1988. The team struggled under the new regime and, to be honest, so did I. I wasn't too impressed with de Mos. Some of his decisions left me completely bewildered. The day before a game against Ajax, he pulled me aside at training to tell me he was going to play me at right-back to shackle Marc Overmars, stop him from getting balls over and combat his pace. I laughed at him and said, 'You must be kidding?' He wasn't happy with my reaction. 'You're quick, you read the game and I trust you,' he said.

When we practised the proposed line-up in training some of the other guys were laughing and wondering what the hell I was doing at right-back! I was nervous going into the game because Overmars was really dangerous and was capable of ripping me to shreds. When we lined up before kick-off he couldn't believe I was marking him.

I wasn't for joking and told him straight, 'If you try to take the piss out of me, you'll find your leg up in the stand!' I got off to the worst possible start as I stumbled after just two minutes and lost my balance. Overmars was away and cut the ball back to Frank Rijkaard and he nearly scored. But thankfully my performance picked up after that and Overmars was subbed after sixty-five minutes. He hardly kicked the ball. I actually played well and Ajax manager Louis van Gaal complimented me on my performance.

Still, it could have gone horribly wrong for me that day and it was just one of a number of examples where I felt de Mos was unfair to me and some of the other players. He used me more as utility player and I was shunted about the team from right-back and left-back to man-marking, although my position was as an attacking midfielder.

He also tried to create a rift between me and Jan Wouters. He told Jan I was talking about him behind his back and Jan confronted me. I told Jan it was utter nonsense. Eventually, thankfully, de Mos was fired midway through his second season in charge. He is the only manager I criticised in public in an interview when I said he wasn't always fair and honest towards the players. I always gave him 100 per cent but I never felt it was reciprocated.

After my critical interview he hit back at me and tried to belittle me by giving it the usual line of 'Who is he?' and 'What has he won in the game?'. He also said I was not tactically aware and strong enough. I thought it was immature of him but it summed him up. If I wasn't tactically aware then why play me out of position against Overmars? I was glad to see the back of de Mos. My career was going nowhere under him and PSV became weaker due to a lack of transfer funds and poor judgement on his part in the transfer market. He arrived in a blaze of publicity and boldly predicted at his first media conference that he 'guaranteed success' to put huge pressure on himself. Big mistake.

Not long after the critical interview appeared, I was in Eindhoven having a sauna with some of the PSV players. We were talking about many things and de Mos featured prominently in our conversation. Incredibly, a couple of minutes later, out of the steam and mist appeared de Mos. He was sitting in the corner and we were unaware of his presence.

Kees Rijvers took over from de Mos for a few weeks and then Dick Advocaat came in during the winter break of 1994–95. Dick built a new team and brought in players such as Phillip Cocu, Jaap Stam and Wim Jonk from Inter. I hoped it was going to be the start of a positive, new era for me and the club. I'd had a miserable three seasons prior to that in terms of success. When times were tough on the pitch I tried to do too much by helping others but I was only doing damage to myself. My own game suffered.

PSV had a fine selection of managers to choose from, but I was glad they opted for Dick as it gave me the chance to work with him again. Progress was made, but we didn't win anything in his first season as he only had a few months to turn things round. It was all geared to getting things ready for the new season. He signed some quality players and one of them was Jaap Stam from Willem II.

The atmosphere in the dressing room also picked up under Dick and I was delighted because I had become seriously disillusioned under de Mos. I knew this was going to be my last chance at PSV and things got off to a positive start as Advocaat made me left-back. I never looked back. We won the league in season 1996–97 after a tight race and I was made captain.

It was a proud moment to receive the Silver Plate on behalf of the club. The journey through the streets of Eindhoven to celebrate with the fans was also really special. I'd waited five years for the moment and made sure I enjoyed every second of it.

The only downside under Advocaat was that we were always the 'nearly men' in Europe. We almost achieved this. And we should have done better in that . . .

We reached the quarter-final of the UEFA Cup in Dick's first full season (1995–96) but we blew it against Barcelona. We drew 2–2 in the Nou Camp in the first leg and it was 2–2 at our place.

Nadal was sent off for the Spaniards and we had a free-kick. The ball struck the wall and they broke up the park to hit us on the counter-attack and win 3–2.

In the Champions League we drew Newcastle, Barcelona and Dinamo Kiev in our section. No problems! We finished second in that section, but back then only one team progressed and there was no safety net of a UEFA Cup place. We were out of Europe. Kiev won the group that year and were an outstanding side. They had Sergei Rebrov and Andrei Shevchenko in their team and were the best counter-attacking team I've ever seen. They were pacy and found it easy to carve their way through defences. In a split second they had four or five players bombing forward in the final third of the pitch.

In the end we were failures in Europe. No excuses. We just couldn't make that final step. Close, but not close enough. During my six years at PSV I won one title and one Dutch Cup. To be honest it was a disappointing total. We also won three Charity Shields, known as the Johan Cruijff Cup.

During most of my time at PSV we were up against an exceptional Ajax side. They had Patrick Kluivert, Edgar Davids, Clarence Seedorf, Danny Blind, the de Boer twins, Jari Litmanen, Kanu and Overmars. The PSV side built by Advocaat was breaking up in 1998. I was at the peak of my career and felt it was a chance to make the break and try something new. I had offers and finally opted for Rangers.

The fans were surprised I left, as they thought I was the one player who would stick around PSV for my whole career. I was supposed to be 'Mr PSV'. In the words of their song for me I was 'Arthur, the King of Philips'. They couldn't it believe it when I decided to leave but things have to move on. I enjoyed being a PSV player and it was an honour to wear their jersey. But the time was right for me to go.

8

DICK'S DUTCH REVOLUTION

On my first day at Ibrox I vividly recall meeting the kit man, Jimmy Bell, in the corridor as I arrived to pick up my training gear. The stadium had the distinct smell of football about it. From the Rangers crests on the wallpaper and on the carpets, it just had a football aura.

Jimmy was the first guy I met at Ibrox that day. He had a strong Glasgow accent and he tried to make conversation with me, but it was a one-way chat! I had no idea what he was saying and three times I had to ask him to repeat what he'd said. I couldn't understand what his question was and I was embarrassed to ask him to repeat himself a fourth time so I just nodded my head and said, 'Yes.' I thought to myself, 'Ah, this is going to be an interesting time.'

Jimmy knew I was struggling to work out what he was saying and he made light of it. To make me feel welcome, he ushered me into his little room which was packed full of Rangers memorabilia. It's an old room, with pictures of players such as Brian Laudrup and Paul Gascoigne on the wall. He had loads of jerseys from European games; he always made sure he got a jersey, whether it was from one of the Rangers players or one of the opposition.

Over the years, Jimmy looked after not only me but also the whole squad. He has a meticulous approach and makes sure everything from your boots to training gear is always in tip-top condition. We were always trying to find something to give him stick about if anything was out of place, but in my five years at

Ibrox I hardly ever had a chance – everything was always perfectly organised. People like Jimmy are irreplaceable and every club should have someone like him in the dressing room. These guys are part of the furniture and are the lifeblood of football clubs all over the world.

All I wanted to do in my first few days was make an impact on my team-mates and the Rangers supporters. I wasn't well known in Scotland but I'm sure many people would have watched me playing for Holland in the 1998 World Cup finals to form their own opinion. I was nervous about my new situation, about this fresh chapter in my life.

My first training session was a bit of a shock because I didn't realise the club didn't have their own facilities and we had to travel by mini-bus to Stepps. Ibrox only had a small gymnasium with a couple of bikes and treatment tables. Of course, it's not always about the facility – the people working inside are the most important facets and Rangers had good people. I had taken it for granted that there would be a training complex at a club the size of Rangers. Of course a few years later, in 2001, Murray Park was built and they now use that as another carrot to dangle in front of potential signings. It's a wonderful facility.

I think it rained most of the first week I was in Glasgow and this didn't make the training sessions too pleasant. I was up to my ankles in mud for most of the time! I remember saying to Giovanni van Bronckhorst, 'What the hell is going on here? This is ridiculous.'

It wasn't just Rangers who struggled to find a decent facility; not too many other Scottish clubs have their own training complex. Beside my house in Hamilton is a small, public park, used by everyone – including people out walking their dogs. I couldn't believe it when I saw Motherwell training there and more or less cleaning up the dog mess before their session started.

Despite the apprehension about the training facilities, I was looking forward to my first game against Shelbourne in a UEFA

Cup tie. I knew that almost 50,000 Rangers fans would be inside the stadium. I felt a mixture of excitement and nervousness in the build-up to the match. My English still wasn't too good and sometimes I struggled to find the right word or phrase to use. I was also just getting to grips with the names of all my new team-mates. I was keen to impress everyone.

As usual, I went through my pre-match routine of putting strapping on my ankles and getting a massage from Marc Stoll. This was not high-profile opposition we were up against, so I was surprised to see such a big crowd. We were 5–3 up from the first leg and I remember getting off to a great start when I scored one of the best goals of my career – only for it to be disallowed. After a one-two, Jorg Albertz played the ball through to me. I was close to the penalty box and could see the Shelbourne keeper coming off his line. I decided to chip the ball with the outside of my left foot and it sailed over him into the net. However, the linesman had flagged for offside because Rod Wallace strayed beyond the final defender. I was gutted. Still, we won 2–0 on the night and I was voted Man of the Match.

I had a nice feeling about Rangers from that moment on. I had good players around me and was particularly excited about the working relationship I felt I could build with Jorg Albertz and Giovanni van Bronckhorst. Both were fine players and had terrific left pegs. We had other quality players such as Andrei Kanchelskis, Sergio Porrini and Rod Wallace. I knew it would take time for us to gel but already I was sure we would get it right and bring success to Rangers.

Colin Hendry was also a new Rangers signing that season and I still remember the first day I met him when he joined from Blackburn Rovers for somewhere between £4 million and £5 million. He was wearing a blue tartan suit and had this big mop of blond hair. He looked like an archetypal big, brawny Scotsman – you know, like the *Braveheart* image – and I think Colin enjoyed trying to live up to that tag.

Dick signed him and I think David Murray was right behind the move to buy him. Hendry was the captain of Scotland and it was good for Rangers to be seen to be paying decent money for that kind of player. It was also good that a player like Hendry signed after a number of foreigners had come in that summer. Maybe Hendry's strong Scottish background was a major factor behind his signing.

He was a leading Scots player, not the most skilful, but he always liked to battle for ninety minutes and loved to get stuck into his opponent. For me, as a Dutchman, I had Hendry down as a typical Scottish footballer – always had his sleeves rolled up and was always prepared to work hard. I had the No. 5 jersey and that was probably the one he craved. The shirts were already printed and there was no way of changing our squad numbers. In Holland the left-back normally wears No. 5 but I didn't realise until I arrived in Scotland that this number is usually reserved for the centre-half.

Off the park Colin was a gentleman and pretty much kept himself to himself. At first, I did find his dress sense a little strange because I didn't appreciate the Scottish culture. I stayed at the Hilton Hotel in Glasgow when I first came over and usually lots of parties and weddings were taking place there. Loads of the male guests wore kilts at these events but at first I used to call them 'skirts' and found it quite funny that men would be happy to be seen wearing them. I thought it was really weird but I now fully understand what it's all about. In fact, Giovanni and I wore the full Highland regalia for an interview with a Dutch television station. We had the full dress as well as bagpipes. The Dutch people thought we were nuts for doing it but I had fun and wanted to respect the dress culture of the country I was living and working in.

It was a thrill to find out new things every day about Rangers, the football club, and Scotland, the country. The Scottish guys in the dressing room were obviously really helpful – the likes of Charlie Miller, Ian Ferguson, Gordon Durie,

Barry Nicholson, Barry Ferguson, Derek McInnes and Scott Wilson were always willing to help us out. On the pitch, Barry Ferguson has lived up to the early hype and I'm delighted he has been able to enjoy such a successful career as captain of Rangers and also leading his country on the international stage. Barry Nicholson and Scott Wilson decided to leave Ibrox for guaranteed first-team football elsewhere and I'm pleased for them that they've gone on to become reliable professionals.

One guy whose career didn't go to plan was Charlie Miller. When I first arrived at Ibrox, I was told he had great talent. He should have been a regular for Rangers and Scotland but just didn't reach the heights his talents merited. He had a wicked sense of humour and was a little bit cheeky but in a nice way. I didn't socialise with him so I don't know what kind of life he had away from the pitch but it has been a talent wasted. I know Charlie's still in the game and has made a decent living out of it but he should have had so much more.

My first league game for Rangers was away to Hearts. It was a Sunday afternoon and the game was screened live on Sky. Because of the publicity we generated and the money Advocaat had spent on players, big expectations were on our shoulders to win this game and go on to lift the league title.

As usual, Tynecastle was packed and there wasn't a seat to be had. The fans were right on top of the players and the atmosphere was unbelievable, like it was a cup final. The game was full of non-stop action and it was a real battle for ninety minutes. There was no time to control the ball, look up and find a pass.

As my first introduction to the Scottish game I quickly learned that no less than 100 per cent in every game, particularly away from home, was going to be required to do myself justice at Rangers. I found the pace of the game non-stop and much quicker than what I was used to in Holland. There were few breaks between play and I didn't get a second to catch breath. We lost 2–1 and it was a bit of a surprise, even though we were full of new players and knew it was going to take a couple of weeks to gel. Still, we had great support from our fans that afternoon and a few of us made a point of going over at the end of the game to applaud them for their backing.

The next shock came just after the final whistle, when the players found out that a national newspaper was set to run a story about Jonatan Johansson and Sergio Porrini being out on the Friday night, forty-eight hours before kick-off. When the article appeared the following day it made the front page and it tried to suggest the pair of them had broken a strict curfew and been out on the bevvy. The truth was, they were out for a meal and coffee. I was also out that night, but not with them. I was in another restaurant. When you are living in a hotel it's normal to venture out for a change of scenery and a taste of some different food, as long as you don't go to a bar or nightclub.

I couldn't believe it had made it on to the front page and had no idea why that kind of non-story should appear as a major headline. Players were upset about the coverage and I knew then I'd have to be careful about every word I said in Scotland. The newspaper coverage on the Old Firm is incredible. In Holland we have two or three pages of sport and that includes football, tennis and other sports. There's more football coverage on a Friday before the weekend games. In Scotland, it's at least ten pages every day and I still can't get my head round the impact football has in this country.

Because of the defeat against Hearts, we felt a bit of pressure going into our next league game at home to Motherwell. My best friend, Michel Doesburg, played for the opposition that day at right-back. Other Dutchmen, Rob Matthaei and Jan Michels, also lined up against us. Van Bronckhorst played on the left-hand side of midfield that afternoon, so it felt strange to have that side of the pitch loaded with players from Holland. I was also really proud of that fact.

I played against Doesburg many times when we played for different clubs. We grew up together and spent very little of our lives apart. Football, in the end, separated us as we had to go different ways in our career paths.

We both couldn't believe we were playing at Ibrox in front of 50,000 people in a league game in Scotland. It just wasn't in any script we might have imagined when we were teenagers playing for FC Beverwijk and FC Haarlem. I had to man-mark Michel at corner-kicks and it was funny because as we were jostling with each other in the box we were laughing and joking.

Rangers took the lead through Rod Wallace but Owen Coyle equalised for Motherwell. It was late in the game and I could feel our fans becoming restless. The last thing we needed was to have just one point on the board from our opening two league games. Thankfully, though, we pulled through with a last-minute penalty from Jorg Albertz.

That was a big weight off our shoulders, to say the least. Before the Motherwell game we had defeated PAOK Salonika 2–0 at home in the UEFA Cup and I could now feel a rhythm coming together in the team. Also, just as importantly, the feeling in the dressing room was good and we were all bonding as a unit. The players were responding to Advocaat's methods well, which wasn't easy, especially for the ones who'd been at Rangers under Walter Smith.

They'd been used to Walter and had had a successful period with him. It must have felt strange to still be wearing the same jersey but having to work with the methods a new man wants you to. That's why it's easier for a new player coming in; he doesn't know anything different about the club and the dressing room and just gets on with things under the guy who's signed him.

We had strong competition for places, at least two and in some cases three guys fighting for every position. It was inevitable some players would move on for one reason or another. Not long into Dick's reign Craig Moore left to join Crystal Palace and Rino Gattuso moved back to Italy to sign for Salernitana.

I always found Rino had a terrier-like attitude in training – he was so difficult to shake off and you had to be beat him two or three times before you were completely away from him. We only had a few weeks together at Ibrox before Rino went back to Italy but it's interesting to see how he developed his raw talent into becoming a Champions League and World Cup winner. What a fantastic achievement for a sportsman.

It's never easy when players leave, particularly when they are popular in the dressing room and with the supporters, but Dick was never one to shirk from a decision he felt was in the best interests of the team, no matter what opinion was held elsewhere.

In late September I started to really feel pain in my knee. I had injured the patella tendon in the knee. Jonas Thern was still at Rangers – signed the previous season by Walter Smith on a free transfer from AS Roma – and he had the same injury. He'd had an operation on it and warned me to be careful as it could end my career if I didn't get it attended to properly.

As the surfaces on the pitches became harder, the injury really started to worry me. I was having to put ice on my knee after the training. The injury started to worsen and eventually it got to the stage where I couldn't train any more – every step was like someone was plunging a knife into my knee, it was agony. Eventually I couldn't play on with it and I was forced to miss a couple of games. The fact was I hated being injured, hated missing games. I was also conscious that I'd been at Rangers a short while and I was aware that some players are accused of being 'money-grabbing foreigners' if they spend too much time on the treatment table. But, whether I liked it or not, the treatment table was to become my companion. If I hadn't taken that route, I would have ended up like Thern – playing a few games and having to retire much earlier than planned.

After my injury was completely healed I played against Celtic and then picked up my first winners' medal for Rangers when we defeated St Johnstone 2–1 in the Coca-Cola League

Cup final at Celtic Park on 29 November 1998. We were playing some great combination football at that time – some of the best football the club had played in years, according to our fans.

We had plenty of players able to score goals – Rod Wallace, Seb Rozental and JJ (Jonatan Johansson). Rod was small but had great body strength and clever movement in the final third of the pitch. Considering he was signed on a free transfer from Leeds United, it was a fantastic piece of business. That said, if Rangers had paid £2 million for him he still would have been a worthwhile signing. Jonatan picked up a bit of a 'super-sub' tag. When he came off the bench, his pace caused havoc and we knew it was just about sliding the ball through for him and he would outpace his marker. He was also a deadly finisher.

Stephane Guivarc'h also arrived at Ibrox just before the final against St Johnstone. He cost £3 million from Newcastle and came with a huge reputation as he had won the World Cup with France just five months earlier. He scored a hat-trick on his debut but despite that fantastic start it never really worked out for him at Rangers.

The competition for places was strong and it kept everyone sharp and focused. We knew we were going to have a good season and no player wanted to miss out. When we played at home we knew we were going to win. Sure, away games weren't quite as predictable, but most of the time we felt quite invincible in the domestic matches. I've heard players claim that winning every week became boring but I absolutely loved it. In many of our games we would be two or three goals ahead and it allowed us to take a gamble here and there on the pitch, try things we wouldn't normally do if the result was tight. It used to drive Dick nuts if we lost possession, but we switched off from his touchline antics during games if we knew we had the three points in the bag.

Getting the first goal was always the hardest because teams used to have at least nine men behind the ball and we had to break down the 'wall' they built in front of us. There's no doubt, Celtic apart, teams who came to Ibrox were only inter-ested in keeping the score down to a respectable number. I got the feeling most sides were happy to leave Ibrox not on the receiving end of more than a three-goal defeat.

I think they were scared of losing by five or six, perhaps denting their confidence for a few weeks after that. Teams would play for ninety minutes at Ibrox and it didn't bother them if they only crossed the halfway line once in either half. Being a striker in the opposition team must have been a hor-rible task. It was a case of get in and get out as quickly as pos-sible, not suffering too much damage. I enjoyed the challenge of trying to break down packed defences. We had a lot of the possession and it was up to us to entertain our fans. It wasn't always easy but I think we managed it more often than not. There's a saying I have picked up in Scotland and I think it was first used by Tony Fitzpatrick when he was in charge of St Mirren – 'Hard work only beats talent when talent doesn't work hard.' It only has ten words but it sums up football per-fectly. Other teams had less quality than Rangers and I sensed they felt inferior as professional footballers. They tried to make up for it by getting stuck in, not giving us a chance to settle on the ball, especially when we were away from home. We might have been a couple of goals up but we couldn't switch off as we were never far away from a scyth-ing tackle.

If you lost concentration there was always the danger of picking up a serious injury. I had to know the pass I was going to make as the ball was coming to me. It was vital to be one step ahead at all times. So, when you are constantly on your guard it is nice to be able to switch off and enjoy a moment.

If you are lucky enough the 'moments' I'm talking about are winning trophies. My first one was the Coca-Cola League Cup and to be honest I didn't even know the trophy existed when I arrived in Scotland. Usually you have a cup final at the end of the season but this game was played in November and I found it all a bit strange to be playing for a major honour in the autumn. We played Alloa in one of the early rounds and I couldn't believe that Ibrox was packed for the game. I remember saying to Giovanni that I thought only around 15,000 fans would turn up.

Now, we knew we were going to beat Alloa but you still have to basically go in and be diplomatic with the truth when you faced the media to preview the game. You have to go through the usual platitudes like 'We will show them every respect because they will be right up for the game and will want to cause an upset' and 'If we don't play to our highest level then we could lose the game as they shouldn't be underestimated'. Of course, what we really wanted to say was, 'With all due respect to Alloa and this competition, we have more important games in the league and in Europe to think about and those are our priority. We should beat Alloa very easily if we feel like it.'

Because Hampden was being renovated, the final was played at Celtic Park. The game wasn't a sell-out, which I found a little surprising, but that might have been partly down to the fact some Rangers fans told me they refused to go to Parkhead because they didn't want to buy a pie and a Coca-Cola there to boost Celtic's funds! We'd beaten St Johnstone 7–0 at McDiarmid Park a few weeks before the final and Alloa wanted to make sure there wasn't a repeat of that scoreline. We went a goal up early on through Guivarc'h but were shocked when Nick Dasovic equalised a couple of minutes later. It was a little tighter than we'd anticipated but thankfully Albertz gave us the lead again and we held on to win. We were all delighted to get the first trophy of the season in the cabinet and were looking towards completing the domestic Treble.

I got a little bit crazy during the celebrations and started to run about the pitch like a Batman character. I had a big flag around my body and a huge Rangers hat on. People were quite surprised at the way I was behaving – earlier that year I was playing in a World Cup finals and here I was, three months later, running around and celebrating like I'd won the World Cup!

It was 'only' the League Cup but it meant a lot to me; it was important to get my first medal as a Rangers player. It also took a little bit of pressure off Dick's shoulders. There was a high expectation level on him from the Rangers fans and other people in Scotland and I suppose some would have been happy to see him fall flat on his face. But he got the initial trophy under his belt and it turned out to be the first of many for him as the manager of Glasgow Rangers.

We had a celebration party back at Ibrox and it was great to see so many happy faces. It was my first cup final for Rangers and in my five years at Ibrox we never lost any of the seven finals we reached. It's great to be on a winning side and never sampling the bitter taste of defeat at a showpiece occasion.

Big game after big game followed and one I particularly remember was our second leg against Bayer Leverkusen in the UEFA Cup. My old team-mates from PSV, Eric Meijer and Jan Heinze, were in the Leverkusen team and we came away from the first leg in Germany with a superb 2–1 victory. It was a fantastic result.

I missed the first leg in the BayArena but came back for the return leg when we drew 1–1. I spoke to Eric and Jan after the game and they couldn't believe the atmosphere inside Ibrox. They thought it was terrific and left with an excellent impression of Ibrox Stadium and the Rangers supporters. I loved the big-time midweek games – the floodlights on and the fans singing the songs. It's what football is all about. I preferred to play football in the dark nights; it was better than the sunny Saturday afternoons. We were winning most of our games and on course for the league title. When you are winning, life is good, so much better. The result from the game can make or break your week. The only downside came at the start of December when Parma knocked us out of the UEFA Cup 4–2 on aggregate.

We gave a couple of good performances against them but it was just not to be. It allowed us to concentrate on winning the league title and the Scottish Cup to complete the Treble. We were full of confidence that we were going to succeed. For me personally, however, the season took a turn for the worse against Kilmarnock on 12 December, when I injured my ankle in a game at Ibrox (which we won 1–0). I stood on a divot, a small crusty bit of turf, and twisted my ankle. There was nobody near me. At first I thought it was nothing too bad and I continued to play on for a few minutes, but I soon realised it was more serious.

After the game I went to hospital for an X-ray on the injury to see if anything was broken, but I got the all-clear. Although my ankle was swollen the Ibrox physio, Grant Downie, put my leg in plaster and told me to give it a complete rest. After a seven-day rest I took off the plaster and I went for an MRI scan at Nuffield Hospital to check if there was any long-term damage in my ankle. The outcome from the scan was that I'd torn the lateral ligaments in my right ankle. Normally that should clear up in a couple of weeks but Grant recommended I wear a 'special boot' to aid my recovery for the next ten days. I was stubborn and asked him, 'Is this really necessary?' The big boot was a pain in the ass to wear – it made me look like an astronaut. But Grant assured me the boot was needed because it would ensure I didn't put any weight on the injury.

I believe my World Cup exertions from the previous summer had finally caught up with me. I'd been playing football almost non-stop for eighteen months – after a long season at PSV, I went straight to the World Cup and only had two weeks' rest before I went to Rangers.

I had nothing inside me to fight with, to win the battle against this injury. Basically, my body told me, 'Enough is enough.' There was a winter break in Scotland that season. I thought the rest would sort me out and I'd be ready to go when the games resumed on 23 January 1999 with a Scottish Cup fixture against Stenhousemuir.

We were in Florida for our winter training camp to prepare us for the second half of the season and I was desperate to get back to full fitness because I didn't want to be accused of being tagged as an 'injury-prone foreigner'. I really don't know if people talked behind my back and criticised me, but I had sort of convinced myself they did and I was determined to prove them wrong. Jonas Thern – who was still struggling with his injury – and I trained with Grant over in the States and it helped to have the Florida sunshine on our backs. I felt I was fit enough to join in with the rest of the boys and, after speaking to the physio, it was agreed I step up my training.

But it wasn't long before I broke down when a pain in my ankle shot right through me. I tried to kick the ball at one point and my studs caught in the dry turf and I knew straight away I was knackered again. I'd been too eager to join the boys in training but I probably needed a longer recovery period.

After I returned from Florida I went to see a Rangers doctor who also worked at Ross Hall and he examined my ankle. I told him about my problems and where I felt the pain. He manipulated my ankle, did some tests and told me that everything looked OK and I could make my return to the team within the week.

Despite what he told me I knew something was not right in my ankle. I went back to Ibrox and spoke to Grant and told him that I didn't believe the doctor's prognosis. Grant also had his doubts and we agreed I should go to Eindhoven for a second opinion with the PSV doctor, Cees Rein van den Hoogenband. I'd known him for six years when I was at PSV and I put my trust in his judgement.

I was examined by van den Hoogenband and after just one test on my ankle he diagnosed syndesmosis. To confirm his diagnosis after ten seconds he asked one of his colleagues to come in and within a minute he'd diagnosed exactly the same condition. I was relieved to get to the bottom of what was wrong with me but couldn't stop thinking, 'Why should I have to go to Holland to get sorted?'

My ligaments were torn and they arranged for me to go in for an operation in Holland to fix my ankle. It was in a right mess but the op was a success. I was very lucky – that operation was the only one I had in my fifteen-year playing career. I was told I would be out for the rest of the season but I had a little feeling inside me that I'd be able to play in the Scottish Cup final on 29 May – providing we made it to Hampden.

Being told I'd be out for the rest of the season was a depressing prospect. But I tried not to let it get me down too much. I was operated on in Eindhoven and was in hospital for two days. I travelled by train back to my parents' home from Eindhoven, a ninety-minute journey. It was wet that day, pouring with rain, and as I got off the train I slipped and fell. I tried to break my fall with one of the crutches and ended up whacking an innocent bystander on the neck. The poor guy thought he was being attacked! I nearly ended up back in hospital for another operation but fortunately my ankle wasn't damaged.

I received most of my treatment on my road to recovery from the Dutch national team physio, Rob Ouderland. After consulting the Ibrox medical staff and asking permission from Advocaat, I stayed in Holland full time during that period to get the best possible attention from medical staff. Had I been at Ibrox I wouldn't have been able to get the round-the-clock treatment I wanted because players with injuries that were not long-term would quite rightly have been given priority over me.

My treatment and rehabilitation programme was in Zeist, the headquarters of KNVB. I started at 9 a.m. and finished at 4 p.m., with three or four full-time physios working there at all times. I had an hour's drive to get there in the morning and the same again to get home. It was tiring but gave me the maximum opportunity to get back to fitness. I had a structured programme; sometimes it involved being in the swimming pool or on the treadmill or a bike. It was a tough slog but at least other injured players from clubs in Holland were there and we

always tried to spur each other on. I would have much preferred to be out on the pitch helping my team-mates and trying
to make a further impression on the Rangers supporters. I only
returned to Glasgow every other weekend to attend the home
games at Ibrox and I became out of sight, out of mind to most
of my team-mates. That I found a little bit disappointing.

Giovanni and Tony called to see how I was doing and if the
operation was a success. Mind you, I think Tony called just to
make sure I was definitely in plaster so that his place in the
team was safe for a few months! The manager and the physio
also phoned me.

It would have been nice to hear from more of the guys, especially the ones I socialised with. But that's footballers for you.
Throughout my career I've always made sure I tried to show
my sympathy for guys who were ill or laid up. As captain of
PSV, I took it as one of my duties to make sure that if any of our
players or members of staff were injured or ill I'd make a personal visit to the hospital to deliver flowers or a basket of fruit,
which is a normal practice in Holland.

I only spoke to the guys when I came back to Glasgow for the
games. I attended most games at Ibrox, watching the boys
defeat the likes of Dundee, Motherwell and Aberdeen to keep
us on track for the league championship. The climax came
when we visited Parkhead to play Celtic on 2 May. If we won
that game, the league was ours. I was still injured but travelled
back to Scotland for the derby. I got my tickets organised to sit
in the Rangers end beside our supporters. It was an experience
I'll never forget. The Celtic and Rangers fans are separated by
police and security staff. It's always a difficult atmosphere –
you just never know what might happen between the fans at an
Old Firm fixture. And that game turned out to be a classic
example of being prepared to expect the unexpected.

As I made my way to Parkhead in a taxi from my house, I
thought about the Rangers players on the team bus and what
they would be thinking about ahead of the ninety minutes.

Jimmy Bell always put on the same CD of different kinds of music to pump things up for every away game we played. I think playing that music was also a superstition of his and the players. When we used to approach Parkhead Jimmy would blast out 'Simply the Best' at full volume. That was a ritual of his for Celtic games. Non-negotiable. The players loved it and we were ready for the battle ahead.

When we got off the bus at the main door at Parkhead the Celtic fans would be there, waiting to give us a lovely, warm welcome! They'd be pointing fingers, shouting obscenities and giving the players a hard time. I used to just smile at them, it never bothered me. But I did used to wonder what made them do such things. Why stand there an hour and a half before kick-off just to get the chance to shout abuse for ten seconds? I found it all very strange behaviour. But if it makes their day . . .

The dressing room would have been a tense place in the build-up to that game, and so was the Rangers end. I had on a baseball cap that afternoon, trying to blend in with the rest of the fans.

As usual, the demand for tickets was unbelievable. There was extra spice to this one because this was to be the first title after losing ten-in-a-row to Celtic the previous season. It was pretty much accepted for a couple of months before the end of the season that we were going to win the league and it was just a matter of when.

Well, when it worked out that we could do it at Celtic Park it was an amazing feeling and an opportunity the boys were never going to waste. I watched the guys in the warm-up and they looked in good shape. They had stature. They had presence. They had a confident look. Celtic? Well, to be honest, their body language had 'inferiority complex' stamped all over it.

It was also a big game for Celtic as they didn't want the humiliation of losing the title to their biggest rivals on their own ground. But they did not get it their own way and we comfortably won the game 3–0 to give Celtic, I'd imagine, one of the worst days in their history. For us to win the league title on their patch really rubbed their noses in it.

Celtic tried to give us a hard time straight from kick-off but the Rangers players were not going to be put off, not on that day of all days. Neil McCann opened the scoring for us and I was really pleased for him. I had played against him when he was at Hearts and he'd always impressed me. He was tricky and was capable of delivering an excellent cross. I think Neil is a Catholic and his signing received a lot of attention because of this. Some fans may well have had reservations about Neil in a Rangers jersey but these were dispelled for good after this game.

After Neil scored, everything went totally crazy on and off the pitch. Referee Hugh Dallas sent off Celtic's Stephane Mahe early in the game and was a figure of hate for the home support. A few minutes later he was hit by a coin or a lighter thrown from the Celtic end. I remember seeing him going down on one knee and I thought he had cramp. Then, of course, there was blood spilling from his face. The Celtic fans were obviously frustrated at what was happening and Dallas was an easy target. During my career I was a complete pain in the ass to referees and linesmen. I never gave them a second's peace and questioned just about every decision they gave against the team I played for. But I felt a lot of sympathy for Dallas that day. No referee deserved that kind of treatment.

Dallas was a top whistler, as he had excellent man-management skill on the pitch and was always good at defusing potentially explosive situations. That day he made a brave decision straight after he was hit by the object, when he awarded a penalty to us down at the Celtic end. Albertz converted it to send us well on our way. I was delighted for Jorg, a player I liked. And he loved scoring against Celtic. He was part of the team that won nine titles and then lost out on ten-in-a-row, so it was great for him to be a winner again.

McCann added our third in the second half. He was on fire that day, perhaps his finest game in a Rangers jersey. Tackles continued to fly in and yellow cards were being handed out all over the place. Vidar Riseth of Celtic was sent off at the death and Wallace was also sent for an early bath by Dallas.

The game was screened live on Dutch television and they would have been pretty shocked by the behaviour of some of the players and the Celtic fans. The football wasn't vintage but they would have been glued to their screens, that's for sure. There was a nasty atmosphere inside the stadium for most of that afternoon. The Rangers fans were up for a celebration and, understandably, primed to wind up the Celtic fans. Bragging rights are everything on a day like that one.

Advocaat was delighted and Bert van Lingen, his assistant, burst into tears. On the pitch the players and some members of staff started a mock version of the 'Celtic huddle'. It was meant to embarrass Celtic.

The Rangers fans had to stay inside the stadium for forty-five minutes after the final whistle and that was not a problem. There was a party the whole of that time, a celebration of winning the league and it felt good to be a part of the league success.

Of course there were days and days of reaction to the so-called 'Shame Game'. It was decided that no more league games between the clubs should take place at the traditional time of 3 p.m. and that 12.30 lunchtime was more suitable.

There was a party back at Ibrox in the evening. It was great and was the perfect end to a day I'll never forget. I only wished I had been able to play a part.

One of a few things I found frustrating about playing football in Scotland was that the championship winners aren't able to have a reception at the City Chambers and parade around the streets in an open-top bus. They can do it in most cities around the world, but not Glasgow. I can understand why it's not possible with the trouble it would cause in the city centre. It would be great to think that society will one day move on and perhaps a generation from now it will be able to happen. Sadly, I have my doubts, but I will never give up hope.

We had to wait for our next home game before being presented with the league championship trophy. All the players and staff were on the pitch receiving their medals, taking turns at holding the trophy aloft and going on a lap of honour, but I stayed in the stands. I didn't want to be on the pitch as it was not my championship and it just didn't feel right. Vidmar had played most of the second half of the season and performed well in my absence. He deserved the credit and the plaudits from the fans. A few of the players tried to push me into going but I wasn't for budging. I received my medal behind closed doors.

It was the same at Hampden Park when we won the Scottish Cup to clinch the Treble. I attended the game against Celtic and was absolutely delighted for the players and supporters but didn't celebrate on the pitch. Yes, I was a part of the team, but I was not a part of the success that day. Despite hoping I would have been fit for that final, the truth is I was never close. And even if I had been, Vidmar had played so well there was no need for him to be replaced.

I was pleased for Rod Wallace when he scored the winner that day. Rod and I became good friends at Rangers. He was always laughing and joking, although he never came across that way in public when he had to speak to the media, which was a part of his duty as a Rangers player he hated.

A lot of the guys didn't like speaking to the newspapers. John Greig had the unenviable task of trying to get players to do interviews and a lot of the time he'd have been better asking a brick wall. Some of us would tell Greigy where to go when he asked and we'd just be winding him up.

The truth is, we would never have seen him stuck. He is the Greatest Ever Ranger and had my respect, although I slaughtered him for not phoning me to see how I was doing after my operation earlier that season. To think I didn't know who he was when he picked me up from Edinburgh Airport for the signing talks! I got on well with him from the moment I moved to Scotland and he was always someone I could talk to and feel comfortable in his company. He is Rangers through and through and I got the impression he loved being part of the set-up during Dick's time as manager of Rangers. Greigy loved the big games, especially the big European nights, and on a few occasions he was more wound up than some of the players. He'd pace up and down the dressing room, looking nervous. Once or twice I told him to sit down and relax.

There was a lot of media attention on the 1999 Scottish Cup final because of what had happened earlier in the month at Parkhead when we won the title. The kick-off was at 3 p.m. and all the players were well behaved. Dallas was in charge again and he handled the match well, although, for once, there was hardly any controversy on the pitch. For an Old Firm game, it was really low-key.

Once again, Celtic never caused us any moments of real panic and we were always in control. I travelled to the game on a staff coach with people like the manager's secretary Laura Tarbet, and Peter from the front door. I had my club suit on. It was a subdued day, with fans and players aware that the spotlight was on them and there was no room for any misbehaviour. We had a great party after the final. We celebrated winning the Treble to the full.

The Treble was an excellent achievement and it was just a pity we lost to Parma in Europe that season. A lot of hard work went in to winning all three domestic trophies and it must have been satisfying for Dick Advocaat and David Murray because a lot of people must have wanted to see the pair of them fail. Sport is about winning. Second means nothing. Advocaat and Murray are winners.

Dick extended his stay at Ibrox just before the Cup final and agreed to sign a two-year extension to his original two-year deal. He announced it immediately after the Cup final and it was a huge boost for Rangers. It also meant the clause I had inserted in my deal allowing me to leave if Dick moved during the initial term of his contract became invalid. It was not a problem for me and I was delighted to stay. I had quickly picked up a good feeling for Rangers, the staff and the supporters. I wanted to stay and the 1999–2000 season couldn't come quickly enough. I was desperate to put the injury torment behind me and help the club achieve more success and actually be on the park this time to do it.

9

ORANJE FINAL

It may not have been the greatest of games or the most dramatic ninety minutes played at Hampden, but the 2000 Scottish Cup final remains one of the greatest memories of my career. The season before we had won the Treble and in 2000 we had already secured the league title by twenty-one points before we faced Aberdeen on 27 May. We were aiming to take our fifth trophy in two seasons under Dick Advocaat. It was a great time to be associated with Rangers. The fans loved us and we could do no wrong.

As a tribute to the Dutch influence at Ibrox and a dramatic show of their appreciation, the Rangers fans made the Cup final a thank-you to us all and it ended up being tagged the 'Oranje Final'. The idea behind the gesture was that every supporter attending the game that day had to wear something oranje or orange, depending which way you wanted to look at it. There was genuine affection from the fans towards the Dutch but there was, I'm convinced, an element who used it as an excuse to wear that particular colour for other reasons we're all aware of. We're not daft!

On the back of that final, Rangers brought out an orange away strip for the next season. Prior to the Hampden showpiece, I'd heard about the idea and read some stuff in the *Rangers News* about it but had no idea what to expect and if the fans would go along with it.

It wasn't until we were making the journey from the team hotel to Hampden that I noticed that just about every Rangers fan had oranje on. Usually they all wore blue. During the pre-match warm-up we could see some oranje as well behind the goal at the traditional 'Rangers End' of Hampden.

In the final ten minutes leading up to kick-off I went through my pre-match routine in the dressing room and I felt great as I checked my boots and rubbed some Vaseline above my eyes and on my knees. Lorenzo Amoruso was injured that day so I was given the armband. As I led the team out the tunnel I couldn't believe it when I looked to my left.

The entire end was a sea of oranje. It was amazing. I thought I was walking out to play for Holland against Scotland in an international game. It was a thrilling sight to see. A beautiful, sunny day and this bright colour at one end of the ground. My brother was over for the game with a few friends and Ronald Waterreus was also in the stands. Ronald likes to play golf, so he combined a long weekend on a few courses in Scotland with the Cup final. After the game he asked what the 'Oranje thing' was all about and Ronald reckoned there must have been more oranje inside Hampden that day than some of the games Holland played in. I agreed.

Ronald is a good friend of mine and, of course, he ended up signing for Rangers in January 2005. Stefan Klos picked up a knee injury in training and I knew Ronald was on the bench at Manchester City and would welcome a move to Ibrox. It required an experienced keeper to replace Stefan and Ronald fitted the bill perfectly. I told the Rangers doctor, Ian McGuinness, about Ronald's situation and he passed the infor-mation on to Alex McLeish. Jan Wouters was also aware of Ronald's predicament and the deal quickly moved on from there. I was delighted when he helped Rangers win the title in 2005. I also thought he played really well during the following campaign, as he kept Klos on the sidelines for most of the season.

During the final I tried to soak up every moment of this spe-cial day. Whenever there was a break in play, for example an injured player receiving treatment, I'd just stand with my hands on hips and look around me. It was a lovely sight. Giovanni van Bronckhorst couldn't believe it either. Dick never mentioned anything to us but he must have been impressed, must have felt proud that his achievements as the manager of Rangers resulted in this incredible show of appreciation from the fans.

As for the game itself? Well, to be honest, I can't remember too much about the ninety minutes. The record books show we won 4–0 through goals from van Bronckhorst, Tony Vidmar, Billy Dodds and Jorg Albertz, but it was never a particularly memorable final.

Games between Rangers and Aberdeen were usually tasty affairs as Aberdeen were always fired up to face us. After an Old Firm fixture, it was a game we felt had the potential to be explosive, a battle, because of the history of the clubs and the way Aberdeen fans treated it. There was always tension on the pitch and in the stands. This final had the potential to be a classic but it lost its edge after less than five minutes when Aberdeen keeper Jim Leighton was stretchered off with a smashed cheekbone after an accidental clash with Rod Wallace. We knew it was serious straight away. It was a shame for Leighton, as it was his last game in football after a glorious professional career.

Back then only three substitutes were permitted and managers tended not to put a keeper on the bench, preferring an extra outfield player. Aberdeen manager Ebbe Skovdahl went with three outfield players, a decision that backfired, but you could understand his reasoning behind it. We also had three outfield players listed as subs. I mean, how often does a keeper get injured, especially in a cup final?

We spoke about it after the game and wondered who would have gone in goals for us had something happened to Klos. It certainly wasn't going to be me and it wouldn't have been Wallace or Dodds because they weren't the tallest! Even if Rod climbed on Billy's shoulders he'd have struggled to reach the crossbar! I reckon Tony Vidmar would have got the nod – he could have used his kangaroo legs to jump and skip around the box! After Leighton left the field the game descended into a bit of a farce as Robbie Winters picked up the goalie gloves. Aberdeen had lost a good striker in Winters, a player with pace who had the potential to cause us one or two problems. As soon as Winters went in goals, we got together and made sure we hit long-range shots and just tried to get everything on target, especially with the likes of Giovanni and Jorg in our side. We also knew set-pieces would be beneficial and had the potential to upset the stand-in keeper.

The goals came for us and we rarely got out of second gear, although it took us thirty-six minutes to open the scoring. But once we got the first, we were confident we'd add to our tally. When we came out at the start of the second half there was no stopping us and we fired in three goals in six minutes. It was a formality, although Winters made three or four decent saves to keep the score semi-respectable. It's always good to win silverware but I prefer it when there is tension and a real fight to the finish. To be honest I'd rather have matches like the 2002 Scottish Cup final, a nail-biter that was won in the final minute when Peter Lovenkrands scored the winner for us to make it 3–2. I also enjoyed the 2003 SPL title success over the 2000 SPL win because it went to the last kick of the ball that year, whereas we knew by the winter break in 2000 that we were going to win the title.

Victory at Hampden that day gave us our fifth trophy out of six in two seasons under Advocaat. It was also the hundredth trophy in the proud history of Rangers Football Club.

We would have loved it to have been another Treble to give us back-to-back Trebles but we were knocked out of the League Cup by Aberdeen in December 1999. Celtic went on to beat Aberdeen in the final of the League Cup that season and they must have been relieved to stop the rot and prevent Advocaat from picking up another clean sweep. They'd never have lived that down. The Rangers supporters would quite rightly have made sure of that.

It was an honour to be captain that day, fantastic to be first up to lift the trophy, especially with it being 'Oranje Day' and the club's hundredth piece of silverware. I was proud to skipper the team but it didn't make the day any more special than previous victories with Rangers. Being the captain did not make me feel like I was the 'main man'.

The celebrations after the Aberdeen game were good and the champagne flowed, but I particularly remember the journey on the team bus along Paisley Road West as we headed back to Ibrox. The streets were packed with Rangers supporters and they gave us a fantastic reception as the bus crawled along the road. It's a tremendous feeling being able to make so many people happy. It was a great part of the job. To know hundreds of thousands of people all over the world are celebrating something you have helped make happen is really special. And 'Oranje Day' was one of the very best, in my eyes.

10

ADVOCAAT: THE BEGINNING OF THE END

In the summer of 1998 Dick Advocaat recruited three fellow Dutchmen to join him at Rangers – myself, Giovanni van Bronckhorst and Bert van Lingen as his assistant. That first season we played really good football, and managed to get the blend of entertaining the fans and winning vital games. We had quality in every area of the pitch and players full of confidence.

There was a real cosmopolitan dressing room with guys from Argentina, Spain, Chile, Holland, Finland, Germany, Russia, France, Italy, England and, of course, Scotland making up the first-team squad. It was the start of a new era at Ibrox. The fantastic nine-in-a-row team of Ally McCoist, Andy Goram, Ian Durrant, Stuart McCall and Paul Gascoigne had all left. I think it was right for Rangers to sell Gascoigne before Dick arrived. I would imagine that the transfer to Middlesbrough, just a few months before Dick was due to start at Rangers, would have had his blessing. Having to work with such an unpredictable character as Gazza would have driven Dick mental.

It was disappointing for that bunch and the outgoing manager, Walter Smith, not to have won anything in their final season together. Celtic had pipped them to the title to stop ten-in-a-row and Hearts had won the Scottish Cup final at Parkhead. Under Advocaat, the expectation level was high. In his first couple of months in the job he spent more than £20 million bringing in players he felt were absolutely necessary to win the league back and to challenge on the European stage. Advocaat believed both were a real possibility. And so did I.

We lifted the Treble in the first season, a fantastic achievement. The league title was won with a bit to spare from Celtic, who had Dr Jozef Venglos in charge that season. We also beat our greatest rivals in the Scottish Cup final that season 1–0 thanks to a goal from Rod Wallace. I didn't know too much about Wallace when he joined at the same time as me. He was picked up on a free transfer from Leeds United and was a prolific striker for us over the period.

But the first season also had its problems along the way. In fact, Advocaat was worried he was going to be sacked after just a few weeks in charge. After the World Cup with Holland, I was given two weeks off by my new manager. I returned to France for the duration of my holiday, to relax.

There I was, sitting by the pool, relaxing, enjoying a Pina Colada. My mobile went off and it was Dick on the line. I thought he was on to ask me how my holidays were going and to make sure I had my feet up, with the long season ahead in mind. I thought he might even be on to offer me an extra few days off! I was wrong on both counts.

'Arthur, it's Dick.'

'Hello, boss, how are you?' There was no time for small talk. The boss got straight to the point.

'Listen, Arthur, I need you to pack your bags and come to Glasgow immediately. We've messed up in the first leg of the UEFA Cup tie against Shelbourne and I need you back to play in the second leg at Ibrox. We can't afford to lose this game. If we lose, I reckon I might not last much longer as the manager of Rangers.'

I must confess I was annoyed at having to cut my holidays short. However, Rangers had paid a huge transfer fee for me and were paying me good wages. Reluctantly, I got my things together and was off to Glasgow a couple of days later.

I was quite nervous on my first day at Ibrox. I think fourteen or fifteen different nationalities were in the dressing room. I thought to myself, 'Jesus, this is a World XI.' The local players,

Charlie Miller, Barry Ferguson, Ian Ferguson, Gordon Durie, Derek McInnes and Scott Wilson, were also there. It was a new season and they hadn't managed to get off to a good start. The Shelbourne result was a worry. Going 3–0 down to a part-time team from Ireland was not what Rangers were meant to be about, but eventually they managed to get their act together and ran in five goals in the second half.

During the first training sessions it was easy to see every player was out to impress their new boss. Every one of them gave 100 per cent. It was interesting to see how players adapted to Dick's training routines. The little possession games we played – 5 v 3, 6 v 4 or 4 v 4 – were always intense. Of course, none of this was new to me. I'd known Dick for ten years. He had no secrets from me. I knew all about his rules and discipline. In terms of football, he could do nothing to take me by surprise, but I know the new regime did surprise the Scottish players and some of the foreigners.

But the most important things the players had to take on board about Dick were that he was honest and straightforward. There was no hidden agenda. He also had a bit of an obsession with good time-keeping. I also hate bad time-keeping – there is no need for it. If you were late even by just one minute he'd be there with his booming 'Yeeees', glaring down at his wristwatch. And that meant another donation to the fines kitty which was usually given to charity at the end of the season.

Dick also instructed us to make sure we had our mobiles off at all times inside Ibrox but there were a few guys who flouted his orders. And I was one of them! The manager caught me out one day when he called my mobile and I answered and couldn't believe it hearing Dick's unmistakable 'Yeeees' on the other end of the line. He started to laugh and said, 'That's another fine!'

Sometimes, of course, he didn't catch some of the players. Football players always find little ways to beat the manager's system! But there was nowhere for them to hide when Dick was angry. Then, he let the players have it – both barrels. He always gave instructions to the squad in English, but when things didn't work out on the training pitch or on a match day, he would yell in Dutch to van Lingen. Yes, believe it or not, Dick had quite a temper on him! He would let it be known he wasn't happy and then he would storm out of the dressing room. The players would turn to me and ask, 'What is he saying?' and I would answer them as best I could. He liked to leave them stewing, it was another way of motivating the players to get even more out of them on the pitch.

Dick also worked hard at Rangers to build a strong team spirit. He wanted discipline in the dressing room, little things like players had to throw their dirty training gear in a hamper and not leave it lying around for Jimmy the kit man.

He also made sure we all ate together every day after training. It was the same when he was manager of PSV. At Ibrox, we'd eat in the Cooper Suite, which was a new scenario at Rangers.

We'd always start at 1 p.m. and had to wait for Dick to say, 'Enjoy your meal.' You dared not lift your cutlery before those words had been uttered. Many of the players started to do impressions of Dick saying his little catchphrase.

The food at Ibrox was always good – pasta, chicken and soup. The ladies in the kitchen – Irene, Tiny, Linda and Mary – were all lovely and they looked after us really well. Now, quite often, we'd be finished training, showered and changed by 12.15. A lot of the boys didn't like waiting around for forty-five minutes until lunch was served and complained of being bored, almost like they were being held hostage. But it forced us to sit together and talk about things, whether it was about football, family life or experiences in Glasgow or the country you were brought up in. It was all part of the process of building up good relations and camaraderie in the dressing room. We were all pretty new to each other and in order to be successful on the pitch, there has to be some kind of relationship off it.

I arrived at Ibrox after the World Cup finals. It was actually quite a difficult time for me because I was one of the last players to get there and already some of the guys had started friendships after training together for two or three weeks.

To prepare for the vital second-leg clash against Shelbourne, we trained on the Monday and headed down to Turnberry Hotel in Ayrshire late in the afternoon to prepare for the game the following night. The hotel was magnificent; I've been back since with Marjon to enjoy it. That night the players were mixing with the friends they had made and others played PlayStation together. I felt a little bit left out, to be honest.

Usually I mix fine with other players but I was wondering what the other guys thought of me. Did they reckon I regarded myself as a superstar? Did they see me as 'Dick's man' because I had been with him at PSV? The best way to make an impression on football players is to do well on the pitch. And I had a good start at Rangers. I won the Man of the Match award against Shelbourne. We won 2–0 and made it safely through to the next round of the UEFA Cup. Oh, and Dick managed to keep his job!

I had to get used to hotels and after that I stayed in the Hilton in Glasgow city centre for three months until I found a house. There was always time to kill and I would go to restaurants in the city or have a coffee in the hotel bar most nights. Colin Hendry, Andrei Kanchelskis and van Bronckhorst had also just signed and they were staying in the hotel too, so on occasion we would go for a coffee or a drink together in the lobby lounge.

It was then I really found out the true size of Rangers and the extent of the feelings the fans had for their club. Wherever I went I was always being asked to pose for photographs and sign autographs. Every person wished me luck and told me not to let down their club. But, to be honest, it made me feel a little bit under pressure. I knew there was no hiding place in Glasgow and below-par performances would not be accepted by the fans.

I was also not allowed to forget that I'd cost Rangers £4.5 million. There was nothing I could do about the fee – the transfer market was absolutely crazy at that time.

Serious questions were asked in the media about Advocaat and his signings after we lost 2–1 away to Hearts on the opening weekend of the league season. I wasn't worried about it. I knew we would take time to settle, take time to get to know each other.

Does he like the ball into feet or over the top? Can he cope with a defender up his backside? It was never going to come together after just two or three games, but we had to make sure it was all in place for when the prizes were handed out. And it was. We won the Treble in our first season. We won everything because we had a good manager and good players. We also bonded well off the pitch and I got to like Ian Ferguson. Fergie's a funny guy and used to take the piss out of the foreign lads and other people in and around the club.

Ian lived for Rangers. That's why he was raging when we lost 5–1 at Celtic Park in the second Old Firm game of the 1998–99 season. All week in training, Ian and the other Scottish lads, like Charlie Miller and Gordon Durie, had been hammering into us that we could not lose this game. Celtic were underdogs and we were expected to win. Headlines appeared every day in the papers about the game and I felt the tension in the city on the Friday, twenty-four hours before kick-off. I thought the rivalry between PSV and Ajax was out of the top drawer but this was something else.

I remember standing in the centre-circle an hour before kick-off, still in my suit and tie, to look at the pitch and get a feel for the stadium. I remember saying, 'Yeah, this is a nice arena,' but one of the guys told me that no compliments towards Celtic were allowed. It was good to see there was no fencing or barbed wire around the arena. The crowd are really close to the pitch – you could almost shake hands with them.

Of course, Celtic play 'You'll Never Walk Alone' at their home games and I had no idea about that. It happens to be one

Eighteen-months-old and I'm already sporting the famous Oranje top

My first ball and even as a three-year-old, I loved to play football

As an eight-year-old, I put up a decent defence against my brother Jeroen

Aged five, with my brother and father

My brother Jeroen (behind me) and Michel Doesburg (on my right) take a sly look at my cards

Beverwijk team photo, 1979.
I'm in the front row, second from left, and Michael Doesburg is in the front, second from right

Haarlem team photo in 1985

Playing for Haarlem in 1989

Firing in a shot in August
1991 for Twente Enschede

Private Numan at my barracks
in Den Bosch in 1989

It was great to play with Romário at PSV. He
was instrumental in getting me there

I am devastated as our Olympic dream is over
and Australia head to Barcelona

Picking up the Johan Cruijff Cup in the Amsterdam Arena in 1996 for PSV after beating Ajax in their own stadium

Celebrating the PSV League triumph in 1997

It was a great honour meeting Nelson Mandela in South Africa

My farewell party in Beverwijk with Marjon

A harsh introduction to my first World Cup as Roy Keane slides in on me in 1994

The Dutch World Cup squad 1998 – from left to right: Van der Sar, Bergkamp, Stam, Cocu, Jonk, Kluivert, Numan, Davids, Reiziger, F. de Boer, R. de Boer

Surging through the tackles of two Argentinian defenders in France 1998

I try to argue my case, knowing full well I'll be receiving a red card

My look of despair says it all as I announce an injury has forced me out of the
Euro 2000 semi-final

Rangers chairman David Murray introduces me to the press in June 1998

Proudly holding the Rangers scarf

My first trophy for Rangers – at Parkhead v St Johnstone in 1998

Giovanni van Bronckhorst wonders what time the fashion police will arrive to arrest us all

As captain of Rangers, it was a proud moment when I lifted their 100th trophy after the 2000 Scottish Cup final

Celebrating with Dick Advocaat after beating Aberdeen in the 2000 Scottish Cup final

A fantastic night as we dump PSG out of the UEFA Cup on penalties in Paris

I can't believe the ref has sent me off against Sturm Graz

I'm so furious I throw my shirt at the fourth official

The pain of another European failure after we fail to beat Monaco in November 2000

Celebrating the Scottish Cup final win against Celtic

I didn't score too many for Rangers but this one against Celtic in 2002 was extra special

Sheer ecstasy as I celebrate that goal

Alex McLeish and I celebrate our dramatic
title win after beating Dunfermline

Ecstatic league winners 2003

The dressing-room is jumping as we start the party after clinching my final league title

The cup final against Dundee and the last
game of my career

Fernando Ricksen, Ronald de Boer,
Shota Arveladze, Mikel Arteta and
Michael Mols give me a lift

Proudly showing off our treble triumph in 2003

Meeting Dick Advocaat and John Greig at Murray Park. Two people I have a lot of respect for

The whole family at a photo session

Marjon and I enjoy a night out at the start
of our relationship

My mum, Marjan, and dad, Hans, proudly show off their first grandchild Britt

In the garden with my two beautiful
daughters, Britt and Maud

Britt gives little Maud a hug

Britt aged three

Maud aged ten months

of my favourite songs – although we used to play 'Simply the Best' at PSV's stadium. The Rangers players gave me pelters for admitting that in an interview. Of course, the fact I liked 'Walk on . . .' made a huge headline in the newspapers in Scotland.

The game was a disaster for us. It was Dick's first Old Firm defeat and we were hammered 5–1. We were in a state of shock. Scott Wilson was given a straight red card by referee Willie Young in the first half for a foul on Lubo Moravcik and we never coped with being a man down. It was in the dressing room after the game that I witnessed the other side of Fergie.

Ian was born and raised in Glasgow, just a few hundred yards from Celtic Park, as a big Rangers supporter. He was furious. He was yelling and shouting, 'F***ing foreigners, you have no idea what it means to play for this club, to lose this game to Celtic.'

He told the guys in the dressing room we were an embarrassment and a disgrace to the Rangers jersey. We had eight non-Scots (me, Niemi, Porrini, Kanchelskis, van Bronckhorst, Albertz, Guivarc'h and Wallace) in the starting line-up that day and I think Fergie was trying to let us all know what playing for Rangers against your greatest rival is all about.

Advocaat stood silent and let Ferguson say his piece. He knew it was best to let him get everything off his chest. Anyway, I think it would have taken a brave man to try to interrupt him! I sat down with Ian the next day at Ibrox and made the fatal mistake of saying to him that he might have overreacted a little bit. After all, it was only a game of football.

He told me, 'No, Arthur, it's not only a game. I hate losing to them. You play for Rangers and you should also hate losing to them. I'd rather beat them four times a season than win the league.' I told Ian that we still had to play them another two times at least, so we could have the last laugh AND win the league. It was a good discussion and I'm glad I had a few moments alone that day with Ian. I might not have agreed with everything he said but it was an education. As soon as I arrived at Ibrox on the Monday after the game I could sense a flatness about the stadium. Peter, the front doorman, was glum. Laura, the manager's secretary, also had a depressed look on her face.

Seeing the reaction to the defeat really brought home Pierre van Hooijdonk's words in France about not being able to cross the divide and play for Rangers. Now I fully understood what he meant and realised he had made the right decision, the only one available to him.

The newspapers, radio and television were full of coverage for days and days about the 5–1 result. The only consolation for us was that we were still top of the league. Of course, we went on to lift the championship that season and complete the Treble. It was a superb achievement. I was delighted for the players, the members of staff and the supporters. I knew how much it meant to them.

I was particularly happy for Dick. There was a lot of pressure on him to deliver success and he managed it. I had worked with him since I was just seventeen and he was a major influence on my career. In my early days as a footballer, Dick taught me to relax and enjoy my football. It's Dick who actually turned me into a left-back and he is probably the man responsible for moulding my international career.

In 1996, when he was in charge of PSV Dick came to me and told me he wanted me to play in the left of a three at the back. I wasn't happy because my preferred position had always been left midfield, or just behind the front two. I had never seen myself as a defender. I let Dick know about my misgivings, but he simply said to me, 'Find me one or two guys who can play left-back and I'll keep you in midfield!' I was stunned and couldn't think of anyone, so reluctantly I was forced to admit defeat and started the season in a back three.

I hated it. It got so bad that I was starting to dislike the game and it got to the stage where I'd rather be sitting in the stand or on the bench than be forced to play in defence. It was against all my natural instincts to sit at the back and man-mark rather than go forward and be creative.

We were struggling under the new system and thankfully Dick saw sense four weeks into the season and changed our system to a 4–4–2 after a heavy defeat to NAC Breda. The team – and my career – never looked back. I started to enjoy the game and grew into the role of an attacking full-back. At the time Holland were over-laden with brilliant midfielders and maybe I would have struggled to get into the team, but the national side were short on quality left-backs and Dick knew I was good enough to make the position my own.

Yet for all our time together I only ever knew him as a manager. I couldn't tell you much about his private life. He always had a rule that he was employed by a football club to do his job as manager and guide the team to win games in the hope it resulted in silverware at the end of the season.

His job was not to party with the players.

At Rangers he was in early in the morning until late in the afternoon. At night he probably went home and put a football video on. He wasn't one for socialising; he was rarely in Glasgow city centre for a meal and a drink. His public face is quite a strict one, which is how he is a lot of the time, but when the door was closed in his office he also enjoyed a laugh and joke.

However, he demanded discipline. In the first two years at Rangers it was fine because we won the Treble in the first season and the Double in the next season. Problems really started in the third campaign. By the time the 2000–01 season started we had lots of Dutchmen at the club, in the first-team squad, the coaching staff, the youth department and even the club doctor. I had a feeling that the microscope would be on the club and that accusations of too much of a Dutch influence at Rangers would start to come out if things weren't going right on the pitch.

Sadly, I was right. And Dick has to take quite a lot of the blame for this. The Dutch people at the club were treated like heroes for the first two years and the Rangers fans even wore oranje Holland jerseys in the 1999–2000 Scottish Cup final as a tribute to the Dutch contingent. We thumped Aberdeen 4–0 that day and I was the captain. I felt so proud. Running out at Hampden that afternoon felt like I was back in my own country for a national team game. I also had a Rangers supporters club named after me – The Arthur Numan Loyal RSC in Milngavie. That is a great honour and I'm still in contact with the club chairman Iain Sinclair to this day. But in the third year it all went horribly wrong and we were looked upon as villains.

Martin O'Neill arrived at Celtic and really kick-started them. They'd had a dreadful season the previous year as we romped to the title by a twenty-one-point margin. O'Neill brought in quality players like Chris Sutton, Alan Thompson, Joos Valgaeren and Neil Lennon. He also inherited the brilliant Henrik Larsson and managed to bring out the best in Stilian Petrov.

Celtic won the first Old Firm game of the 2000–01 season 6–2, a result I found totally embarrassing. Bert Konterman and Fernando Ricksen made their debuts that day and it didn't go well for either of them. Bobby Petta gave Fernando a torrid Old Firm debut that day and it was no surprise he was subbed less than twenty-five minutes into the game. Fernando wasn't happy at being hooked but Dick replaced him for his own good.

Fernando had cost over £3 million from AZ Alkmaar but was still a young player, only twenty-four at the time. He was highly rated in Holland and also had the chance to sign for Ajax at the same time Rangers were after him. That game was a huge turning-point for Celtic. I was injured and watched the match from inside the stadium with my parents, but I could tell Celtic were really up for it. We'd never known a Celtic team like it. We were meant to be the dominating side and thought we'd win the game, but they blew us away that afternoon.

We managed to pick ourselves up a little bit and won the next Old Firm game 5–1 at Ibrox. It was Tore Andre Flo's debut and he scored to get his Rangers career off to an excellent start. There was enormous pressure on him with the £12 million price tag from Chelsea and I think he buckled under the strain – although I believe the transfer fee was a ridiculous amount of money to pay for him. He was often the centre of attention and if he didn't score at least a goal in every game then he came in for abuse and was labelled a waste of money. Every time his name was mentioned in the press or on television it was always '£12 million striker Tore Andre Flo'. It was an intense pressure to be under.

Fernando and Bert also struggled and they didn't cost anywhere near Flo's fee. In particular, I felt that Fernando needed help and guidance during the early stages of his Ibrox career because he had arrived from a small club in Holland and it is a big adjustment to make when you come to Glasgow – both on and off the park.

I offered him advice, to show different things to improve him as a player and as a professional. But it was clear he wasn't keen on taking my advice and we had a couple of arguments about it. He was diving in at training and some of his tackling was a little over the top. I told him to relax and calm down a little. But he was too stubborn to listen and made it quite clear he wanted to do it his way. The truth was, at that time, Fernando was struggling to cope with the pressure of being a Rangers player and I only wanted to see him succeed. He just wasn't for listening, at least to me, so I left it alone. It was a pity because he was making an impact for all the wrong reasons in his first year or two at Rangers and he struggled to fulfill his potential.

However, he has been a good player for Rangers in recent years and I was delighted to see him winning the PFA Player of the Year in a joint award with Celtic's John Hartson in April 2005. He's had his problems since with new Ibrox manager Paul Le Guen, but I hope he gets his issues resolved and again shows the kind of form that made him a Dutch international.

In fact, I reckon that if he had a more focused approach to his football development he could easily have become our country's right-back for many years. Holland are struggling at the moment for a decent right-back and Fernando would have fitted the bill and could have enjoyed playing for national coach Marco van Basten. But because of Fernando's behaviour off the pitch he's received negative headlines.

Of course, we all received criticism during our time at Rangers. We knew at the start of the 2000–01 season that if things didn't go well then Advocaat would be accused of having too many Dutchmen at the club. We just knew the Dutch would get the blame from the press, media and the supporters.

But the truth is that a lot of the players were under-performing that season – not just the Dutch boys. We also had a bad run of injuries and Dick wasn't able to pick a settled side. The Dutch players spoke about it during pre-season and knew there would be no escaping the abuse if results didn't pick up. I can handle criticism but to blame everything on the Dutch was wrong, totally out of order.

Even so, the anger I felt from that criticism was nothing compared to what I felt when Davie Provan asked me questions during an interview for Sky at a press conference inside Ibrox that was open to all the media. I came into the press room after a defeat to face the music. A lot of players hide from the media after a loss, but I feel it's my duty to try to explain things as best I can at the particular moment.

Out of the blue, one of the questions Provan asked me was, 'Are the foreign players just coming here for the money?'

I was gobsmacked. I was angry and remember saying to myself, 'Stay calm, Arthur, stay calm.' I don't know if Davie was trying to elicit a reaction from me but I wasn't taking the bait and I answered him in the most diplomatic way I could. What I felt inside, and I wanted to say and do to him was altogether different. I had to stop myself from getting up from the press table and slapping him in the face.

I was really pissed off. I felt insulted and thought Davie should have known better than to ask that kind of thing. I'll never forget that question. This kind of thing became normal. Almost every day negative stories about the Dutch were being given to the pressmen. It was made out that our influence was too big and that the people from my country were in total control of the club. It was nonsense, absolute nonsense.

What was true was that some players had fallen out during Dick's third season in charge. But this is normal at a football club. Players weren't happy at not getting a game every week. Jorg Albertz was a fans' favourite but didn't start as many matches as he wanted because of the competition in midfield with Barry Ferguson, van Bronckhorst, Claudio Reyna and Tugay. Some other guys were unsettled at being on the bench or up in the stand and that's when stories of unhappiness started to appear in the papers. Yes, things were not perfect, but I felt the stories were exaggerated. I went through it before with the Dutch national team and all the negative stuff came out at different times.

Fall-outs do happen. My goodness, I had plenty during my career. At Rangers I used to argue with Barry Ferguson in every game. We were room-mates but that didn't stop us having a go at each other. Shouting at your team-mate is sometimes necessary – when I got abuse from my manager or a team-mate I would roll up my sleeves and be determined to shut them up. Neil McCann played in front of me at Rangers and I would shout and bawl at him, but I would always do it with respect and with the right meaning behind it.

One of my biggest dressing room bust-ups happened to be with Lorenzo Amoruso. Alex McLeish was in charge and it was half-time during a UEFA Cup game. Before the game, Lorenzo was told by the manager to stay away from the free-kicks within shooting distance and leave it to either Ricksen or Barry Ferguson. However, not surprisingly, he disobeyed the instructions and took a free-kick that flew wildly over the crossbar and hit some vehicles in the car park! People in the high-rise flats were complaining!

The players weren't happy with Amoruso but no-one would speak up. At half-time, I told him he was out of order and that he should do what the manager instructs him. Lorenzo was having none of it, he became all defensive and accused me of picking on him, jumping on his back for the sake of it. It was typical of Lorenzo to react like that.

At half-time in the dressing room he threatened to kill me! We were shouting and bawling at each other, nose-to-nose. I expected McLeish to say something to Amoruso for blatantly disobeying his pre-match instructions but I don't think he said anything to him. After the game, we forgot about it and moved on, which was the best thing because we changed beside each other every day. However, I do always feel it is better to be honest with your team-mate. Lorenzo is a proud Italian and was honoured to be captain of such a great club, but when Dick decided to relieve him of his duties he took it personally and started to become depressed about the situation. After losing the captaincy, Amo was never the same with the boss and their relationship suffered because of it.

There were also problems between players when Advocaat was in charge. I remember in November 2000, Ricksen and Andrei Kanchelskis started fighting in training one day. They had a big argument over a tackle between them. Andrei threw the first punch and Fernando retaliated and I have to say some great blows were exchanged! Advocaat and some players stepped in to break it up. We trained at Stepps at the time and Advocaat sent Kanchelskis back to the bus to wait for the rest of the squad, which I felt was wrong. He should have sent both players away as they were as guilty as each other. Kanchelskis wasn't happy and was shouting 'Dutch assholes' as he left the training ground.

Of course, the incident came out in the papers and once again Advocaat was accused of favouring the Dutch. It was the last thing we needed and that's why he should have sent both of them away. It was in situations such as that one where he failed to make the right call that Dick didn't help himself. At that time the atmosphere in the dressing room wasn't good. However, I have to stress it wasn't as bad as the press and media were making it out to be.

There were cliques and little groups – but that's normal at every club. The Dutch had a clique and the Scottish lads had a bond. I think this is quite normal because it's easier to speak to people in your own language. If we were only talking to our countrymen and ignoring the rest then that would have concerned me but that was not the case. I think that some of the lads who didn't understand Dutch or Italian might have thought they were being spoken about, but that was never so. What concerned me most was that some players like Sergio Porrini and Kanchelskis were happy not to see their names on the squad sheet on a Friday afternoon for the game the following day.

That kind of behaviour was just typical of the dressing room in the 2000–01 season. Results weren't positive and the atmosphere was not as good as it should have been. Dick took the biggest kicking out of anyone else at the club from the press and media. It became too personal and went too far. Criticism is part of the game but that kind of stuff is out of order. It is disrespectful. One day he is a hero and the next day he is a dud. There was never any middle ground at Rangers.

Because we were not winning enough games and Celtic were going well under O'Neill, our performances were suffering and it was no surprise Celtic won the Treble that season, 2000–01. In the summer of 2001 we moved to Murray Park, our brand new, state-of-the-art training complex. The players were delighted with the facilities. When I signed for Rangers, I had no idea they didn't have their own training complex. It's something that David Murray and Dick must have forgotten to tell me! To be honest, having to board a mini-bus at Ibrox and then go on a twenty-minute journey to Stepps was out of order. I suppose in the summer it was fine but in the winter it was a complete disaster. All crammed into the mini-bus, the journey back every day wearing soaking wet training gear was not pleasant. It was even worse if you'd picked up an injury at training that morning.

Thankfully, after some forceful pressure from Dick towards Murray, the club now has Murray Park. To be honest, some sort of similar facility should have been in place at a club the size of Rangers at least ten years earlier. The players, manager and chairman felt Murray Park would be the launch-pad for a successful season, the chance to regain the league title from Celtic.

Celtic wanted to win the title more than we did that season and it showed. We were determined not to allow it to happen the next season. I really wanted it to be a good campaign for Dick's sake as well as the staff, players and fans of Rangers.

In 2000–01 I noticed a difference in Dick as Celtic were going towards the title. He was very tense, not his usual self. In his final season, 2001–02, I really felt sorry for him. Things were not going his way and he decided to step down from being team manager, taking on the role of Rangers' Director of Football. After leading the team into Europe beyond Christmas with the win against Paris Saint-Germain in the UEFA Cup, he felt enough was enough. Alex McLeish took over as manager.

As much as I felt sorry for Dick, I don't believe he was blameless for his downfall. I felt he was sometimes too strict with us and things might have been different in the dressing room if he handled things better. The players used to go out for meals and drinks and go-karting sessions, it all came naturally. Latterly, on the odd occasion we did go out together, it was almost forced rather than something we were all up for as a group. When the club is winning everything is great at a football club. When defeats happen regularly it takes its toll on everyone connected with the club. I noticed the entire place was down. A Monday morning after a defeat was particularly bad. Jimmy our kit man was depressed, the kitchen staff struggled to raise a smile and, of course, the supporters were unhappy.

During this depressing period Celtic were doing well, which just made it even worse. The Celtic supporters popped up all over the place and loved to rub it in to the Rangers fans. To be honest, up until 2001, I barely knew that Celtic supporters existed! When we were winning they were nowhere to be seen. They soon appeared from the closet, though!

Along with Advocaat, the players held meetings at Ibrox to try to get to the bottom of what was wrong inside the dressing room. Why do we not seem to be all in this together? Is it the tactics? Is it totally down to the manager? Are we to blame? Often, more questions than answers came out of those sessions, but the bottom line was we knew the most effective way to sort it out was to win games. However, what helps you win games is having a good team spirit, wanting to do well for one another and the manager.

A decision Advocaat took because he thought it would help the mood in the dressing room was to replace Amoruso as skipper with Barry Ferguson. I was vice-captain to Lorenzo and under normal circumstances should have taken over from him. But I thought it was a sensible idea NOT to give me the armband.

It was not the first time I had turned down the chance to be captain of Rangers. When I first signed for Rangers Dick offered it to me because I had been his skipper at PSV Eindhoven and he knew what I was about. He knew he could trust me 100 per cent to be professional on and off the pitch. But I reckoned it was best not to accept his kind offer. It was an honour to be asked but I felt it was best to get myself settled at the club and find out exactly what Rangers were all about. It was at that point Dick turned to Lorenzo. Lorenzo had been at Ibrox for a year prior to that, having been signed by Walter Smith from Fiorentina in the summer of 1997 for around £4 million.

Looking back, I still think it was the right decision, both times. However, having been at Rangers for five years, if I'd known back in 1998 what I know now about the club then I would have given more consideration to being captain of such a massive institution. I know I would have been very proud to skipper the club, to follow in the footsteps of great, and successful, Ibrox captains such as John Greig, George Young and Richard Gough.

At Dick's second time of asking, my reasons for not accepting were totally different. I was ready for it and I don't think too many people in the dressing room or supporters would have disagreed with the selection, but it just wasn't right. It had to be another player. It had to be a non-Dutchman. With all the negativity towards the Dutch at that time, there would have been war if I was given the nod. I spoke to Advocaat about the situation and he agreed. It was the best thing all round that it was given to a Scotsman and Barry fitted the bill perfectly. Not only because he was Scottish; he was a top performer on the pitch too. Amoruso wasn't pleased and got a little depressed about the whole situation for a while. But Rangers is a massive football club and must always be bigger than any individual. Barry was delighted to be appointed skipper, although I know he did find it daunting for the first few months, which was to be expected. I think the captaincy helped mature him, though, and he grew into the role and it helped him develop as a player and a person.

Things picked up for a while after that but it still wasn't good enough. Advocaat was coming under more and more pressure and the dressing-room atmosphere was still not as good as it should have been. And it was not all down to the fact that there were so many Dutch people at the club.

The good thing for Dick was that he was allowed to leave having taken us into Europe beyond Christmas. We played Paris Saint-Germain – a team packed with talents like Ronaldinho, Jay-Jay Okocha, Mikel Arteta and Nicolas Anelka

– in the UEFA Cup and a win over the two legs would see us into the New Year for the first time in nine years since Walter Smith's fine side lost out in controversial circumstances to Marseille in the latter stages of the Champions League.

Our tie against PSG ended up going to a penalty shoot-out over there after two goalless draws, although we had a chance to clinch it in extra-time but sadly Ronald de Boer missed from the spot. With so many Dutchmen involved with Rangers, we were dreading the thought of jinxing the penalties! I remember all the players standing in front of the bench at the end of extra-time and Bert van Lingen looking for volunteers to take the penalties. After a deep breath I was brave enough to say to him, 'Bert, put me down for the last kick.' Now, by that I meant the last kick of sudden-death. I wanted to be the tenth taker, but Bert thought I meant the final one of the first five.

I was sitting in the technical area, untying my bootlaces, when Bert came over. 'Arthur, what are you doing? Come on, we need you out there on the pitch beside the other four guys.' I then realised Bert had misunderstood me. It was too late. The referee had been given my name on the list of five and there was no going back.

I was bricking it as I walked up to face Lionel Letizi, who ironically is now at Ibrox. All I could think about was not missing the kick. I knew if I missed and we crashed out then I would have been as well packing my bags and going back to Holland for good. I knew the press and media would want to blame the Dutch.

After Ronald's miss in extra-time Bert Konterman failed in the shoot-out, so I was dreading being the THIRD Dutchman to miss a penalty in Paris! All I could see was the negative headlines about the Dutch influence at Ibrox. I had missed in a penalty shoot-out against Borussia Dortmund the season before and didn't want the same thing to happen again.

Lorenzo and Russell Latapy slotted away two penalties.

Then it was my turn to take a kick and I remember standing, waiting to make the forty-yard trudge to the penalty area. Should I walk? Should I run? Should I jog? All these silly things were going through my mind.

It's hard to put into words exactly how I was feeling. But one thing's for sure, I was nervous. It's easy to slot away a penalty 99 times out of 100 in training, but when it comes to a match situation it's all about getting your nerves under control and not necessarily about skill. As well as the skill you have to add in factors like the tension, what's at stake and the crowd. All these things influence the outcome and I still believe practising penalties on the training ground can't prepare you for a shoot-out at the end of 120 minutes.

I put the ball on the spot and for the whole time I made sure I didn't make contact with the eyes of their keeper, Letizi. As I walked back I also decided I was going to place the ball with my left foot down my left side, low to the keeper's right.

For some reason I changed my mind in the run-up and ended up hitting it powerfully across myself and to the left of the keeper. It made its way to the side of the net – a well-taken penalty if I do say so myself.

Well, talk about being relieved. I've watched it a few times on video since and the emotion on my face is clear to see. I was drained and just let it all out. I ran to the jubilant Rangers fans, clenched my fist and screamed, 'Come on!' Barry then scored the winning penalty and we had the chance to celebrate an excellent victory and an achievement to be proud of.

Dick was going absolutely bonkers on the pitch. I'd never seen him looking so happy and animated, although I guess – as was the case with my own feelings at that moment – it was just pure and utter relief. He had it all planned. He waited for the right moment before he stepped down. I think there were other things he wanted to achieve at Rangers before he chucked it. Getting to the second stages of the Champions League would have been one thing and bowing out as the title winning manager possibly another.

Overall, I felt quite sorry for Advocaat in the end. He changed things at Ibrox. He brought in quality players from all over the world and had the team playing some attractive football both domestically and in the European arena. He also played a huge part in the development of Barry Ferguson. Dick's input has made Barry the fine player he is today. Dick also insisted on a training ground being built that matched the stature of the club.

In my opinion, he deserved to leave Rangers with a positive send-off but it never happened. From where I've been standing, he's been remembered for his time at Rangers as the man who wasted £12 million on Flo and brought too many of his countrymen to Ibrox.

It's cruel to overlook the Treble he won in his first season and the Double in his second season. Yes, he made mistakes, but all managers do. Dick knew he was stepping down after the PSG game to become the Director of Football at Rangers. I was aware of the speculation but Dick never confirmed anything to me during any private moment together. Yes, I had known him longer than any other player at Rangers, but it didn't get me any inside knowledge.

The first I knew about the move was when Dick called all the players together for a meeting at Murray Park. He informed us about his new role and that Alex McLeish would be taking over as the next manager. Although it wasn't completely out of the blue, it still came as a bit of a shock to me.

A couple of days after the announcement, I went to see him at his office. I told him that I thought he'd made the right decision but that he wouldn't enjoy his new role. Deep down, we both knew that, if a job offer came in, he would take it. I didn't think he'd last two weeks as Director of Football because he can't stand still for a minute, can't switch off from being a football manager.

He lasted a little longer than two minutes but it wasn't too long before he accepted an offer to take over as the national coach of Holland again. For the first few weeks of his role as Director of Football, he was happy to be out of the firing line. It had been a tough period for about a year and it took its toll on him and his family, especially when the criticism became personal rather than constructive. He put a brave face on things, seeing him wandering around Murray Park in his new role. But he deliberately kept his distance from the players, which was the right thing to do as he wouldn't have wanted to be accused of interfering in McLeish's team.

But I was under the impression he was frustrated. He'd be sitting in the stand watching a game, and he'd spot something that needed to be changed tactically but had no power to do anything about it. All he could do was mention it to McLeish after the game or the following day, providing, of course, the new manager asked for his opinion.

However, it was the right time for him to go. The last straw for most of the players was after a defeat in October at St Johnstone and Dick absolutely slaughtered the players in his interviews after the game. He called us shameful and said, 'It was hopeless. We're talking about top players – top internationals, top Scottish players – but I didn't see any of that out there tonight. I can't accept it any more. I am totally sick of it. Too many players in my team have big heads. During the week they have too many things on their mind and when it comes to the game they are not focused. They like to look good in their nice white shirts with their nice red shorts but that has nothing to do with winning. Things will change.'

Dick said the players were more interested in golf and playing with PlayStations than they were in turning out for Rangers. The players felt that Dick shouldn't have gone public with that kind of criticism. I got the feeling there was no way back for him with several of the guys after those comments. It threw oil on the fire.

Because the place had more unhappy faces than happy ones, Dick could not do his job properly. Too many negatives surrounded Rangers. So it was in the best interests of the club that a fresh face was introduced. There was irritation in the dressing room and on the training pitch and that had to stop. There was little tolerance level in the dressing room at half-time and players were too confrontational with each other.

Also, in Dick's latter days, there was no spark on or off the pitch between quite a few of the players, which, to be fair, is the case in dressing rooms all over the world. So it was best for all concerned that Advocaat stood down as manager. I wish it could have ended under happier circumstances, but that's football. It can be a rewarding business to be in, but also a very cruel one.

11

GOING FULL CIRCLE

After sixteen years playing at the highest level, I would never have predicted that season 2002–03 would be my last in the game. My final campaign was like a cameo of my career – dramatic, controversial but hugely enjoyable. When I started the season away to Kilmarnock on 3 August 2002, I didn't think that by the end of that campaign I'd be hanging up my boots and walking away from football.

In the previous season Celtic had won the title with a good bit to spare and we knew we'd have to be in tip-top form to have any chance of keeping up with them, never mind actually winning the SPL. We drew 1–1 at Rugby Park. Yes, it was early days, but we already felt up against it.

My body was getting older – I was thirty-two at that time, thirty-three in December. I played my last game for Holland in a friendly against the USA at the end of the previous season. I was taking some painkillers for problems with my right knee and some other bits and bobs on my body. I felt it was right to quit the international scene and concentrate on Rangers. I desperately wanted to be a winner that season and felt I'd jeopardise my own ambitions at club level if I continued to represent Holland. Instead of flying and travelling about with the national team I would use that time to rest my body and prepare for Rangers games.

I decided to tell Dick Advocaat about my decision soon after the Kilmarnock game but had other things to attend to first. Against Killie I tried to play my usual game, which was to overlap and offer an option to the midfielders and attackers. Jan Wouters shouted some instructions to me in Dutch and I disagreed with him but followed the instructions given from the bench. He told me to stay at the back because all of the defenders were pushing forward and losing focus on their defensive duties. But my natural instinct was pushing me forward and I had plenty of space to exploit, as Kilmarnock gave me acres to exploit down the left-hand side.

We drew 1–1 and I was pissed off in the dressing room after the game at starting our season off with only a point. After the game McLeish asked me and Jan what we were arguing about and we explained the situation to him.

It niggled at me all weekend and I was still raging as I drove to Murray Park on the Monday morning. I was angry we dropped points. I was irritated in training and that's when it hit me how long and difficult a season it was going to be.

Straight after training, I went to Advocaat's office and asked if he had some time to see me after I'd had my shower.

He immediately suspected that I wanted to talk about my Holland career and he said, 'Is it something to do with the national team? I expected this already.'

I made it clear I wanted to retire but he told me to have another think and give it a couple of days before making a final decision. But my mind was made up and nothing could change it. I also maintained I wanted to make my decision about my international career myself. I didn't want to quit Holland because I was too old or not good enough to make the team after ten years being involved in the national side.

I played forty-five times for my country and was in the squad at the World Cup finals in 1994 and 1998 and part of the European Championship squads of 1996 and 2000. My many happy memories were locked away. It was time to move on, let a younger player come in.

It was also important to make the decision at that time, at the start of the campaign to reach the 2004 European

Championships in Portugal. It wasn't ideal for Advocaat as there was no natural left-back to take over from me; but he respected my decision.

In the UEFA Cup that season we were put out by Czech side Viktoria Zizkov on away goals. Disgraceful. We were in control of the home game and should never have thrown it away. Our next game was a trip to face Celtic. And, to be honest, it was the last thing we needed. They'd won their midweek UEFA Cup tie and were favourites to win the latest Old Firm derby.

The day after our UEFA Cup exit we were really down but picked ourselves up after McLeish held a meeting to lift the spirits. We were all depressed but had to snap out of it for the big derby ahead. And quickly. McLeish reminded us of the positives going into the game – he still had not lost to Celtic since he took over as manager of Rangers. That was sweet for him and it no doubt rankled with Martin O'Neill. We were also unbeaten in the opening nine league games, the only points dropped being on the opening day at Kilmarnock.

That said, there's no doubt the feeling was just to get out of Celtic Park without losing. Celtic were formidable opponents at the time. They had top players in Henrik Larsson, Chris Sutton, John Hartson, Alan Thompson and Stilian Petrov. And with Bobo Balde and Johan Mjallby in their team, we just simply couldn't match them in the air. Celtic were more powerful, more physical than us. In fact, when all their big men arrived in our penalty area for set-pieces, it was like having the Royal Air Force attacking us! We had to play to our strengths and as much as they had a height advantage, we played better football than them.

Our tactics were spot-on and we exploited their system of adopting a back three. We liked to get the ball on the deck, pass it around and get it into wide areas and in between defenders for Peter Lovenkrands and Claudio Caniggia to take advantage of the space and freedom on the touchline with their explosive pace. O'Neill came across as being stubborn with his rigid

3–5–2 formation. It worked a treat for us and we couldn't believe he continued to use it in the games against us. I think he moved to a back four for the start of the 2003–04 season, but by that time we'd caused them plenty of damage.

Along with our pacy wide players, we had Barry Ferguson, Ronald de Boer and Mikel Arteta bursting forward from the central midfield area to support our central striker and it worked beautifully. Arteta was a skilful player who could create chances from midfield and was good going forward, but asking him, like Barry, to track back and pick up his man was a different story. I, and others, would tell Arteta to defend, but he couldn't handle being given instructions. We were only telling him for the good of the team – constructive criticism, if you like, because the defence was getting killed when runners weren't being tracked. Arteta seemed to take it personally and would sometimes go into his shell instead of responding positively.

We all make mistakes, we all sometimes aren't capable of reacting in the best way to advice and instructions. Goodness, I made plenty of mistakes during my career.

I enjoyed the games against Celtic. Neither side had any secrets from each other – we knew them inside out and vice versa. Many fine individual battles took place on the pitch. I regarded Celtic players as the enemy for ninety minutes, but never had a problem with any of them when we met off it.

Lorenzo Amoruso was always fired up for Old Firm games and, generally, played well in them. He would always rise to the occasion. I don't think Larsson, Sutton or Hartson enjoyed being up against him. However, when he felt he was playing well he tended to get carried away with himself and thought he was Franz Beckenbauer. If only he had cut that nonsense out of his game!

He made mistakes but was rarely, if ever, willing to accept blame. If he made a bad pass, he would look down at the pitch and kick a bit of turf with his boot. Or he would point a finger of accusation at a team-mate. He thought he was so important

– too important, to be honest. He felt compelled to tell every player in the dressing room where they were going wrong. Frankly, he would have been better concentrating on his own game. In the end, players just switched off from him, his 'advice' going in one ear and out the other. On a few occasions I had to tell him to mind his own business when it came to matters about how to play football.

Craig Moore was a great centre-half to have in our team, particularly for games against Celtic. Oz was never afraid to batter his opponent. Sometimes it wasn't legal, but it was always effective. Larsson tried to keep out of Oz's way but never got a moment to himself as Oz was constantly breathing down the back of his neck.

In Celtic games I always felt I had to concentrate more on my defending, because Celtic always played with a wide player. Didier Agathe was normally my direct opponent and he had the pace to destroy defenders. I had to match up to him, keep tight, prevent him from turning to have a one-on-one against me. I handled him pretty well during our battles over a period of three seasons. I had a psychological edge over Agathe in games before a ball was kicked and that was priceless.

I think Lovenkrands had the same advantage over Mjallby, Balde and Joos Valgaeren. He loved playing against them, as they couldn't cope with his pace. Usually, he scored against them. It got so bad that Celtic supporters sent letters warning him not to score. The sentiment and tone of the letters were threatening and he told me about it. To be fair to him, Peter never allowed the threats to get to him and continued to be a pain in the ass for Celtic. In fact, in the same week that he recieved the letters, he scored two goals against Celtic in the Cup final when we won 3–2.

If anything, Peter used the letters as an incentive to spur him on. That afternoon early in the 2002–03 season we left Celtic Park with a draw and we were still top of the league. We worked really hard to get the point, although we'd taken an early lead after a mistake by Celtic keeper Rab Douglas. In the end we came back to score through Shota Arveladze to make it 3–3 and weren't too disappointed with the outcome.

Old Firm games were vital that season and we won the next one 3-2 at Ibrox. During the game I injured myself when I slid in to clear a ball off the line and Agathe came crashing into me. It was an all-or-nothing tackle to prevent a goal as I slid in and Agathe hit me full on my knee. I was in a lot of pain, but adrenalin got me through it. I was out for a few weeks with bruised bone and ligament damage, but it was worth it because we won the game.

That was an important win. With the way the season ended up, every point, indeed every goal, was vital. We were unbeaten in the league for the season up until Boxing Day when we lost 1–0 away to Motherwell. It was a crazy defeat and McLeish was raging after the game. At least we still had a little gap over Celtic, as we'd managed to take fifty-seven points out of a possible sixty-three up until that game in Lanarkshire.

There was a winter break that season and it was a welcome rest for us all. Celtic were still in Europe, in the middle of their UEFA Cup run that took them all the way to Seville, and it was good for us they had other concerns away from the SPL. We enjoyed a nice winter break in Dubai for a week. We had some good training sessions and took part in a friendly against Bundesliga side Energie Cottbus. We also had time to relax and some of the boys enjoyed a round of golf on a beautiful course.

I started my contract talks in Dubai and they weren't going to plan. My contract expired at the end of that season and I was keen to agree terms on a new one as quickly as possible. I was disappointed that didn't happen, but I put negotiations to the back of my mind and didn't let any negative thoughts get in the way of my priority of winning the Treble. I was still going to give my all, but of course a few cynics questioned my commitment because an agreement hadn't been reached. I found that insulting. Apart from wanting to do well for myself, my team-

137

mates, the management and the supporters, I was desperate to show the men upstairs they had made a bad mistake by not sorting out a new deal.

Our first game back after the winter break was a Scottish Cup tie away to Arbroath. The dressing rooms were small and a few of the boys had to wait outside as others got changed. The treatment table was set up in the shower area. It was the type of game, on a cold winter's day, where you just wanted to go in, get the job done and make sure no one was injured or booked. We cruised through to the next round after a 3–0 win and marched on to the last sixteen after beating Ayr United 1–0.

March was a crucial month to our season. Since that defeat at Motherwell we'd played seven league games and taken maximum points. That took us up to another visit to Parkhead and we went there on 8 March as league leaders. We lost 1–0 to a Hartson goal but still remained top. McLeish's seventeen-month unbeaten run against O'Neill unfortunately came to an end.

Just eight days later we met again in the CIS League Cup final. Celtic also had the chance to make it to the next stage of the UEFA Cup.

Our motivation was still having the chance to win the Treble, although I would have preferred to be in Celtic's shoes with the chance of Euro glory. Regardless, something had to give that afternoon at Hampden. Celtic were getting all the attention, as the final was sandwiched in between their 'Battle of Britain' UEFA Cup ties against Liverpool and we just got on with things quietly.

The first test was to win that day and we were delighted to emerge victorious by 2–1. It was the first step towards the Treble. Once again Lovenkrands was on the scoresheet. Neil Lennon was red-carded for Celtic and Hartson missed a penalty in the final minutes when we were 2–1 up. I was injured and missed that game.

Caniggia really proved his worth and showed what a class act he was most of the season but came to the fore at the crucial stages. Although he was nearing the end of his career, there was hardly an ounce of fat on his body. He ate the right things, attended the gym regularly and only sipped heavily iced, still water. Of course I used to wind him up, saying the reason he was still so fit in the twilight of his career was because he missed eighteen months after testing positive for drugs. He took it in good spirit.

Old Firm games happened often in the final few weeks of the season and we were still top of the league when Celtic came to Ibrox for the first one after the league split. We were eight points ahead but they came to our place on a high after they had beaten Boavista to reach the final of the UEFA Cup. Larsson scored the winning goal in Portugal, to prove once again what an outstanding striker he was. He caused Rangers much heartache over the years and there's no doubt he was a key figure in the success Celtic had during his seven years in Scotland.

The Celtic fans arrived at Ibrox with beach balls and sombreros to celebrate the fact the UEFA Cup final was being played in the sunshine city of Seville. I could see the funny side and managed to have a laugh. At that point remember saying to myself that I wanted to make sure I had the last laugh and they would be unhappy at winning nothing. They beat us 2–1. It was still in our hands but we were only five points ahead of them with four games to play. They had five fixtures remaining.

It was even worse after our next match when we drew an incredible game 2–2 away at Dundee. Barry Ferguson missed two penalties and it was only when Arteta finally scored from the spot after our third penalty that we managed to scrape a point. Ronald de Boer faced the other way when Arteta stepped up to take it. He couldn't face it any more.

I thought we'd lost the league that day. When you're awarded three penalties in one game and still don't win it, what does that say? At that moment my feelings were natural. I'm sure I wasn't the only one to have serious doubts about our title hopes.

We had three games left and beat Kilmarnock 4–0 at home and then won a tough match at Hearts 2–0 to somehow keep us in the driving seat – but only just, one goal better off to be precise. Our last game was at home to Dunfermline and Celtic had to travel to Kilmarnock, which on paper looked the tougher fixture.

Because of my contractual situation I knew this would be my last game at Ibrox. It was so important to win the league. I didn't want to leave on unhappy terms. The entire build-up to the final-day drama was fantastic. The newspapers, radio and television all gave full coverage of this last-gasp Old Firm shoot-out to see who would be crowned champions. I knew both sides would win their respective games – it was just a case of by how many goals? We stayed in the Glasgow Moat House Hotel the night before the match. It was a Saturday and it was quite busy with fans from both sides. We had dinner and a few of the lads sat about the hotel foyer drinking coffee and convincing each other we'd score more than Celtic the next day.

As usual, I roomed with Barry Ferguson that night and I think he sometimes must have found me a pain in the ass to share with. Just before an Old Firm game in our hotel room we'd sometimes wind each other up by jostling and pretending to make sliding tackles. I was always up early, whereas Barry preferred a lie-in. I would be up, curtains open and in the shower, much to Barry's annoyance. He would shout at me, 'Dutch asshole, get back to bed!'

I'm a nightmare to room with and even I'd hate to share with me! I don't like any light in the room, it has to be completely pitch black. If I see a little bit of light shining under a hotel room door I have to put a towel down to keep the light out. I can't even sleep if I can see the little red stand-by light on the TV.

But what really drives me mad is any kind of noise. There has to be utter silence. I remember, in a World Cup qualifier with Holland, Frank de Boer lost the plot with me because the incessant tick-tock from a clock in the room was driving me crazy. Usually, I'd just get the clock in question and throw it in a drawer or wrap it up in a towel in the bathroom. But this clock was fitted into a bedside cabinet. I spent forty-five minutes pulling the cabinet apart, trying desperately to prise the clock out. Frank was raging and my antics probably confirmed his opinion as to what a weirdo I can be! Still, I wasn't caring because I managed to rip out the offending clock, throw it away and grab myself a decent, silent night's kip!

The final day of the season was going to be an emotional and nerve-racking one. My brother Jeroen and some friends came over for the game. Alex McLeish didn't need to deliver a team-talk that day. It was not necessary – motivation took care of itself. I knew we'd beat Dunfermline – I just didn't know if we'd score more than Celtic.

The atmosphere at the warm-up was unbelievable. It was also a little tense. We just couldn't wait to get started and it was a relief when Barry was finally tossing the coin with referee Stuart Dougal to get the final day of the league campaign under way. The BBC broadcast both games on different channels that day to give the armchair fans an afternoon to remember.

Out on the pitch, the players didn't have the benefit of a remote control to flick the channel or a radio glued to our ears, so we had to rely on the fans to keep us informed of events in Ayrshire. We took an early lead through Mikey Mols. It settled us down and I expected us to go and score a few more before half-time. It didn't work out that way.

In fact, Dunfermline equalised through Jason Dair when he rifled a shot in from about twenty-five yards. A worrying silence descended on Ibrox when that shot hit the back of the net. It was vital we scored before half-time and regained the lead. Thankfully, Caniggia obliged after Amoruso somehow managed to cross the ball from a tight angle on the left wing.

There's no doubt in my mind that going in at the break with a lead that day was significant. If we had gone in at 1–1 it may well have been a psychological blow big enough to cost us our chance of going out and getting the five or six we felt we needed to clinch the title. It would also have given Celtic an extra spur to know we weren't doing the job properly.

The dressing room was buzzing at half-time and Neil McCann came on in the second half, making an immediate impact. He changed the game for us. Dangerous until the last whistle, he sent over some great crosses. Shota Arveladze made it 3–1 and then Ronald de Boer added a fourth. That was Ronald's nineteenth goal of a quite magnificent season for him. His goals and all-round ability were a key factor in our title success that season.

Advocaat signed Ronald a few days after we lost 6–2 to Celtic in August 2000. He cost around £4 million from Barcelona. I knew about the deal about a week before it was signed and sealed. Ronald phoned me from Spain to say that the clubs were negotiating and he wanted my opinion on what it was like to play for Rangers and about the quality of life in Scotland. From that first telephone conversation between us I got the impression he was a little reluctant to come to Ibrox. I had won a Treble in my first season with Rangers and a Double in my second season. We had just lost to Celtic and knew it was going to take incredible consistency to win the title for the third time.

I told him, 'This is a fantastic club, with great fans, very passionate about football. I'd love you to come and join us.'

I was positive and honest and said, 'You're probably lying on a beach just now in Spain and you won't get that here. It's pouring at the moment and it does so almost every day. But I know, if you come here, you will come for the football, not a holiday.'

I was genuinely excited because Ronald was a world-class striker and it would be a magnificent coup for Rangers to sign him. I also had a slight concern, as it meant another Dutchman coming to the club and I could see the writing on the wall and the finger of blame being pointed in the Oranje direction if we didn't keep the league away from Celtic. The same thing was happening at Barcelona at that time as things weren't going well at the Nou Camp for Louis van Gaal. Having so many Dutch players and coaching staff was cited as the root of their problems.

As the negotiations continued I kept it all to myself. Manchester United also wanted Ronald but he would have been going to Old Trafford as a squad player and that's what he was at Barcelona. Ronald loves parading his talents to an audience and I told him to be mindful of that when making his decision.

I said to him, 'It's a difficult choice but a nice one to have. United are one of the biggest clubs in the world but you will end up feeling frustrated there, just as you are just now at Barcelona. You will play every week at Rangers if you perform well and you will enjoy it. Come and help us in our fight against Celtic.'

His father-in-law, Rob Cohen, who is also his agent, called me as well and his main concern was about the lifestyle in Scotland. Naturally, he was thinking about the kind of life his daughter and grandchildren would have.

A fee was agreed and Ronald arrived for his medical. I was delighted he'd signed. He was guided by my advice and totally trusted my opinion. Ronald was superb for us and his ability to turn players with his back to goal was just incredible. Mols was also excellent at that aspect of his game. But Ronald could be frustrating to play with, too – he would sometimes lose possession and, instead of tracking back to win the ball again, he would be standing berating himself. He'd always been that way. We'd be arguing about it during the game and some of the Rangers supporters also didn't like Ronald's reluctance to chase back as they thought he didn't care.

When we were together at Twente Enschede he was exactly the same. He was young then, about twenty, and would yell at himself when he lost possession. He had a lot of self-confidence and couldn't get his head round it when a defender had the audacity to take the ball off him, or when he gave it away needlessly.

During team-talks at Twente the manager, Theo Vonk, would stand up and do a take-off of Ronald. He'd pretend to be Ronald on the pitch, after losing the ball, and shout, 'How can I, the great Ronald de Boer, with all this talent and skill, lose the ball? Tell me, how can this be?' We'd all be pissing ourselves. Ronald could see the funny side but there was also a message in there for him from the manager.

I think just after Ronald scored against Dunfermline, Celtic went 4–0 up at Kilmarnock and at that point were top of the league. I knew this as I was continually asking the fans during the game what the score was at Rugby Park. Thankfully it only lasted a couple of minutes, as Stevie Thompson put us 5–1 ahead. That was a crazy few minutes; we also hit a post and Dunfermline keeper Derek Stillie was pulling off some great saves. Alan Thompson also missed a penalty for Celtic just about that time. There was a huge cheer at Ibrox when the news of the missed spot-kick filtered round the ground.

It was a day with more twists and turns than an Alfred Hitchcock movie and at times the tension must have been unbearable for the fans. We were then awarded a penalty with about two minutes to go and Arteta had the balls to volunteer to take it. I was nowhere to be seen at this point. Penalties were not my forte! Arteta kept his nerve and tucked it away. At that time he was still a young boy and deserved major credit for scoring such an important goal. If he'd missed it? My God . . . I watched him take it and then I ran away to celebrate myself on the pitch. I charged up and down the length of the Govan Road stand to share the moment with our supporters. The league was ours. What an incredible feeling.

I'd never been involved in a day like it during my whole career. I didn't draw breath for the entire ninety minutes. It was some way to bow out of playing at Ibrox. It could have been a disaster, but turned out to be one of the most memorable days of my life.

Celtic had lost their fourth trophy of the season. With ten or eleven weeks of the campaign to go, they had the chance of the domestic Treble and the UEFA Cup. They ended up with nothing. It must have been soul-destroying for them.

Sutton said in a post-match interview at Rugby Park that he wasn't surprised we had scored so many goals against Dunfermline, as he expected them to lie down to us. Utter garbage. And insulting to the Rangers players who had to give everything they had to score six times. Also, Scott Wilson and Barry Nicholson, two ex-Rangers players who played for Dunfermline that day, put the boot in a few times to our players. Not for a second did they hold back. Sutton's comments were completely out of order, but I can also appreciate he must have been feeling dejected after winning nothing from a season that promised to deliver so much. At the end, he won f*** all! Everyone at Ranger was delighted to see him in so much pain and taking the loss so badly.

It was also great for McLeish's assistants, Andy Watson and Wouters, to win another trophy and their 100-per-cent record remained intact the following weekend when we beat Dundee 1–0 in the Scottish Cup final. It was five out of five. Perfect. An incredible achievement.

The Treble of 2003 felt much better than the Treble of 1999. I had played my part this time, so felt worthy of accepting my medals. It was just a great shame that a contract wasn't agreed to keep me on as a Rangers player. But nothing could sour my memories, or the pride I felt, from that brilliant Treble success.

12

ALEX MCLEISH: DEFYING THE ODDS

I had a positive feeling about Alex McLeish's appointment as soon as he was announced as our new boss. I didn't know him but I'd always been impressed by his Hibs side whenever we faced them or when I watched them on television. They played good football and I liked the fact they always tried to be positive.

With respect to Hibs, though, moving to Glasgow Rangers was a huge step for McLeish. He was fortunate that he inherited a top squad of players. The problem was that the chemistry and camaraderie weren't right. The players welcomed a new face, some fresh air into the dressing room. It felt like a fresh start, a new beginning, and was just what the club needed. It was also a perfect opportunity for some guys who had been out of favour under Advocaat to impress the new boss and stake a claim for a regular place.

Like the way all good managers operate, I'm sure McLeish would have done his homework on Rangers before he took over the reins. Like most observers, he must have wondered why a team, with guys like me, Ronald de Boer, Claudio Caniggia, Michael Mols and Barry Ferguson, were underachieving so badly in the league. Great players they were but, simply, as a group we had little confidence and too many divisions in the dressing room. McLeish had to mould us together again and bring a smile back to the dressing room.

The new gaffer took time to speak to us on an individual basis, assuring us all that this was a fresh start for every player and there would be no favouritism. Even Russell Latapy was told there would be no agenda against him and things would be starting from a clean slate. Latapy had let McLeish down a couple of times during his spell at Hibs and McLeish decided enough was enough and let him leave Easter Road. Latapy was a fine footballer but sometimes he might have enjoyed the occasional night out and, in my opinion, he let it creep into his professionalism.

The players weren't the only ones who had to prove themselves – McLeish also had to show he was up to handling the pressure of managing a club the size of Rangers. Could he cope with the pressure of having to win every game? Could he handle the players? He'd never won a major trophy as manager during his time at Hibs and Motherwell and there seemed to be a few Rangers fans uneasy with his appointment. However, that was not the case in the dressing room – he had the respect of the players and the squad made him feel welcome.

McLeish didn't change too many things when he first took over from Advocaat. When we had a three o'clock kick-off we would still meet at 1 p.m. in the Cooper Suite. Advocaat was strict and regimented in many ways; in contrast McLeish was much more relaxed – at times too relaxed, to the point where we didn't know what our day-to-day schedule was. Sometimes he gave the player an inch too much and they took a mile. His team talks were good and he knew what he was doing when it came to tactics. In his very first meeting with the players he told us that he knew we all had ability and that the squad was blessed with excellent players. He said, 'I don't need to tell any of you how to kick a football. At this moment, my job is about getting the confidence back, getting you all to play as a team and wanting to win for each other.'

McLeish didn't arrive with a magic wand but he did manage to get things together, slowly but surely. He had teething problems, like taking two games to dispose of Berwick Rangers in the Scottish Cup, but on the whole he was making a good impression.

We were out of the league race when he arrived at the start of December, although we had to put a public face on and say we still had a chance of catching Celtic. Realistically, we knew our best chances of silverware lay with the two domestic cups. We drew Celtic in the semi-final of the CIS League Cup and it was a game we were all looking forward to. McLeish wanted to get off to a positive start by notching a win against our oldest rivals and take us towards a trophy.

We stayed at the Moat House Hotel in Glasgow the night before the game and after we'd had dinner, I sat in the lobby lounge having coffee. I always liked to have a massage and I also went to the medical room for treatment from the physio, Davie Henderson. Now, Davie is massive fan man, Rangers through and through. The results we'd had that season depressed him and he was desperate for a win against Celtic the following night to cheer him up.

I was lying on the table and Davie kept going on about this Celtic game. He reminded me that, if we lost, they'd be certs to go on and win the Treble, which would have given them back-to-back Trebles in O'Neill's first two years in charge. Henderson went on, 'If they do that, this Rangers team will always be remembered as the side that lost two Trebles to Celtic. That would be a horrible thing to go through life with. But, if we can win this game, then it might be the turning-point for the next couple of years and we can put this bad eighteen-month spell behind us.'

Davie's words never left my head the entire night and into the following day. What he told me was pretty obvious but it was the way he said it, the way he hammered home the impor-tance of being successful and not being too bothered about being second best to Celtic. His words were always, 'get f***ed in about them.'

Going into the game, I was really fired up and totally pre-pared. In my own mind and body I felt as good as I ever had going into a game of football. I was also convinced we could win the game and I could feel an air of confidence around our dressing room inside Hampden.

Within seconds of kick-off my confident mood took a battering – I had the worst start to any game in the whole of my professional career. With less than sixty seconds on the clock, I tried to pass the ball back to Stefan Klos but didn't notice Henrik Larsson running on my blind side. Larsson intercepted and rounded Klos. His shot was going in but Lorenzo Amoruso made it back and cleared off the line. If that had gone in, it could have been the end for us. I was so grateful to Amoruso – he really did save my ass. Thankfully that was my first and last mistake that night and we lifted ourselves after that initial scare and went on to win 2–1.

Bert Konterman scored with a wonder-goal from twenty-five yards to take us through to the final. I was delighted for Bert, as he had so few things to smile about during his time at Rangers. He was always singled out for criticism but he never complained, he just shrugged his shoulders and got on with it.

We defeated Ayr United in the final and it was great to get our hands on a piece of silverware again. It took a lot of pressure away and McLeish couldn't have asked for a better start to his Ibrox career than winning a trophy less than four months after taking up the post.

We were on a roll now and wanted to follow our CIS Cup success up by winning the Scottish Cup. We met Celtic in the final and we were determined to make it a double cup success. The Scottish Cup was our big chance to redeem ourselves and we managed to beat Celtic 3–2. The scoreline wasn't a true reflection of the run of play that day – we absolutely humped Celtic and deserved to win by more.

Peter Lovenkrands scored in the last minute to give us the win but we should have made life easier for ourselves that afternoon. Still, it was a dramatic way to end the season and beating Celtic like that made it special and all the more memorable. Yes, I enjoyed that afternoon, really enjoyed it. To see the

Rangers fans with their heads held high again and feeling the good times were on the way back made the whole day so sweet. I was delighted for them because they had been through a rough time. It also underlined that we were a good squad and getting things to gel again was all that was missing from making us into a decent team. It must have been satisfying for McLeish, satisfying to win the silverware and also to silence the critics who had questioned his appointment. His Ibrox reign was off to an excellent start.

I was also pleased for Andy Watson. Andy came with Alex as his assistant, to work with Jan Wouters. I detected Andy was a little nervous during his first few weeks at Rangers and was keen to earn the respect of the players. He was enthusiastic and worked hard and the players enjoyed working with him.

After a few weeks at the club I spoke to Andy and he told me it was a fantastic honour for him to be at Rangers. He was also keen to find out what the players thought of him, to know if he had been accepted. I told him just to be himself, be the same as he was at Hibs. If he hadn't been doing his job right at Easter Road then Alex wouldn't have brought him to Ibrox. I told Andy to remember that at the end of the day it was still a bunch of football players he was working with, we were all human beings, it's just that we were more experienced and better players than the ones he had worked with at Hibernian.

No matter the club you work for, I think it's important for a member of the coaching staff to be strong, not to show any sign of weakness. A dressing room can be an unforgiving place and there are some players who will take advantage and seize on someone's weakness if they sense a vulnerability. Alex, Andy and Jan are now away from Rangers after it was agreed with David Murray that a parting of the ways was best for all concerned in the summer of 2006.

Murray brought in as McLeish's replacement Paul Le Guen, the highly rated French coach who has an excellent CV and, on paper, looks to be a fine appointment. He won three titles in a row with Lyon in France and had several big European clubs interested in recruiting him. So for Rangers to land him is a major coup and Murray should be applauded for his capture.

McLeish had a torrid final season at Rangers and from as early as September people were calling for his head. He won the league title on the last day of the season in 2004–05 when Nacho Novo's goal defeated Hibs and Celtic lost 2–1 to Motherwell at Fir Park and that bought him a bit of time after yet another last-day drama. He just couldn't get the results he required after that and the league form wasn't good enough, with unacceptable results against the likes of Falkirk, Livingston and Aberdeen at crucial times of the season. Celtic – now under the leadership of McLeish's good friend, Gordon Strachan – went on to win the league and Hearts finished second. It meant, of course, that Rangers didn't even get a crack at the Champions League, something that is unforgivable in the eyes of the supporters and the men in power. They had to be satisfied with a place in the UEFA Cup.

I sometimes wondered what must have been going through Alex's mind when the pressure was really on him. He appeared on the back pages most days, mainly for negative issues. It must have been torture, even worse for his wife and family. It puts tremendous strain on a person having to cope with pressures and intrusions from all angles. It's that type of thing that always makes me think twice about getting involved in management.

The one thing that must have kept him going, made him feel it was worthwhile, was the run in the Champions League campaign to make it to the last sixteen – the first time a Scottish club had progressed that far in Europe's premier competition. McLeish and his players made it through the group stages as runners-up to Inter Milan, ahead of Porto and Artmedia Bratislava. It was something the side I played in never managed to do, to play in the last sixteen of the Champions League.

151

Ultimately Villarrreal knocked Rangers out but they came agonisingly close to progressing, drawing 3–3 over two legs to go out on the away-goal rule. The way it all came to an end for Alex wasn't the way it should have happened. Like Advocaat, he achieved so much at Rangers but I imagine he'd have preferred to leave under different circumstances. Rangers could have handled McLeish's situation better. From November onwards, his future was the subject of constant newspaper speculation. Was he staying, was he going? At that point Murray should have come out and publicly backed Alex but he waited too long – more than a month – before standing by his manager. It was an awful situation to leave McLeish in and if I'd been in his situation I would probably have walked away.

After we won the Treble in 2003, I remember saying to Alex, 'You need to think about your future. Things can only go downhill from here. You've won five trophies out of five – it can't get any better for you. You're losing a lot of quality, experienced players and under the financial restraints it's unlikely you'll be able to replace them with guys of an equal calibre.'

Alex didn't agree, but in a way, he didn't disagree either. However, I suppose it's a huge wrench to walk away from a club you've supported all your life in the midst of a successful period.

When Alex's time officially came to an end in May 2006, he hired Mr Singh's Indian restaurant in Glasgow and took all the players and members of his coaching and back-room staff out for a farewell dinner. I'd been away from the club for three years but he still invited me. Michael Mols was also asked along and it was a nice gesture from him. It was good to mingle with my old team-mates again, although only a few remained from my time at Ibrox, such as Barry Ferguson and Bob Malcolm. My friend and former PSV team-mate Ronald Waterreus was also at Rangers by this point, after he signed from Manchester City in January 2005 (after Stefan Klos picked up a serious knee injury in training).

That night I had a blether with McLeish and he brought up the conversation we'd had three years earlier when I told him it might be the ideal time to walk away from Rangers with a Treble in the bag and his managerial credibility at an all-time high. 'When you said I should think about my future, perhaps you were right.'

13

PLEASURE AND PAIN

David Murray's appointment of Dick Advocaat as manager was a bold and original move. The Rangers chairman had watched Walter Smith's nine-in-row team dominate Scottish football throughout the 1990s. But it wasn't enough for the Ibrox owner.

And when Walter left Rangers it was time for a new era and Murray wanted the club to continue their stranglehold on the Scottish game but also make an impact in Europe. The Champions League was Murray's Holy Grail and he gave Advocaat the funds to recruit some top-class players to make it happen.

When I signed for Rangers I didn't know if we would be in the Champions League or the UEFA Cup the following season, because the title race in Scotland was tight between the Old Firm clubs. Celtic pipped Rangers to the title, so we had to settle for the UEFA Cup.

We beat Shelbourne, PAOK Salonika, Beitar Jerusalem and a very good Bayer Leverkusen side to set up a mouth-watering clash against Parma. The Italian side were high-quality and packed with accomplished players like Juan Veron, Fabio Cannavaro and Gigi Buffon. We were the underdogs but were quietly confident as we had come through an intimidating atmosphere away to PAOK with a 0–0 draw following our 2–0 first leg victory.

The first leg against Parma was at Ibrox and our packed stadium was jumping that night as we fought out a 1–1 draw with

Rod Wallace grabbing our goal. It was a game we could have won but Gordon Durie missed a great chance near the end, although Antti Niemi also pulled off a great save from Fiore to prevent them taking a lead back to Italy.

We knew we had to score over there to have any chance of going through and that is always the downside of conceding at home. The tie was played on a cold December afternoon and was broadcast live on television back in Scotland.

We had to remain solid at the back, soak up the pressure and hit the Italians on the counter-attack and our game plan worked a treat as Jorg Albertz gave us a first-half lead. Sadly we couldn't maintain our advantage and individual errors cost us as, first, Sergio Porrini was sent off for two yellow-card offences, then Lorenzo Amoruso gave away a penalty for a needless handball. There's no explanation for Lorenzo's actions. Players just lose their minds for a few seconds, we see it happening all over the world all the time on the highest stages. I've been there myself, but I was lucky to get away with it in a game for PSV.

Despite taking that lead, we eventually lost 3–1 overall and, disappointingly, we were out and heartbroken not to have stayed in Europe beyond Christmas. In the fall-out from the Parma game certain sections of the media suggested that match-fixing may have played a part in the game because of the red card and the penalty – both Italian players from Rangers involved – but that was nonsense. We never believed for a minute Sergio or Lorenzo would get involved in anything as underhand as that. If anything, both these guys would have been fired up and more motivated to raise their game back in their homeland.

Sergio was gutted at the final whistle, because when you have been red carded and the team loses, you feel like the scapegoat and the loneliest man in the world. I know, I've been there.

Parma went on to win the UEFA Cup that season, defeating Marseille 3–0 in the final. Funnily enough, during my five years at Rangers, sides that knocked us out of Europe tended to go on and reach the final.

The following season we got the perfect revenge on Parma when we knocked them out of the Champions League qualifier. We took a 2–0 lead to Italy with goals from Tony Vidmar and Claudio Reyna and managed to scrape through to the group stages after going down 1–0 in the return leg.

We were drawn in the group stages with Valencia, Bayern Munich and PSV Eindhoven and I particularly relished the chance to play against my former club. I'd been widely criticised by many people in Holland for leaving PSV to join Rangers. They said I had taken a backward step as Rangers were not as big as PSV, so I was desperate to prove them all wrong – the press, the Dutch public and some people at PSV.

I was nervous and tense for our third group game in Eindhoven at the end of September. It felt strange being in the away dressing room in the Philips Stadium, although the PSV fans made me welcome and the hard-core ones even belted out my song, 'Arthur, the King of Philips'. To be honest, I expected a warm reception after the years of service I committed to them.

We played really well that night and won 1–0, and the added bonus was my delight at proving to the Dutch that Rangers were a strong team. The other pleasing aspect of that win was the fact that Albertz grabbed our goal with six minutes left. Jorg was not enjoying the best of times under Advocaat during that period, as he couldn't hold down a starting slot and he seemed to take out his anger and frustration on the ball with his goal that night.

I reckon I played well and made a telling contribution up against Dennis Rommedahl – the 'Danish Roadrunner'. He has frightening pace but I kept him in check. At the final whistle I threw my Rangers top over the fence to the PSV fans. I felt ecstatic at coming away from PSV with a win but I didn't want to over-celebrate and rub it in to the home fans. I kept my emotions in check, but inside I was overjoyed. The victory against his old team must also have been sweet for Advocaat. Eric Gerets was in charge of PSV at that time after he succeeded Sir Bobby Robson.

In the home game against PSV a month later, Advocaat made a surprise selection when he gave a start to Derek McInnes to man-mark Luc Nilis. He is a top player but Derek didn't give him a sniff that night as we ran out comfortable 4–1 winners. Ruud van Nistelrooy also played but had a quiet night, although he scored from the penalty spot when we were 2–0 up. He had a lethal partnership with Nilis so we deserved credit for keeping them at bay. Amoruso, Neil McCann and a Michael Mols double gave us the win.

Our final group match was away to Bayern Munich in the Olympic Stadium and a draw would have taken us through to the next stage, with the Germans needing a win to progress. When we played Bayern at Ibrox in September they escaped with a 1–1 draw but didn't deserve to take a point – we played well but couldn't hold out as they equalised with a deflected free-kick in the final minute. They should never have been awarded the foul in the first place. The referee got it wrong when Alexander Zickler collapsed to the deck after I challenged him at the edge of the box. I didn't touch him. It was a shocking decision by Polish ref Ryszard Wójcik and my anger was compounded when Michael Tarnat scored for Ottmar Hitzfeld's side.

Only needing a point was a decent position to be in, but it should have been more comfortable for us. We lost both games to Valencia and I don't think many people were aware of their strengths, deluded by their form in the Spanish league. However, in Europe, as is the case with a lot of teams, they were excellent and topped the group. They never stopped there and went all the way to the Champions League final that season, although they lost 3–0 to Real Madrid in Paris.

In the Olympic Stadium we got off to a dreadful start as Bayern took the lead with a penalty after just ten minutes. Thankfully we never crumbled after that early setback and we showed character and class to fight back. We hit the woodwork three times that night in one of the best performances away from home I was involved in with Rangers. We played the Germans off the park but just couldn't score against a star-studded team that included Lothar Matthaus, Markus Babbel, Giovane Elber and Bixente Lizarazu.

Sadly we couldn't grab the goal our performance merited and the disappointment of failing to qualify was exacerbated by the crushing injury to Mols, who damaged his cruciate ligament during the game. Bayern keeper Oliver Kahn raced at least forty yards from his goal to challenge Mikey for a ball and the striker hurdled him to avoid contact but landed awkwardly and his knee gave way. It was a nightmare for him and his family and a severe loss to the team. He had signed for us for £4 million that summer from FC Utrecht and although he was a relatively unknown quantity in Scotland, he was an instant hit with the Ibrox fans with his mesmerising ability to twist and turn defenders with his back to goal.

He was on fire in his first few months and the Ibrox fans took to him straight away, just the way he was with the Utrecht crowd. As well as his football ability, Mikey's smile endeared him to the fans. The Rangers shops even used to sell a Mikey mask and at Ibrox we used to look up to the stands and see the unmistakable Mols grin looking down at us from hundreds of faces.

Unfortunately the smile was wiped from his face after that horrible night in Munich. Mikey was out for a long time, longer than we all anticipated as his operation and recovery didn't quite go to plan. I don't think he was the same player when he came back; he never truly felt 100 per cent because there were always the psychological doubts gnawing away in his mind. He was damaged, physically and emotionally, and badly needed a run of games to have any chance of getting back to his old ways, but he never managed to sustain a period of games under Alex McLeish. However, I was delighted for Mikey when he managed to bounce back and play a significant part in the Treble-winning season of 2003.

A lot of players seem to be unlucky with injuries when they come to Rangers. Daniel Prodan never kicked a ball after his £2.7 million move from Steaua Bucharest because of a recurring knee problem and was accused of being a chancer who was only here for the money. But that accusation was completely inaccurate, as I can vouch for his commitment and dedication. Daniel was in the gym every day at Rangers in an attempt to get fit and he used to train at Esporta in Hamilton on his own. He also brought over his personal trainer from Romania but nothing seemed to work for him. He was very unlucky and Daniel was depressed that he never got the chance to show Rangers what he was capable of.

Murray and Advocaat were dejected we never made it through to the next stage of the Champions League as they both badly wanted it to happen and knew how important it was to the club. They always knew domestic success would happen but they knew success in Europe was pivotal in raising the club's profile. Trying to make an impact on the biggest stage of all would have to wait for another year.

The only consolation from failing to qualify from the group stages was having the parachute of the UEFA Cup but we were knocked out in the next round by Borussia Dortmund after a penalty kick shoot-out. We didn't play well in the away leg and let them come back to level it 2–2 on aggregate after we'd taken a 2–0 lead at home. Their keeper, Jens Lehmann, was the hero for Dortmund and had a habit there of saving penalties, long before his penalty saves for Germany against Argentina in the 2006 World Cup finals. Amoruso scored against him in the shoot-out but the German No. 1 saved kicks from van Bronckhorst, myself and Reyna to give them a 3–1 win on penalties.

We were back in the Champions League the following season, 2000–01, after winning qualifying ties against Kaunas of Lithuania and Danish side Herfolge. The draw for the group stage was kind to us and we had to face Sturm Graz, Monaco and Galatasaray. With that draw we felt we had an excellent chance of finishing in the top two and that belief was cemented after our first two games when we defeated Graz 5–0, then dumped Monaco 1–0 away.

The result against the French was superb and Advocaat pulled off one of his selection surprises when he played Tugay at sweeper. Tugay is a good footballer, with great vision and a good brain, and he used that intelligence to perfection that night as he passed the ball well out of central defence. That was what we needed that night in the Principality.

Giovanni van Bronckhorst scored our winner with a fine shot to prove what an important player he had become at Rangers. Gio was signed by Dick for around £5 million from Feyenoord; as with me, many questioned his decision to move to Ibrox. However, it was perfect for him for the next stage of his development as he possessed fine skill but had to add battling qualities to take him to the next level. Playing in Scotland moulded his game and made him more complete as a footballer.

Gio got his move to Arsenal, although sadly it never quite happened for him at Highbury as a midfielder. I remember joking to him that the moment might come when he'd have to move from midfield to left-back, but he said, 'No way. Never in a million years.' Well, he ended up playing that position and won the 2006 Champions League with Barcelona in that position as well as playing there for Holland. I'm delighted he developed from a boy into a man and that he has enjoyed success in his career.

We had back-to-back games against Galatasaray and after losing 3–2 in Turkey we were held 0–0 at Ibrox. It left us with seven points, joint top with the Turkish side. Our next game was away to Graz and it would lead to the angriest I've ever felt as a footballer. The sole reason for my rage that night was referee Lopez Nieto, who, in my opinion, was a total son of a bitch and a pure disgrace that night.

In the first half, I was on the sidelines receiving treatment for an injury but was ready to come back on and waited for his signal. The ref caught my eye and waved me back on but, almost immediately after I won possession, he whistled and stopped the game. He came over to me and claimed I was not given permission to re-enter the field of play and yellow carded me. It was utter bollocks. I went to see him at half-time but he waved me away and stuck to his story. I told him I thought he was a f***ing liar.

He gave me a second yellow card with about five minutes left but it was for a nothing tackle. He could maybe have whistled for a foul, but to book me again was shocking. I walked off in disgust, tore off my jersey and threw it at the fourth official. Advocaat was there to stop me because I couldn't get to grips with the two yellows. It was lunacy.

I was furious and tried to get to Nieto after the game and went to his door fully intent on giving him a 'Glasgow kiss'. I was held back by van Lingen, but I told Bert to leave me alone as I had to get this off my chest. I said to Bert, 'I don't care if this is my last game in European football. I'm going to have him. F*** him.'

UEFA don't normally deal with appeals when it's for two yellows, but all credit to them for hearing my case. The television cameras proved Nieto waved me back on and my sending off was rescinded. I didn't need to attend a hearing and a lot of the credit for that has to go to Campbell Ogilvie. He was with Rangers then and is a highly respected figure within UEFA's corridors of power.

Campbell was excellent at his job and in December 2000 accompanied me to Hampden for an SFA disciplinary charge after I made comments to the newspapers in the aftermath of our 6–2 defeat to Celtic at Parkhead in August. I wasn't playing that day but felt Jonathan Gould tried to get Barry Ferguson sent off when he sprinted out of his goal to have words with the referee after Barry made a tackle. Barry was sent off, but I was quoted in the paper as saying I felt the decision was wrong. I was hauled up to explain my comments and the whole set-up was an absolute farce and an embarrassment to the Scottish game. Campbell instructed me not to say anything stupid and just to accept whatever punishment came my way.

I can't remember for sure, but six or seven people sat on this disciplinary panel and they had the article in front of them and asked if my comments were accurate.

'Yes. Every word and every letter,' was my curt reply.

A lady on the committee said to me, 'Well, you might be able to get away with comments like that in Spain, but not here, Mr Numan!' Incredible!

One of her colleagues quickly corrected her and informed her I'd never played in Spain and was, in fact, from Holland. She hadn't done her homework properly – maybe she thought I was Ronald de Boer! I was charged with bringing the game into disrepute and received a warning letter from the SFA a week later.

During the hearing they made me feel like some kind of petty criminal, but the truth is, I was hauled up there for bugger all. I couldn't help but think to myself that the time and money wasted on bringing the committee together would have been better spent, financially and energy-wise, trying to improve youth development and facilities in Scotland.

I was able to play against Monaco in our final Champions League game at Ibrox. A win would have taken us through to the next group stage, a draw would have given us the safety net of the UEFA Cup and defeat would have seen us finish bottom.

Goals from Kenny Miller and Mols had us 2–1 up with a few minutes to go and we were convinced we were going to progress until we stupidly gave away possession, which led to a free-kick. The French scored from the set-piece and we knew

we'd blown it again. It was unbelievable and to do it in front of
our fans made it even harder to take – much worse than the season before in Munich.

It was unrealistic to think we could ever win the Champions
League but we should have done much better. With the talent
we had in the squad, it shouldn't have been beyond us to reach
the second group stage or the last eight. Instead we were close,
but not close enough. It is one of my biggest regrets in football
that Rangers failed to make the grade in the Champions League
under Advocaat. You can blame injuries, tactics, stupid mistakes from individuals, bad defending and poor finishing – but
ultimately the bottom line was, we were out again.

We made it to the last sixteen of the UEFA Cup the following
season when Advocaat guided us there but stepped down after
we beat Paris Saint-Germain. McLeish took over for the game
against Feyenoord when Rangers were still in Europe for the
first time since Walter Smith's fantastic team of 1993.

After we drew at Ibrox we lost 3–2 in de Kuip with Pierre van
Hooijdonk scoring directly from two excellent free-kicks. We
missed a few decent chances that night as Mols and Neil
McCann came close to putting us through to the quarter-final.
Later that season Feyenoord made it to the UEFA Cup final in
their home ground and lifted the trophy after a 3–2 win against
Borussia Dortmund. It was tough getting knocked out by
Feyenoord because we all felt we had a really good chance of
going all the way that year.

I have decent memories from Europe but unfortunately the
bad outweigh the good. It should have been much, much
better.

14

WHY I LEFT RANGERS: DESERT STORM

When I signed for Rangers from PSV Eindhoven in the summer of 1998, I put pen to paper on a four-year contract. During my third season we extended it to tie me to the club until June 2003.

When a player is in the final year of a contract, he wants to know as quickly as possible what is happening – will I be staying here or will I be going?

It's no secret that Rangers had to address their massive debt problems during Alex McLeish's reign and the days of spending £20 million to bring in a handful of players had come to an end. At its peak, Rangers were, perhaps, carrying a debt of around £70 million and the only way that was going to be reduced was by bringing down the wage bill in the football department, spending little money on new players and moving on players with a market value.

David Murray took a back seat from the day-to-day running of the club and stood down as chairman in July 2000. He was still the owner of Rangers but must have felt that he wanted a rest away from the pressure to let others take on a more prominent role. Murray was replaced by John McClelland. Martin Bain became Director of Football Operations and took a much more hands-on role at Ibrox.

McLeish had to trim the squad in a bid to cut back costs. Kenny Miller was the first to go and he joined Wolves for £3 million. Tore Andre Flo also left a few months after that. Jorg Albertz, Claudio Reyna and Tugay were also big-name casualties towards the end of Advocaat's reign as the financial purge started. Big changes were being made and it was a signal of the shape of things to come.

At that time, this kind of downscaling wasn't unique to Rangers. It was happening all over Europe – in Italy, England, everywhere. At Ibrox our squad might have been worth £100 million when transfer fees were going through the roof, but when it all started to fall apart then the squad was probably worth less than half that amount. Clubs had overspent in transfer fees and had paid players far too much money for ages. Now they were – literally – starting to pay the price. And it was a heavy one. Football clubs were millions and millions in debt and the banks ordered them to tighten the reins and dramatically reduce their spiralling debt. It was a simple case of downsize or face the prospect of going bankrupt. It was a shock at first but we all knew the gravy train would come to a shuddering halt at some stage.

With the desperate financial situation Rangers found themselves in, I knew, when my contract was running out and we were to start negotiations on a new one, that I would have to take a pay cut. I was prepared for that, it wasn't a problem.

We were out of European competition early and only had the domestic scene to concentrate on. During that campaign we also had the pleasure of a winter break, which I think is an excellent idea for the Scottish game. We headed off to Dubai to a winter camp for the chance to train in the sunshine and play a bounce game against German side Energie Cottbus. It was all very relaxed and everyone was in a good mood, enjoying the great weather and pleasant surroundings of that fascinating place.

It had been on my mind for a while what was going to happen with my future and I thought that being in Dubai might give me a clearer indication, since Bain and McClelland were there and it was a chance to have a chat about what we were thinking. I did want to stay and Rangers knew that. I was prepared to sign a new deal that would have more or less taken me to the end of my career in top-flight football. Also, Marjon was pregnant with our first child and we didn't want the stress of moving to a new club and a new house at that time.

Later in the week, I was asked to go to McClelland's hotel room for a meeting with him and Bain. McLeish was not present. I was just dressed in a short-sleeve shirt, shorts and flip-flops. As soon as I walked into the room I could sense an atmosphere – something just didn't feel right. I was the first player at the club out of contract they were dealing with under the new wage structure because of the debt.

I had met Bain from dealing with him for sponsorship matters at the club but I didn't know McClelland. He and Bain looked tense to me. Their body language told me they were preparing to give me some bad news, news that I would find difficult to accept.

They explained the situation of how Rangers were in serious debt and that they were struggling financially. However, they wanted to keep the good players at the club and that I fitted into that category. I told them that I was happy to stay and had never expected to still be at the club after five seasons; I'd expected to be away after two seasons to continue my career in England, but I'd grown to love the club and Scotland and wanted to stay for one more year at least.

I then said to them, 'I understand the financial situation and I'm prepared to take a cut of 25–30 per cent.' I was relaxed and was just being honest with them and thought that would save a bit of time from negotiating back and forward before a solution was found. I'd had five great years at Rangers and the club had always treated me well. I wanted to have it all sorted by March, which I didn't think would be a problem because the two contract negotiations I'd had in the past with Murray were sorted quickly: it was boom-boom and my name was on the dotted line.

However, this was different, totally different and I was taken aback by the offer made to me by Bain and McClelland. After the initial small talk about the weather and stuff was out the way, they put a deal in front of me. They knew they couldn't offer the terms I was looking for, in many ways the deal I deserved. Bain was doing most of the talking about the money and he said, 'Arthur, we can offer you a basic wage of £5,000 per week.'

I was numb – I just didn't expect that kind of offer. I thought it must have been a mistake and I replied, 'Can you repeat that, please?'

He did and it was the same figure. So, I was not hearing things. I thought they were taking the piss with that offer. I was a player with forty-five caps for Holland and someone who had helped Rangers win leagues and cups in my five years at Ibrox. But they made me feel like I was a seventeen-year-old kid with just a handful of games under my belt.

They could tell by my reaction that I was far from happy. I felt it was an insult, a slap in my face. They began to apologise for the deal and reminded me that this was just the first offer, there might be a little room for improvement.

I left the room bitterly disappointed. I got the impression Rangers thought they could get away with offering me a drastically reduced deal because they were relying on my loyalty to the club. They knew I was content at Ibrox, Marjon and I were expecting our first child in July and we were both settled and happy in Glasgow. I reckon Rangers took me for granted and expected me to settle for almost anything they offered. I was even more disappointed with that offer when I later found out that it was £5,000 per week gross. I thought it was net as Rangers had always put net figures to me in the past.

The bottom line was, I was going from a salary of £550,000 net to £144,000 net. I have documents from Rangers with the offers they made me.

Bain came out the room after me and said, 'I'll do everything I can to get you a better deal. You're a great player and a good influence on the young players at the club. I might be able to find a sponsor to help finance a better package for you.'

I knew they had money to spend on new contracts. Peter Lovenkrands was given a new, lucrative deal just before I had signed and I knew how much he signed for because he asked me for advice on the offer made to him by Rangers. I also knew Barry Ferguson had picked up a couple of decent wage rises. Good luck to them and I didn't grudge either a single penny. Younger guys obviously have a re-sale value and Rangers knew if these guys flourished they could make millions from them in the transfer market. Realistically I knew I was coming towards the end of my career and had little re-sale value to the club.

I was in a bit of a daze as I headed back to my room. Barry Ferguson was sharing with me and he was the only player I told that I was going for a contract meeting that day.

He was waiting for me when I got back and asked, 'How did you get on? Everything sorted out?'

I told him that it was far from cut and dried and that I didn't think it was going to be resolved. I said, 'It's not fair to give you exact figures but I've been offered a new deal at a wage cut of around 75 per cent.' At that point I hadn't worked the exact percentage figure of what I was going to be down every week.

Barry was gobsmacked and said to me, 'That's ridiculous. What kind of direction is this club taking?' Barry was just as surprised as I was. He is a guy who grew up a Rangers fan and it was hard for him to contemplate his team having to make such drastic financial cuts. He was the captain of the club and was worried by the level of player he might have beside him the following season.

In our room together, I would sometimes ask Barry about his future plans. He'd just signed a new deal at Rangers but I told him he was still young with a great career ahead of him and I could see him playing for one of the top clubs in England. He has the quality to become one of the best midfielders in Britain. I told him I thought he had the potential to become as good as Roy Keane. It looked as if Keane was coming to the end of his career at that time and it seemed to me that Barry had all the attributes to follow in Keane's footsteps.

Barry had been at Rangers all his life and I thought it would move his career forward if he tried something new. Although he was playing for a great club like Rangers, I reckoned he needed a new challenge to take his career on to the next level. I thought that, if he played in the Premiership for a couple of years, he could then return to Ibrox a more experienced player who could pass his expertise on to the youngsters.

With all respect to Blackburn, I believe Barry made the wrong choice when he moved to Ewood Park – to me, moving to Rovers was not really a step up. In my view, he was good enough to play for a club at a much higher level – Chelsea, Manchester United, Arsenal or Liverpool.

Barry was captaining Rangers and winning trophies almost every season. He was playing in the Champions League and 50,00 fans at Ibrox adored him. He wanted to move on but I believe he made the wrong choice although perhaps his decision was hastened by the situation at Ibrox, where Rangers were being forced to buy players who were not as good as the guys Barry had been used to playing with.

That night I phoned Marjon, my father and Joop. They could tell by my voice that I was extremely disappointed and agreed that I was right not to accept the new deal. I was disappointed for the rest of that trip in Dubai but kept my head down and focused on the training and getting myself sharp again for the second half of the season. I had just turned thirty-three and felt I had plenty of good games at the top level still left in me.

McLeish was keen to know how the meeting had gone. It was also encouraging to hear he was desperate to keep me. Whenever we had a conversation he made it clear he wanted me to sign a new deal as soon as possible, although he appeared to be a little bit in the dark about what was going on because he only ever had questions for me about the situation. He wanted me to stay but I knew he didn't have much power when it came to the money side of things.

McLeish knew I was a good influence on the younger players. Lovenkrands was a case in point – the fact I played behind him and talked him through games with his positional play, helped him get his new deal.

When I was twenty-one and had just joined PSV Eindhoven our keeper, Hans van Breukelen, was a senior member of the squad and was regarded as the father figure in the dressing room. He was good to me. I learned things from him about being a good professional on and off the park. My first few weeks at PSV were pretty daunting, though, as some of the senior guys were hard on me to begin with. When I first joined it was almost like an initiation process. They could have made my life more pleasant for that first month.

But I kept my head down, took my dumps and started playing well for the team. It was almost like I had to go through this test to show I was good enough – and strong enough – to play for PSV.

Young players need to see older, wiser heads beside them. Stevie Hughes was a player who benefited from that at Rangers during his early days of trying to make the transition of going from the reserves into the first team. Hughes listened to advice and all I could do was point him in the right direction. It was up to him – as it is with all players – whether he took it on board.

On my return to Glasgow from Dubai, I spoke to Joop again and asked him to arrange a meeting with Rangers within two weeks. He spoke to Bain and we agreed to more talks at Ibrox on 27 January.

We met and a new offer was put to me, this time for a basic wage of £300,000 gross for the year. There was decent appearance money on offer of around £3,000 per game, increased after I played a certain number of matches. I wasn't happy with so much of my package being based on appearance money because I could have picked up an injury or they could sit me up in the stand rather than pay me for playing. I remember in December 2002 I bruised bones in my leg after a goal-line clearance in an Old Firm game. I was out for four weeks so I knew that injuries in football can happen at any time in any circumstances, so there was no way I would accept a deal that included clauses dependent on appearances.

I'd asked for a basic salary of £525,000 gross and expected us to meet somewhere in-between. But Rangers made it clear there was no room for negotiation – this was their final and maximum offer.

I sat in the Ibrox boardroom with Joop and we asked to be excused for a few moments to go into another room to discuss the terms. I was angry and said to Joop, 'Why did they waste our time and bring you over here to make that kind of offer? This contract has to be right and I don't feel it is. I'm not going to sign just for the sake of it. I think Rangers are trying to call my bluff but I'm not going to bow to their demands. That's it, I'm finished with Rangers.'

I knew then it was over but things dragged on for a few more weeks. In a final attempt to make something happen we asked Rangers again but they were not for budging. On 13 February at 3 p.m. Martin Bain sent a fax to Joop saying there was no increase on the second offer and I had until 6 p.m. that night to agree to the deal. I found a three-hour ultimatum to be insulting. So I said to Joop, 'F*** them.' I didn't accept the contract and Rangers moved on to chase other targets they had mentioned they would go for to replace me at left-back if I didn't sign.

Jerome Bonnisel and Dan Eggen were with us on trial in Dubai and these players were brought to my attention as possible replacements if I left. The following day, Bain informed us that the offer had been withdrawn and that the club would move on to find my replacement. In the very same fax, he also wanted to control what the club said to the media and also the way I portrayed our negotiations. I resented that suggestion by Bain. Did the club feel they had something to be frightened of? I refused to be a puppet but had no intention of rocking the boat. During the five or six weeks that had passed up until mid-February, the press were always asking me what was going on and I never once gave anything away, never spilled the beans.

However, I like to be as honest as possible and I felt I had to tell the truth after we defeated Hearts 1–0 at Ibrox on 15 February. I was invited up to the Chairman's Club after the game and once the formalities were out of the way Andy Cameron interviewed me for the benefit of the guests. I reckon around a hundred people were inside the room, sponsors and VIPs.

Andy asked me, 'So, Arthur, what can you tell us about your contract, what's happening?'

I had nothing to hide, nothing to feel guilty about. 'Unfortunately I will not be signing, Andy. We can't agree on new terms and I will be leaving at the end of the season. I hope to go out on a high by winning the league.'

McClelland was in the room at the time and I think he was surprised I was so honest. The others inside the room were also surprised.

It didn't take long for the news to spread and the following day I received many phone calls from the press asking about my situation. I was also honest with them.

I still had a huge desire to finish my Rangers career on a high and desperately wanted us to win the Treble. I'd made my mind up and knew I was leaving but while I was still with the club I was fully committed and would always give 110 per cent.

On 22 February we played in a Scottish Cup tie against Ayr United at Somerset Park, a match we won 1–0. It was the game that Ayr United striker James Grady accused Amoruso of spitting at him and it caused controversy for weeks. But there were fireworks in the dressing room before kick-off as well, involving myself and Murray.

The Rangers owner doesn't usually attend away games but he came to this one at Somerset Park. Now, I think Murray is good company and he sometimes liked to come into the dressing room to have a laugh and a joke with the players. I never had a problem with that because I would give him back a bit of banter which he always took in good spirits. But there was a more serious side to this visit and he said to me, 'You've not agreed terms. But you didn't speak to me.'

I wasn't for keeping my mouth shut and told him, 'And I'm not going to speak to you about it. Sorry – you had your chance and you blew it.' I was very serious with him. Other players and members of staff were in the dressing room at that time.

I felt let down by Murray and the other people in power at Rangers. Towards the end of the season Murray had another go at trying to keep me. We were in an office inside Murray Park and he asked me if I'd sign again. Far too much water had passed under the bridge by that point and, in a jokey type of way, I said to him, 'David, you can offer me double the amount of money that I'm on just now and I still wouldn't sign.'

I don't think he liked my reply but I wanted to make it absolutely clear to him that my decision was not purely down to cash – it was more about the manner in which they dealt with me, the way they went about offering me the new contract. For a player who'd never caused them one minute of trouble, never attracted a negative headline for off-field behaviour, I should have been treated with more respect.

I was determined to make sure I finished my Rangers career on a high – to be able to leave with good memories and show the club they were letting a very good player leave the club, one that would be difficult to replace. At that time I was looking at other offers. Feyenoord were very keen for me to sign and I was flattered. But I didn't have a good feeling about going there. Feyenoord were not my club and I would have felt uncomfortable playing for them.

Guus Hiddink phoned to ask me to go back to PSV and it was something I considered. But Hiddink made it clear I was going to be a squad player for him and I thought that at only thirty-three years old I had more to offer and still wanted to play every week. I didn't expect to walk into the PSV team but I knew I was good enough to play every week. I asked for two or three days to think it over and during that time Frank Arnesen called me. Frank was Director of Football at PSV at that time. He said that Guus might not have explained the situation properly. Frank felt I would be coming to play at left-back.

From my contacts at PSV I got a feel for the type of deal I would be offered and the financial package was excellent, much better than Rangers' offer. I thought long and hard about it, discussed it with Marjon, my dad and Joop, but came to the conclusion that I had enjoyed six years at PSV, had been the captain too, and felt it was best to keep those memories intact. When you go back somewhere you run the risk of undoing the good work from the first spell and I didn't want to do that.

During this period, every Rangers fan I bumped into asked me why I wasn't signing for the club. I gave a polite response and said that these things happen in football, but I really wanted to say exactly how I felt. Most importantly, I just wanted to make sure that the fans knew I was not being greedy.

You know, I had retired from international football after the first league game of the 2002–03 season when we drew 1–1 with Kilmarnock at Rugby Park. We'd lost the league the season before and I didn't want to be part of that again. So, I chucked Holland – something that really disappointed Advocaat, who was back in charge of Holland at that time. I wanted to give my all to Rangers but, in return, they showed me little respect.

Looking back on it now, I think I made a mistake by saying to them in that first meeting in Dubai that I was willing to take a 25 or 30 per cent pay cut. I should have kept quiet and let them do the talking. But it still wasn't acceptable to me for them to offer what they did. I'd much rather Rangers had said to me that, because of the downsizing, they would not be able to keep me and that they had little money to offer, hardly worth their while wasting ink to put it in writing.

Now, I know for sure that, being a loyal Rangers player, I would have said to them, 'Let me be the judge of that. Offer me what you can, regardless of how big or small the offer is, and I'll look at it.' That way I would have been a bit more prepared and would have understood more of what the financial situation was. But to go from £550,000 net to £144,000 net was too much of a boot in the tender area.

I know that to the average man in the street, whether it be in Scotland, Holland or America, anything like £5,000 a week is a lot of money and, yes, I agree. However, to take such a drastic cut in one hit was too much. But it wasn't just the players that were being hit. In fact, in many ways, I was lucky still to be offered a deal. Just before the negotiations between the club and myself, many members of the Ibrox and Murray Park staff were made redundant and given just a couple of days to clear their desks. It was hard to watch secretarial staff and other colleagues lose their jobs. There was fear all over the place, a look that asked, 'Am I going to be next?' The players were also uneasy. My situation became public knowledge and Mols and Caniggia knew it was only a matter of time before they suffered the same fate.

I had sympathy for McLeish. He wanted to keep me, he told me so on several occasions and kept trying to persuade me to change my mind. He really had no say in the financial matters. In the end he had to do quite a lot of bargain-basement shopping and, in my honest opinion, the club ended up bringing in players to replace me that weren't fit to tie my shoelaces.

Mistakes were made all over the place in the transfer market during a period of a year or so in which guys such as Emerson, Nuno Capucho and Egil Ostenstad came to the club and made only a negative impact on the pitch.

Thankfully, I had the chance to go out on a high. We won the League Cup and lifted the SPL title on the last day of the season when we defeated Dunfermline 6–1 to win on goal difference from Celtic. That was an unbelievable day, the most dramatic I was ever involved in. Celtic were down at Kilmarnock that afternoon and actually went top of the table for about three minutes. We won the league with one minute of the season to go, thanks to a penalty from Mikel Arteta.

The Treble was there for us and we had to face Dundee in the Scottish Cup final at Hampden Park on 31 May 2003. I ended my first season at Rangers with the Treble and wanted to finish my career at Ibrox exactly the same way, then go on holiday and look at my options. First, I had the Scottish Cup final to negotiate. Oh, and before that, I had loads of parties to attend.

The day we won the league turned into a seventy-two-hour bender. We were out on the Sunday night and that rolled into the Monday. We had to report to Murray Park on Tuesday for training and a couple of the boys turned up with their club blazer and tie on as they'd not been home from the Sunday.

It was no surprise it was the Scottish boys like Barry Ferguson, Bob Malcolm, Mo Ross and others like Craig Moore and Michael Ball. We just had a bath, sauna and massage and then it was my leaving party after we'd finished. I hired a Japanese restaurant called Yen in Glasgow city centre and we had the place to ourselves. I thought it was a nice thing to do, to share some food and a few drinks with my team-mates and members of staff before my time at Rangers came to an end. I paid for the do myself which is the normal thing in Holland. If a Dutch person has a party and invites a group of friends it's up to that person to pay for everyone else's fun. It's part of our tradition so I found it a bit strange in Scotland when someone invites you to a party and you still pay for food and drinks! I think you call it going Dutch! But that's not the way the real Dutch do it.

Andy Watson and Jan Wouters came to my party but McLeish didn't. I went to see him the day before the party and told him it was best for everyone if he wasn't there. It was nothing personal. We had a Cup final four days after my party and it was best for him not to see how much alcohol was being

176

taken! It was also better McLeish wasn't there because players never relax properly when the manager is around.

Unfortunately, Barry Ferguson and Craig didn't make it to my farewell. They were both still feeling merry from the previous couple of days and I think Barry was also moving house that day. I was disappointed that the lads I'd got really close to at Ibrox weren't at my big send-off.

We all had a great night and it was just as well we were off on the Wednesday! Not surprisingly, when Cup-final day came, we could have been in better physical condition as I'm sure some of us were still sweating out the alcohol.

Goodness only knows how we managed it but we won the game 1–0 and Amoruso scored the goal in his last game for the club. It was a poor game but it was just about winning the Cup. Dundee boss Jim Duffy and his players were up for it and they played some good stuff – they just couldn't score. One of my memories from that day is at half-time when Michael Mols asked to be taken off. He was shattered. Not a kick of the ball left in him. He just looked at McLeish and begged, 'Please can I be taken off?' It was very honest of him. McLeish granted Mols' wish and subbed him. I was nervous before that game because I knew it was going to be my last appearance for the club and we had the chance to win the Treble. Dundee brought on Nacho Novo in the second half and I was up against him. He was full of running down the right wing. I became tired in the second forty-five and struggled to keep up. I had to come off with cramp in my left calf. I received a great ovation from the fans as I left the field for the last time.

I sat in the technical area for the last fifteen minutes and savoured every moment. To be honest, it was the perfect way to end my Rangers career. The blue, white and red flags and scarves were in the air and it was a joy to watch, to sit back and soak it all up.

We celebrated at the end and I made the most of it. I had mixed feelings. I was happy because the Treble had been won

but I was sad that it was all coming to an end. I had goose-
bumps as I waved cheerio to the fans, clapping them as I made
my way round the Hampden track. Some players lifted me on
their shoulders and a banner was made for the fans that read,
'Thanks for the memories.' It meant a lot to me to be valued
and respected by the Rangers fans. Football supporters can be
hard to please, unforgiving in many ways, but it said enough to
me that they cheered my final moments and mourned my
departure.

My five years at Ibrox had flown past. I was proud to have
worn the Rangers jersey and to have helped the club to win ten
domestic trophies, including three SPL titles. I could have
stayed on but wouldn't been comfortable with the contract I
had signed. I also wouldn't have wanted to overstay my welcome and undo all the good work I had put in during my time
at Ibrox. The older you get the more likely people start to mut-
ter that 'Numan's legs have gone'; or if you are injured quite a
bit then they say, 'Numan is only here for the money.' I didn't
want either accusation hurled at me. I'm glad I'm remembered
positively.

In the dressing room after the Dundee game, Amoruso was
crying. He knew he was also leaving and he was in an emotional state. Lorenzo had one year of his contract to run but the club
were selling him to Blackburn Rovers for £1 million. I was
much more relaxed because I was making my own decision
and was comfortable I was doing the right thing. I went on holiday for a few weeks after that, spending some time in Spain
and Holland. For the first two or three weeks I never really
thought about football. I knew Joop was working on things in
the background, keeping my options open.

I came back to Glasgow about five weeks later and on my
return to the airport a few photographers were there, waiting
for my arrival. A story had started to surface that I was going
to sign for Rangers again, but I assured everyone that was pure
speculation and it was never going to happen.

PSV and Feyenoord were still chasing me. Espanyol also made it clear they wanted me to join them. San Jose also got in touch to offer me the chance to move to America. It was something that appealed to me but the timing was just wrong. Marjon was due to give birth and I wanted to be there to share the special moment of the birth and the early days of being with my child. That would have been impossible if I had to move to America because they were going to a training camp in South Korea for three weeks. It was just not a good idea for me to sign.

The more time passed, the more I lost interest in the game. I had little motivation, although I was still running and keeping myself in good condition. The idea of retiring from football crossed my mind but I never thought I'd do it. I felt I had two good years left in the game and people whose opinion I respected told me the same.

However, I remember when I decided to call it a day. It was at the end of September and I was in Marbella on holiday with Marjon and Britt, our new baby daughter who was only about eight weeks old. I was watching television and there was coverage of some of the teams playing and training. It hit me then that I wasn't missing the game and was simply enjoying being a father. I still kept fit and in good shape but I was struggling to get myself motivated for a fresh challenge.

As the summer dragged on I realised I began to miss football less and less and my motivation to get back into the game was fading. I had finished with Rangers on a high by securing the Treble and wanted to be remembered as a player who quit the game at the top level.

I felt that if I signed for a new club I wouldn't be 100 per cent motivated and I've always been a guy who gives every team I've played for my full commitment. I didn't want to cheat the fans or myself by going to a club that I knew my heart wasn't really in. I told myself that my time was up. I was going to retire from football and never go back. I told Marjon about my decision and she was surprised but gave me her backing. I phoned my dad, Joop, my brother Jeroen and Michel Doesburg and they were all surprised. They told me I was being ridiculous and shouldn't rush into a decision like this. But I hadn't rushed it – I had taken my time.

When the news became public there was disbelief in Holland and Scotland about my announcement. Jaap Stam, Marc Overmars and Edwin van der Sar got in touch to say they were surprised and that I would regret it. But I had no doubts about my decision. All during my career I made decisions that took a lot of soul-searching but knew it was the right thing to do, from going to a tribunal when I transferred to PSV, to moving to Scotland to play for Rangers, to retiring from international football. I'd never regretted any of those calls and I was confident I'd look back some time down the line and not regret my decision to retire altogether from football.

I had been involved in two World Cup finals and two European Championships, I had won league titles in Holland and Scotland and I had played with some great players and been selected by some top managers during my career – guys that are held in high esteem throughout the world, such as Louis van Gaal, Frank Rijkaard, Dick Advocaat and Guus Hiddink. I'd had a wonderful career and I felt it was right to bring it to an end.

At that time Britt was only a few weeks old and it was great being able to see her every day. It was a fantastic experience to become a dad and I enjoyed every bit of it. I still do. When you are a footballer, you are on the road a lot and it can limit the amount of quality time you get to spend with your children. After Britt's birth I soon realised I wasn't wrapped up in the game as much as I was before. And maybe that was in the back of my mind and influenced my decision to walk away from football. I didn't want to miss out on Britt growing up. I wanted to share the special moments with Marjon and our daughter and I was in the fortunate position that I could do that without needing to work.

Football was a big part of my life and I still enjoy watching the game and doing media work. But I do not miss the involvement of being on the pitch. Since I retired I have only kicked a ball a few times. I've had countless invitations to play in games and to go here and there, but I refuse almost every request. That doesn't stop the kids in my street ringing the doorbell, as they can't take no for an answer! I suppose I never thought I wouldn't miss the game – but I really don't. It was a huge part of my life for over twenty-five years but I've been able to switch off from it very easily.

Rangers had tried to get me to go back during that summer before I retired but there was no way I was going to return. I also had an offer to go and play in Qatar and I could've earned unbelievable money for eight months over there, but I declined the offer.

I was sad it didn't work out to stay longer with Rangers but that's how football can be. When the talks broke down I told Murray not to underestimate the older, more experienced players and what they bring on and off the park. Rangers should have looked at the bigger picture in terms of the playing staff. They didn't and the club suffered as a result.

However, everything in life happens for a reason and things have worked out well for me. I like the freedom of not being tied down to a full-time employer. I still enjoy going to watch Rangers and want to see them continue to be successful. I have no hard feelings towards the club. I still visit Ibrox regularly and always get a warm welcome from everyone involved at the club. I just wish they had handled my contract situation in my final season with more professionalism and respect.

15

RELIGIOUS DIVIDE

When I arrived in Scotland to play for Rangers I was aware of the fierce rivalry between the supporters of Rangers and Celtic. What, however, I had no idea about was the religious element to it all. Just before my arrival in Glasgow, Pierre van Hooijdonk spoke about it to me when we roomed together in the 1998 World Cup in France, but it's something you have to see at first hand to get any sort of grasp on the whole situation.

So I knew that Rangers originated from a Protestant side and Celtic from Catholics. But I could never have imagined how deep some fans allow their feelings to run about the whole situation. As a foreigner, this was a new experience to me. There is certainly fierce rivalry in Holland, especially between Feyenoord and Ajax, but it's on a different scale to the Old Firm's.

I still find the situation that exists between some of the Old Firm supporters to be bizarre, although there definitely appears to be more awareness nowadays about trying to stamp it out. I do not know the history surrounding it all and, to be honest, I really do not want to know every detail. I respect the views of both sides, as long as people believe in them for the right reasons.

A lot of the songs from both sides have nothing to do with football. I remember when I was injured during my first season at Rangers, I was up in the main stand watching a game. The fans in the stand around me starting chanting, 'Arthur, Arthur, give us a song!' Eventually I gave in and stood up on my own and started to sing a song I thought the fans would be happy to sing.

So I started to sing 'Hi-ho, hi-ho!', waiting for everyone around me to join in, but instead I got strange looks and sniggers. I thought I was singing the first line to 'Hello, Hello . . .' and when I looked at the reaction of the crowd I knew I'd made a fool of myself.

The next day, in the dressing room, some of the players, including Ian Ferguson, Charlie Miller and Gordon Durie, lined up like the seven dwarves and shuffled along the dressing room singing, 'Hi-ho, hi-ho, it's off to work we go . . .'

I have no idea the background to the 'Billy Boys', I don't know what they are about and I do not understand it all, but I admit I enjoy the tune and the atmosphere of a lot of songs the supporters sing.

I find it difficult to understand what 'The Sash' is all about. I do not know why Rangers fans are referred to as 'Orange bastards'. Likewise, I'm not really sure what the word 'Fenian' means or why it is applied to Celtic supporters. I think it means a deregotary term towards Catholics, but does it? I have asked a few people from both sides if the divide and had different answers from all of them. What I do know is the background to Rangers, the football team. I know about their great achievements in football and the trophies they have won and that is good enough for me. I'm really not interested in songs about the IRA or the UVF.

In many ways it is easier for me as a foreigner to talk about this kind of thing. I remember in 2001, I think it was about that time, when Rangers had to send a player to the Glasgow City Chambers for a conference about bigotry and sectarianism. I find it an extremely difficult topic to discuss and talk about because it is so sensitive. There are so many wrong things you could say about it and so few right answers that people from both sides will agree with you on.

None of the Scottish players in the dressing room was keen to go to the City Chambers to attend, as they felt they'd be in a no-win situation. As a foreigner I couldn't give a qualified opinion as I was unaware of the history, but at least if I did say something that was out of place I, and Rangers FC, had the excuse that I was foreign. So I went.

The newspapers, radio and television were there and I was very diplomatic when I was interviewed about the situation. I said, 'What can I say about something that's been going on for more than a hundred years?'

Martin O'Neill attended on Celtic's behalf. The media jumped all over him, the chance to ask him about it and also the chance to get him to speak about Celtic's on-field displays, which were good at that time. He, too, found it difficult to give an answer because with an issue such as that one, words can come back to haunt you. He ended up having a bit of a run-in with a BBC reporter over the questions he was asked and it ended up being shown on television. It made the headlines for a few days afterwards.

It was exactly for that reason the Scottish players at Rangers didn't want to go and I think it was the correct decision for them not to attend. It was not also just about the Scottish boys; I think that Lorenzo Amoruso and Sergio Porrini felt they shouldn't go either, as they are Catholics from Italy. They were well clued up on what they could and could not do in Glasgow and when wearing a Rangers jersey. Shota Arveladze wasn't quite so on the ball as them and he had a strange experience when Rangers played a pre-season friendly against Lingfield in Northern Ireland. Shota was a sub and he blessed himself as he came on. He didn't mean to cause offence, he was just doing it for luck. It was totally innocent on his part. But the fans from Northern Ireland weren't too happy and Shota was booed for when he touched the ball. Shota had no idea what he was being booed for until it was explained to him. Again, it's just another example of not being able to please all of the time when it comes to sensitive issues.

I know that UEFA are involved in the whole situation now and they want to stamp anything that causes offence out of the game. Great strides have been made tackling racism in the past twenty years and they want to do the same with sectarianism. But where do you draw the line? My feeling is it almost impossible for a football club to make sure 50,000 or 60,000 fans are impeccably behaved for ninety minutes. There will always be a few morons inside a stadium.

Rangers and Celtic are making genuine efforts to get rid of the idiots and they should be applauded for that. But this is a battle neither club will be able to win in the space of a year or two. This will take time, a long time, but I believe things are improving and maybe will continue to get better. I believe fans now think twice before singing a sectarian song – and that is positive.

As long as the kids are being educated in school about it, and parents are being reponsible about it all, then things will be on the up. Schooling is so important. I grew up without any specific religious beliefs, although I do believe there is a God. I actually attended a Catholic primary school, Holy Heart, when I was eight years old. It was because the school was right on the doorstep of my family apartment. I was there to learn and there to enjoy myself.

I would sometimes have to attend Mass with the school and some of the stories told were quite interesting. Because I'm not Catholic, I didn't receive Holy Communion and I used to sit and wonder what it was all about, what my classmates were going up the aisle to receive. But the fact I was not Catholic did not cause any aggro. This was simply because what religious beliefs you had were of no importance to kids in Holland. It didn't matter. We all got along well and were only interested in playing with each other. We played in the same school team.

Kids need to play together and we have to hope that in this country, whether you wear a blue top or a green top, it shouldn't matter. Yes, there can be rivalry and you can laugh and joke about it with each other, but it should never be too serious. It should never lead to violence. Too many people have been killed or seriously injured in Scotland, Northern Ireland and Ireland because of religion and that is very sad. Innocent people should not be lost to this world under such circumstances.

The more campaigns from the Scottish Executive and the Old Firm clubs, the better. The more it is highlighted, the better chance there is of the situation improving. I'm a parent and all that every parent should want is for their children to grow up in as safe an environment as possible. Going to a football game should be a pleasure, it should entertain you, leave you with a smile on your face. It should not be about hatred and should not have you worrying if you will come back from a game in one piece.

And that does not only apply to Old Firm fans. Other clubs' fans have a duty to behave more responsibly. Take Aberdeen – sure, there might not be the religious element attached to their club but they have a hatred towards Rangers FC and their supporters. The songs I've heard them singing during their games against Rangers were really offensive. They must be brought to task over this. Lots of Old Firm players are singled out for 'personal treatment' on and off the pitch from rival fans. I've been called an 'Orange bastard' many, many times when I've been in Glasgow and other places, but most of the time I could laugh it off. I can handle that kind of thing. What I still can't quite understand, though, is men in their forties and fifties getting so worked up about it all. For a grown man to shout abuse, veins sticking out of his neck, face the colour of a plum, is quite unbelievable. I can sort of understand teenagers having a go, perhaps trying to show off to their friends or whatever, but men of much more advanced years? They try to get you annoyed, force a reaction out of you. I've been fortunate that I've not had to endure too much, so from that point of view I do have sympathy for guys like Barry Ferguson and Neil Lennon who have to put up with it all far too often.

I also know Peter Lovenkrands was assaulted a couple of times in Glasgow. I lost my temper on one occasion on a night out in Glasgow. I was on a stag do and it was a '70s-theme fancy dress. Typically, I had the big afro wig on and the flairs. I was in a bar having a drink and I got a phone call from Michel Doesburg to come and see him in another bar. He was with Dunfermline by this stage and was having a drink with some of his team-mates. But two guys stole my wig and I chased them. It was stupid of me to give chase – I should have stayed put – but I'd had a few drinks by this point.

I ended up in an alley, just off Sauchiehall Street. I confronted them and politely asked for my wig back. I asked several times. The guy kept a hold of it and came towards me. He grabbed my shirt and ripped a few of the buttons off. He told me if I reacted in any way he would call the newspapers about me. They were Celtic fans. A few things were going through my mind and I had a quick decision to make. I thought of the time the PSV fans attacked me outside the stadium and I ended up worse off.

This was a two-on-one situation and didn't look too promising for me. I feared getting hammered by the pair of them. So I punched the guy right on the nose, the one who wouldn't give me my wig, grabbed the wig off him and ran like hell. I tore down Sauchiehall Street, grabbed a taxi and went straight home. I'm not proud of my behaviour on that occasion but felt I had to make the first move to protect myself.

Then there was the time I played for Holland against the Republic of Ireland in a 2002 World Cup qualifier in Dublin. On the day before the game our training session was open to the public and Giovanni van Bronckhorst and I took some pelters from the Ireland fans, a lot of them wearing Celtic tops. We didn't expect the red-carpet treatment over there and of course, van Hooijdonk was loving every minute of it and enjoyed pouring oil on the fire!

During the game I was booed every time I touched the ball. Then Jason McAteer elbowed me in the face. It split my eye open and I had to get it stitched up. He got some cheer from the Ireland fans for doing that to me. They were delighted to see a Rangers player on the receiving end of something like that.

Players and ex-players can also continue to do their bit and we all have to aim for harmony. You know, the football players can cross the Old Firm divide and more fans have to be willing to do the same. Giovanni van Bronckhorst and Henrik Larsson are great friends. There have been many more relationships like theirs over the years and I'm told that the Rangers and Celtic players from the 1960s and 1970s used to socialise a lot together.

For example, if I need my hair cut I always go to Pele in Glasgow city centre. There's great banter in there as the owners are on either side of the Old Firm – Fraser follows Rangers and Michael supports Celtic. I know players from both sides of the Old Firm go there and there's always a joke or two flying back and forward.

I've attended many charity functions with former Celtic captain Tom Boyd for St Andrew's Hospice and we've helped raise money for good causes. I've always got on well with Tom at these events and that goes for all the Celtic players, past and present, at a number of occasions.

On a lighter note, when I was out and about at functions or parties, something I found amusing when I first came to Glasgow was the 'funny handshake'. Now, I had heard of the 'Glasgow kiss', but this? When I had it a few times I thought, 'What the f*** is going on here?' I now know it is a Masonic handshake. I'm used to it now and I understand and accept it.

The things I've written about this are only my opinions. I don't have solutions. I hope the situation gets better but I have my doubts that it will totally disappear because it has been going on for a hundred years. It might take something like UEFA deducting points from a Champions League game or closing down the ground for a game for it all to come to a complete halt. However, for the sake of the players, management and the well-behaved fans, I hope that never happens.

We can only hope the situation improves as it has been doing in recent times. If people from both sides are pulling all the time to meet in the middle then that's all we can ask for.

16

TASTE OF ORANJE

All young footballers dream of the day they pull on their country's colours and win their first international cap. For me that momentous day arrived on 14 October 1992 in a World Cup qualifier at home to Poland. But what I thought would be one of the greatest moments of my life and one of the highlights of my career turned into a personal embarrassment.

I was twenty-two at that time and starting off on the road to what I thought would be a long and successful international career. We were 2–0 down to Poland and I was made the early scapegoat when Dick Advocaat replaced me with Gerald Vanenburg after thirty-nine minutes.

It was not the way I had envisaged my Holland debut!

Since I was a schoolkid I had dreamt about the moment when I pulled on the famous Oranje jersey. From when I started out at senior level, mixing my studies with four days' training a week at FC Haarlem, to when I became a full professional at Twente Enschede, I wanted the feeling of playing for my country in a full international so much.

When I got my move to Twente I wanted to improve and, through hard work and determination, I achieved my goal. After just eighteen months there I got a transfer to PSV Eindhoven; it was a quick, meteoric rise for me. I played well at PSV for the first two or three months and my performances were starting to get noticed by certain parts of the media who mentioned me as a possibility for the national team.

PSV started well in the league, they'd qualified for the Champions League and I was contributing to our success by playing well on the left-hand side of midfield in a 4–4–2 formation. I was feeling good and knew I was playing well, but was taking nothing for granted as far as getting selected for Holland was concerned, even though Advocaat was in charge and he knew all about my strengths. One day after training, Hans Westerhof, the PSV coach, asked to see me and I thought he wanted to talk about the way the team was playing and discuss my role. To my complete surprise, he said, 'I have good news for you, Arthur. You have been selected for the Holland squad for the World Cup qualifier against Norway. Well done. It is an honour for you and for the club.'

I felt ecstatic and was immediately on the phone to let Marjon and my family and friends hear the good news.

When the squad was announced a couple of days later it was something else to see my name in the newspapers and on television alongside Marco van Basten, Ruud Gullit and Frank Rijkaard of AC Milan and Ronald Koeman of Barcelona. Real superstars of world football. I was going to get the chance to train with them and hopefully play alongside them in the same team.

One of my first times when I went down for breakfast at the team hotel, I was shy as I sat across from van Basten and Gullit. In fact I was a nervous wreck and normally I have bread sprinkled with chocolate first thing in the morning. But because I wasn't myself and they were all talking among themselves, I was too shy to interrupt and ask them to pass me the chocolate sprinkles. So rather than simply ask them, I had cheese instead – what an idiot!

The squad met up at a hotel and before I'd even had a chance to hook up with my team-mates the media pounced on me as they were desperate to speak to the new boy in the squad. I was asked my opinion on the fact my PSV team-mate Vanenburg was not in the squad for the Norway game. I told them I was surprised at Vanenburg's exclusion, as he had been playing well at club level, but Advocaat reserved the right to select the players he wanted. It was an honest opinion, not meant to be controversial or confrontational in any way. I thought nothing more of it.

We arrived in Oslo and before we headed out to train, Advocaat called a meeting in the dressing room. He said, 'There are two things I'd like to talk about just now and the first is Arthur Numan.'

I thought he was going to introduce me formally to the rest of the squad. I couldn't have been more wrong.

No, on the contrary, wee Dickie gave me a dressing-down in front of my new team-mates! He continued, 'Numan has found it necessary to speak in public about my squad selection. I want to remind you all that I'm the manager and I can choose the players I want to choose. It's disrespectful to me to say something about my selection and it's also disrespectful to the person you are speaking about that has been left out.'

I wanted to curl up into a ball. God, my first meeting with the national team and I'd already upset the manager. I could feel the experienced players looking at me as if to say, 'Silly young fool.' It really upset me and no matter how innocent or uncontroversial I thought my answers were, it was on my mind throughout training that day. It was a lesson learned and a difficult way to learn it. I'd never experienced a hard time like that before. It taught me a valuable lesson about speaking in public and Dick was absolutely right in the point he made about it being unfair on the guy who was included in Vanenburg's place. Gaston Taument was in the squad ahead of him.

At least Dick didn't hold any grudges. I was back in the squad for the next game, against Poland, and Vanenburg was also included. We met at a hotel for the build-up and as I was one of the new boys who was about to make his first appearance (I'd not got off the bench against Norway) I was one of the players put up to interview with the media. Bearing in mind what had gone on previously, I was much more careful what I said that time.

International gatherings can be long and boring, particularly in the hotel. Back then, there were no personal DVD players or iPods that allow you to go off on your own with a movie or some music for company, so a lot of the time was spent in the hotel foyer drinking tea and coffee, playing cards or having general chit-chat. Well, for a young player, it felt like an eternity of waiting around. I deliberately kept myself to myself, mostly mixing with the PSV players and the other young guys in the squad, just sussing out the lie of the land.

The last thing I wanted to do in front of the superstars was to come across as a Billy Bigtime. In general, senior players have no time for young guys with a big-headed, over-confident attitude. You have to earn the right to be respected in football, at least that's the way I always looked upon it.

Sadly, too many young players don't have that attitude. I'm all for young players with a bit of cockiness, but too many play a handful of first-team games and all of a sudden think they've made it. Too many of them swagger about and don't keep working hard enough to continue their progression and education in the game. They quickly forget what helped them to a first-team spot in the first place. In Holland we have the saying, 'Het is moeilijk om aan de top te komen, maar moeilijker om er te blijven,' which, roughly translated, means 'It's hard to reach the top but staying there is even harder.'

I didn't set out to be liked by the established players in the Dutch squad at that time but I wanted them to see I had talent and was willing to work hard. After my climb to PSV in club football, this was another step up the footballing ladder. It was a great experience training with some of the players that won us the European Championships in 1988 and the European Cup at club level. Perhaps, though, I tried too hard to impress my new colleagues. After every training session I came off the pitch absolutely knackered. I gave 100 per cent and then some in every session. I used up a lot of energy in the eight-v-eight practice games.

Training was never 'friendly' and it was full of competitive tackles. Koeman, van Basten and Wouters took no prisoners. They were also special players; to see them up close was an education, the way they controlled the ball, kept possession with one-touch passing and always appeared to be one step ahead of their opponent. They were mentally sharp, all the time. I also noticed there was always a lot of yelling and shouting between the players. Plenty of arguments took place. Wouters never left you in any doubt about what he thought of your performance.

I roomed with Rob Witschge, who was the left-back. It was a deliberate move by Advocaat to put us together, as he knew we would be playing down that side together against Poland.

We were well prepared for the game. Advocaat had made sure we all knew what was required of us tactically, when we were in possession and when our opponents had the ball. We were shown video clips of the Poles and after losing our first qualifier against Norway we knew how important a win was in this game.

The team was announced the morning before the game and I was delighted to be on the starting list. Advocaat came to me beforehand in the hotel and told me to take it easy on the pitch, not to try too hard. Basically, keep it tidy and do the simple things. I was probably running around like a headless chicken in training and Advocaat felt a word in my ear was appropriate.

Wouters also gave me some advice. As I said, he wasn't afraid to speak the truth. He was a senior pro with a wealth of international experience and I was only starting my cap career. Whether you were new to the squad like me or a veteran like van Basten, Wouters never held back. He was constantly on my back during that game against Poland, in the De Kuip Stadium in Rotterdam. I remember from a throw-in he received from me, the ball bounced just in front of him and he gave me dog's abuse for it. Although he was yelling and shouting it didn't effect my game and in hindsight I realised he was just trying to keep us all sharp and on our toes.

I remember when we played together at PSV some of the younger players couldn't handle Wouters ranting at them and that affected their game to such an extent that one young player pleaded with him to stop moaning at him. I suppose, in many ways, he was a madman on the pitch, because he's an out-and-out winner. Yet, off the pitch he is a quiet character. We had played well and created plenty of chances but we just couldn't score.

Before we knew it Poland were 2–0 up and I was subbed in the thirty-ninth minute. I could see Vanenburg warming up and I had a feeling I was going to be the one to make way for him. When my number was held up on the substitute board I was fuming with Advocaat, calling him names under my breath as I jogged off the pitch. The rage then turned to a mixture of deflation and embarrassment. My body was slumped on the touchline. I don't think I could have felt any worse even if I'd gone fifteen rounds with Mike Tyson.

I was in the shower at half-time and Dick made a point of coming to see me. He told me it was nothing to do with the way I was playing, it was just a tactical switch. We eventually fought back and drew the game 2–2. After the game the president of the Dutch FA came into the dressing room to present me with a little silver rabbit, a memento to mark my debut. Every Dutch international gets one after their first cap. After my twenty-fifth cap I received a silver plate, which had all the games I had played engraved on it, along with the date and scoreline.

Thankfully my second cap was much more memorable than my first, although this time I came off the bench with ten minutes to go as we won a World Cup qualifier away to Turkey 3–1.

We qualified for the 1994 World Cup and I was desperate to be included in the squad but was feeling insecure about my chances. I couldn't help but have negative thoughts. In the end Advocaat selected me in the twenty-two-man squad but I knew I was going there as a player in the category of 16-22, not the first-choice eleven.

There was a feeling we could do well in America but the plans were thrown into chaos just before we were due to fly out to Canada for our final warm-up game when Gullit walked out on the squad. He had a disagreement with Advocaat. The precise details I'm not 100 per cent sure about, but it may have been that Gullit wasn't happy with the formation we were to adopt, or his role within that formation. Perhaps he was unhappy about both.

The whole Gullit thing came right out of the blue. The players did not see it coming. In the friendly games we played in Holland before we departed, Advocaat tried different formations and there wasn't any sign of unrest. We played Scotland in one of our warm-up games in Utrecht and beat them 3–1. I came on as a sub at the start of the second half.

Gullit had his issues with Advocaat and he quit. He left the team hotel, near Amsterdam, and never returned. It was obviously a huge story and dominated the headlines for days, not just in Holland but throughout Europe. The Dutch press followed Gullit to get his version of the story but he never spoke out and kept his feelings private.

We lost a world-class player, the player every footballer supporter identified the Dutch team with. He had the big hair and the big reputation. It was a great pity he wasn't there to help us. To this day, I'm unsure if he has ever had any regrets about his decision.

Advocaat called a team meeting shortly after Gullit's walkout and told us to forget about what had happened and concentrate on our preparations for the World Cup. It was just typical of our nation. Something sensational, negative, always happens in and around the time of major tournaments. If only we could make life easy for ourselves.

As if that wasn't enough to deal with we also had a major problem on the way to the World Cup on one of our flights. A Dutch journalist stupidly informed a fight attendant that he had a bomb in his bag! He was fooling around, although it was a silly prank to try. The flight attendant immediately told the captain and the plane made an emergency landing. Dick was fuming. I remember him shouting, 'This is the World Cup, not a holiday camp. I'm never allowing the press to fly with us on the team plane again.'

Another member of the press pack happened to be a nervous flyer and he took a few drinks to settle his nerves. He was also on medication at the time, but rather than the alcohol having a sedative effect on him it actually turned him into a madman and he started going crazy on the plane! He was literally foaming at the mouth – and so was Advocaat for a different reason. Once again, Dick's face was a picture and the veins were popping out of his neck! When we eventually landed safely in the States I started to realise what being part of this squad meant to me.

It was great to be a part of my country's World Cup hopes. We had a mixture of youth and experience in the squad. The experience and knowledge came from Koeman, Wouters and Rijkaard. We also had some promising young talent in Marc Overmars, Brian Roy and Frank de Boer.

Training was very competitive and Advocaat liked to play matches between his first choice and the rest. I was in the 'reserve' team all the time and we would have the third-choice keeper or the physio Rob Ouderland, who played at a good level, in our side. We were always fired up, desperate to do well and give the manager some selection headaches. We did that by sometimes beating the first eleven in training.

We faced Saudi Arabia in our opening game and won 2–1, but had to rely on a Taument goal with only three minutes remaining.

Our training camp was in Orlando. It was a private base on a golf complex. The houses on the compound were sensational, fancy bungalows with big gardens and swimming pools. We would train every day but the Florida heat was unbearable. It was like playing football in a sauna. We had to stop every fifteen minutes to take fluids in.

I remember Rijkaard really struggled with the heat and humidity. After one game, he told Advocaat he did not have the energy to start the next game and asked to be put on the bench. Even the warm-up in games used to take its toll. You had to take it very easy. For our quarter-final clash against Brazil at the Cotton Bowl in Dallas there was no roof on the stadium, so there was no shaded area on the pitch. The sun was beating down and the players were gasping for breath under the searing afternoon heat.

It was important to relax, get plenty of rest between games, and I used to enjoy going out on a boat on a lake to do some fishing with Overmars and Ed de Goey.

Once or twice Advocaat allowed us out of the complex to go out and relax. It was fine for us because none of the players were recognised when we ventured out. The Americans just haven't taken football on board the way people expected them to. They went for it big time in the 1970s, when they brought out Pelé, Franz Beckenbauer and George Best to play, but it never quite caught on. They were then given the World Cup but that again failed to catch their imagination ahead of basketball and baseball.

When we went downtown to watch a game it was actually difficult to realise the World Cup was actually taking place there! No football was being shown in the bars or restaurants. There were maybe ten different channels available in some of the bars but it was basketball and baseball that the punters were watching. Many of the locals seemed to have no idea about the World Cup. When watching it with us they knew next to nothing about the rules and would often ask us what the offside law was all about and what a yellow card was for.

Yet, the organisation of the tournament was first class, as you would expect from a country such as America. The facilities were superb. If football really did take off in the States then they would have an outstanding chance of becoming world champions. With its population, ability to produce skilled sportsmen and excellent facilities for training, they really would be a country to be feared.

My only appearance in the 1994 World Cup was against the Republic of Ireland when I came on as a sub with about twelve minutes to go. The game was played at midday and I remember being knackered after a few minutes. I won a free-kick down at a corner flag. I deliberately stayed down to get some treatment, to catch my breath and get some water. I also knew the television cameras would zoom in on me, so it would give my friends and family the chance to see me on television to prove I was actually there!

The other aspect of this game that sticks in my mind was a number of hefty challenges between myself and Roy Keane. If you were unlucky and Roy didn't win the ball in a tackle, he certainly seemed to get the player instead!

It was a bonus to get on and play some part in the 2–0 win. I knew 1994 was going to be my chance to sample the occasion and take mental notes of everything involved to make sure my preparation for the 1998 World Cup would be top quality, and for Euro 96 before it.

We were knocked out by Brazil at the quarter-final stage and it signalled the end of an era, a generation of top, top players who had achieved success by winning Euro 88 in Germany. It was time for a new group of players to come together and try to maintain their success. It was a big ask but there was quality coming through in the form of Clarence Seedorf, Edgar Davids and Patrick Kluivert. Advocaat resigned shortly after the tournament and was replaced by Guus Hiddink.

Hiddink has had a remarkable career in management. He had successful spells in charge of PSV Eindhoven and Holland. And he also led South Korea to the semi-final stages of the World Cup. When he became manager of Australia, he took them to the 2006 World Cup finals in Germany – their first time in the tournament for thirty-two years – and got them out of the group stages to qualify for the last sixteen. They were only knocked out after a controversial penalty decision went against them when playing Italy.

He is one of the most respected managers in the world and one of his strengths is being able to get a group of players to come together, gel on the pitch and have a good atmosphere off it.

It must be a difficult job being in charge of a national team for a tournament when you have the squad together for a four- or five-week period, especially when you're expected to bring together a disparate group of strong-willed, opinionated Dutchmen.

When we were in France two years later for the World Cup Hiddink made small but important adjustments, such as making sure we all ate with different people at meal times, encouraging us to mix to improve our team spirit. We'd had too many cliques at Euro 96 and Hiddink didn't want the same scenario developing again. His plan worked because we achieved much more in France than we did in England, basically with the same group of players.

Hiddink employed Rijkaard as one of his assistants alongside Johan Neeskens and Ronald Koeman and that was a good choice of backroom staff. Neeskens had the respect of the entire squad and every time he spoke we listened. Rijkaard was also good to have around, particularly for players like Davids, Seedorf and Kluivert, as they could go and talk to him if they felt the need.

I was a squad player in Euro 96 and didn't get stripped for a single minute's action. I sat next to Stam in the dugout and he, too, never left the bench throughout that tournament. I accepted that but knew I deserved to be in the team for the start of the 1998 World Cup qualifying campaign. Hiddink left me out of our first game of that campaign, away to Wales, and I decided to have words with him. It seemed to work, because he played me in every game after that.

It was my feeling that Hiddink preferred Winston Bogarde and wanted him to play. But he couldn't justify putting Bogarde in ahead of me. I knew, though, that I had to play well for every minute of every game or else he would have the excuse to leave me out. I think Bogarde had more credit with Hiddink than I did.

At that time I was playing really well for PSV. I was comfortable in the left-back position and always looking to overlap to join in the attack. It was something I excelled at, an aspect of my game that the coaching staff and fans began to expect from me. But when I played for Holland under Hiddink I was more reserved and concentrated on my defensive duties. I didn't join the attack as often, as my priority was to defend and make sure I was solid and not doing anything stupid.

Although I earned most of my caps – twenty-one – under Hiddink, I did not enjoy some of them as much as I should have because I felt my natural game was sometimes being suppressed.

I read a Dutch football book, *Hard Gras*, and there's a chapter where Hiddink talks about the situation between Bogarde and myself during the World Cup. Hiddink says Rijkaard also has a lot of sympathy for Bogarde and before the Holland–Mexico match Frank even told the manager it would be nice if Bogarde started the game. Hiddink echoed Rijkaard's views becuase he thought Bogarde worked hard in training and should be rewarded for his efforts. But he picked me because he felt I 'didn't fail' and he didn't want to change the defence. Using the term 'didn't fail' told me everything about the situation. Would it not have been better to say I played well or made a positive contribution? With Hiddink in charge, I was always under pressure and felt my head was on the chopping block waiting for the guillotine.

France 98 was a superb tournament for the Dutch and I thought we could have beaten France in the final if we had managed to overcome Brazil in the semi-final penalty shoot-out. We had a couple of other disappointments during our time out there when Bogarde broke his leg in training and Wim Jonk's close friend Harry Kwakman died in a car crash. I also got to know Harry as he came to the PSV home games. Wim was given the heartbreaking news about the tragedy after one of our training sessions and it really hit him hard. Understandably he was down and depressed after that. He didn't attend the funeral but wrote a lovely, moving poem about Harry that was printed in the newspaper.

Euro 2000 was my fourth and final major finals with the national team. I arrived for the pre-tournament training camp in Switzerland with a groin injury and there was a concern on my part I might not make the squad. Rijkaard was now the coach and the finals were being held in Holland and Belgium. From the camp in Switzerland, three or four players would be left out and would miss out on the final party that returned to our base in Hoenderloo.

I was put through some training schedules by the medical staff to prove my fitness and it wasn't going well. I could manage some things but not everything. However, I had an inner determination to make this squad. Dutch journalists were dismissing my chances of making it due to injury and that really pissed me off. But through hard work and determination I did eventually make the squad.

Bogarde was also struggling with an injury and did not make the squad, so Giovanni van Bronckhorst and Bolo Zenden were filling in at left-back in the warm-up games. Rijkaard pulled me aside a few days before our opening game against the Czech Republic and said that Giovanni would start the tournament at left-back. He also made it clear that if Giovanni was suspended or didn't play well, I'd be in.

I was disappointed but had a feeling that would be the case and I had no complaints about sitting on the bench. I had only had one warm-up match and hadn't played enough games with the team to merit my inclusion, whereas Giovanni had – although it was difficult for him to step back from midfield into a more defensive role.

Giovanni was booked in our opening game against the Czechs and cautioned again in the next match against Denmark. We won both games (1–0 and 3–0) but were criticised for our performances, especially when it took a lucky last-minute penalty decision to beat the Czechs. So I knew I would start our final group game against France. I was so excited. The game couldn't come quickly enough. Our facilities were good and once again all the preparation was excellent. The team manager, Hans Jorritsma, was responsible for all that stuff. He was a former hockey player himself and went on to become Pakistan's national team coach for years and they lifted the Champions Trophy – hockey's equivalent of the World Cup. Hiddink appointed him before France 98 and it was a great idea to utilise his experience and know-how.

Hans goes around to check hotels and facilities before major tournaments and always gets every aspect of our preparations spot-on. If any player had a problem – and believe me there are always many – Hans would sort it out. Whatever you wanted, it was never an issue. He was a real Mr Fixit.

The only complaint I had about our camp for Euro 2000 was that it was like Fort Knox. The complex contained houses and it was four players to every unit, with each player having his own room. Surprise, surprise, I was in with Marc Overmars, Pierre van Hooijdonk and Jaap Stam. Much of the time the house was just one huge mess and it would have been nice to escape from it now and again. But because we were the home nation there was no chance of us being allowed out. This wasn't like America in 1994 when hardly a soul knew who we were. Once or twice, however, the management did allow us to go back home to see family and friends.

Our final group game against France was significant. Both nations were already through and the only issue to be decided was which of us finished top. There was talk in the newspapers before the game that the French team would be happy to qualify as runners-up as they would play their next game in Belgium, where they had a big support. If we ended on top we stayed in Holland.

However, there was no suspicion on the pitch that France were happy to lose. They were the world champions and wanted to put down a marker to us, one of the host nations. We won 3–2 and there was no evidence the French laid down. It was a cracking game and I felt I turned in a decent performance, just pleased to get through my first ninety minutes of the championships unscathed and be part of a victorious side.

We played Yugoslavia in the quarter-finals and that game goes down as one of my most cherished from the forty-five times I represented my country. Everything just clicked into place and we romped to a fantastic 6–1 win, with Kluivert grabbing a superb hat-trick. Our supporters were terrific and created a great atmosphere and a fantastic sight to witness – a sea of Oranje.

I felt good in the game, in fact I was flying. I even had a chance to score! When I felt a tweak on the sole of my foot, I just passed it off as a touch of cramp. I played on, didn't want to come off. I was enjoying the match so much and, after missing the first two games of the tournament, there was no way I was volunteering to come off. However, the niggling pain in my foot just wouldn't go away and only my adrenalin got me through the last twenty minutes.

We won the game comfortably, totally destroying Yugoslavia with our ball circulation and movement. I don't think many teams could have lived with us that night. After the match Rob the physio examined my foot and decided to put ice on it. I'd been given new boots only a couple of days before, and the pitch was dry and hard and maybe that didn't help. We liked to play our football on short grass, sprinkled with water just before kick-off. The weaker football nations prefer long turf on a bumpy pitch to stop their opponents zipping the ball about.

I went back to base camp after the win but the pain was persistent. When I woke up in the morning it was still sore and I didn't feel comfortable. I went back to see Rob and the doctor and they said I had to get it checked out properly. We informed Rijkaard and after breakfast drove to Amsterdam for a hospital scan.

The scan showed I had torn my tendon. It was an injury volleyball players usually get from the way they land at the net after a jump. The first thing I wanted to know was if I'd be fit to play against Italy in the semi-final. The doctor dropped the bombshell that there was no way I could play. It was just too dangerous and, instead of being out for four or five weeks, I could end up being sidelined for up to six months and would require an operation to stitch the wound back together.

But I wasn't taking 'no' for an answer and asked them about the possibility of taking an injection to allow me to play – just whatever was necessary to get me fit for the semi. I had missed the semi-final of France 98 against Brazil because I was suspended and here I was being told I couldn't play in the semi-final of Euro 2000 because of a foot injury.

This was more than likely going to be one of my final chances to play in a game with so much at stake and the thought of missing out was tearing me apart. There was a temptation on my side to take an injection but I was getting no encouragement from the medical staff and knew that Rijkaard wouldn't put me under pressure to play.

So, when I thought about it, I knew that by playing on I'd probably miss out on the prospect of Champions League football and the chance to play a part in winning back-to-back titles. Celtic had just appointed Martin O'Neill as manager that summer and were determined to mount a bigger challenge than the previous season when we romped to the title by twenty-one points.

I had missed a lot of my first season at Rangers through injury and couldn't go through that again. The thought of working on my own to regain fitness and having to sit in the stand and watch the games was too much. No, it wasn't for me. Also, Rangers had invested a lot of money in me with a transfer fee of around £4.5 million and were paying me excellent wages. I had a duty to the club, Advocaat, my team-mates and the supporters to be fit and available for the new season. I looked at the bigger picture and made the right decision. So I accepted the medical advice and now had to come to terms with the fact Euro 2000 was over for me. To go from such a high the previous evening to being totally deflated the next day was one of the worst feelings I ever experienced in football.

On my return to the training camp the press were hovering around asking why I wasn't taking part in training that morning. I walked straight onto the training pitch to tell Rijkaard the news. The injury was too severe and complete rest was required. Rijkaard was really sympathetic towards my situation. I faced the press later that day and it was hard to sit at a desk, behind all the microphones, and try to explain how I felt, my disappointment at losing out yet again. It was such a difficult thing for me because I was so upset about the whole situation. It was the end of my tournament and I was distraught. I could feel the colour draining out of my face as I sat there answering the questions. I kept asking myself, 'Why me? Why this strange injury?'

Mentally I didn't feel ready to pack my bags and leave the base. I wanted to stay with the squad for the Italy game, play my part in some way no matter how small or insignificant my input would be. I asked Rijkaard if I could hang around and he agreed. It was good of him to agree, but he knew I was not a troublemaker and would not have a negative impact on the squad.

I sat on the bench for the semi-final against Brazil in France and I was back on the bench for the semi-final of Euro 2000 against Italy. I was there purely as a fan now and I badly wanted us to beat Italy, but I still can't believe we failed to beat them. The Italians had Gianluca Zambrotta sent off after half an hour and then Frank de Boer missed a penalty four minutes later. Incredibly, after an hour we missed another penalty – this time Kluivert was the sinner. It was unbelievable drama. Italy almost scored in the final seconds of the game to snatch victory and I felt we had to score in extra-time because I knew we wouldn't win the game if it went to a penalty shoot-out.

Of course, as is always the story with us, we lost on penalties. Frank had the courage to take another one but missed again. Jaap Stam and Paul Bosvelt also fluffed theirs. We were out. Once again, spot-kicks finished off our chances and we were home earlier than expected.

But, really, to miss FIVE in one game was – even by our standards – unbelievable. Crazy, in fact. No scriptwriter could have made that one up. I went over to Stam after the game. We were on the pitch and I looked up at him. I had an ironic smile on my face, trying the lighten the moment, and asked him what the hell he was doing with his penalty. 'Did you try to hit it all the way to Old Trafford?'

The serious part was that we had missed another golden opportunity to win a tournament. In 1998 I reckoned we would have had a 50:50 chance of beating the French in the final. Yes, they beat Brazil but they faced the Brazilians at the perfect time as they were knackered after the semi-final against us and also had the problems with Ronaldo to contend with the day before the final.

We would have had an even better chance of beating France in the Euro 2000 final. In front of our supporters, I would definitely have backed us, just as long as it didn't go to penalties! That generation of players was good enough to win something. That crop of stars followed on from the Gullit, Rijkaard and van

Basten era and created a new belief – players that the public looked up to and believed in. We just never made the final step, the biggest step of all.

We couldn't maximise our potential. Bottom line, I suppose, was we weren't good enough. Good, yes, but simply not good enough. Story of my career in many ways. Yet, in the cold light of day the difference between success and failure was really only down to a couple of penalty kicks. Instead of Barthez, Zidane, Vieira and Blanc, it could have been van der Sar, Numan, de Boer and Bergkamp.

In the aftermath of the Italy game I started to ask myself if I could have made a difference. After the Brazil game in 1998, I thought if I had not been suspended and Overmars had been fit to play, we could have won. But our first-choice left side of the team was wiped out and that was bound to have a negative effect. After the Italy match, I thought that if I was playing I could have helped create more chances with my overlaps down the left.

Eventually, on both occasions, I had to switch off. It was doing my head in, I was taunting myself. I had to accept defeat. Live with it. But it will always haunt me and whenever I see any of our games from those tournaments on television the old feelings and thoughts come back. But I'm sure I'm not the only one from that fine generation of Dutch footballers. Dennis Bergkamp, Davids, Kluivert, Seedorf, Stam and the de Boer twins will all be exactly the same.

As a footballer it's a huge regret of mine not to have played in a World Cup final or a European Championship final. Had I played in one it wouldn't have made me a different or better person, but it would just have been lovely to look back on.

But penalty shoot-outs killed us. It's another hard-luck story and there are players all over the world with hard-luck stories. Rarely are the ones who score remembered, only the ones that missed. I felt for David Trezeguet when he missed France's penalty in the World Cup final in Berlin in June 2006.

Being able to switch off from what is at stake. In the end it's the definitive way to decide a game of football and it's also a necessary evil. It's just a pity somebody has to miss, has to be the fall-guy. Losing games doesn't just hurt the players; managers are also left depressed. The defeat to Italy left Rijkaard distraught. After the game, on the team bus, outside the Amsterdam ArenA, he was in tears. He sat alone at the front of the coach and couldn't keep his emotions in. It wasn't for show, it was a genuine breakdown. He was overcome with emotion and it was caught on camera by a television crew. His tears weren't witnessed by the squad and we were also unaware he had resigned immediately after the game. His decision to stand down came as a complete shock to all of us.

Due to my injury problems, I only played five times under Rijkaard during his two years in charge, but he made a good impression on me, despite his lack of managerial experience at the time. Regardless of the circumstances, he was always very relaxed and switched on. He was calm and composed. Being in charge was his first job as head coach and he handled it well.

He would often stop training to make a point and whatever he said always had significance to it. He wasn't the type of guy to speak so he could hear the sound of his own voice. His words had a purpose and were always sensible. He had the total respect of the players.

Rijkaard was promoted from being one of Hiddink's assistants at France 98 to the main job. He was held in high esteem by the men in charge of the Dutch FA. Of course, his appointment was a big gamble because the fact he was an outstanding, and successful, footballer didn't guarantee he'd be the same as a trainer. Right from the off he gave himself a good chance by selecting his assistants well, surrounding himself with the experienced and legendary figures of Ruud Krol and Neeskens.

After his resignation from the Holland job Rijkaard took over at Sparta Rotterdam. He signed the likes of Aaron Winter but things just didn't work out for the new manager and Sparta ended the season relegated. He was out of work after that until he was a surprise choice as manager of Barcelona. Now, with a decent CV but not too impressive, where was the logic in giving him the top job at the Nou Camp? From the outside looking in, he struggled in his early days in Spain but they stuck by him and gave him the time all managers need. And standing by him paid off big-time in May 2006 when he led them to glory in the Champions League final after a 2–1 victory against Arsenal in Paris. Victory with two former Old Firm players, van Bronckhorst and Henrik Larsson, in the team!

We were distraught to find out he'd been in tears after the Italian game at the Amsterdam ArenA. We went back to training camp afterwards, had something to eat and then headed straight to the bar for a few drinks and an in-depth chat about the match. The penalty misses, the drama, the resignation – it was a lot to take in in one day.

The worst feeling comes the day when the realisation's definitely there that the tournament is over and your team is not going to win it. You shake hands with your team-mates and then you get into the car and drive home. There was an emptiness inside me after that tournament. After I returned home it took me a while to adjust because I had been in a routine for a couple of weeks with the team. Now, I was back with Marjon and I suppose I couldn't have been easy to live with because the depression was there for a few days. We went on holiday more or less straight away and that is always the best thing to do. A change of scenery is the perfect antidote.

In 1998 I didn't pay much attention to the World Cup final between France and Brazil. It was different in 2000 and I was more of an interested spectator when France took on Italy because the tournament was on my doorstep. The French were triumphant and achieved an incredible double of being World and European Champions at the same time. Credit to them for that, it was a remarkable achievement.

I only played five more times for my country after that summer. Under Louis van Gaal we didn't qualify for the 2002 World Cup in South Korea and Japan and that was a massive blow to football in Holland. It was shocking.

Advocaat was in charge when I announced my retirement from international football in August 2002. I felt it was time to give others a chance and I wanted to give my all to Rangers. My body was getting older and it was taking me longer to recover from injuries. Rangers paid my wages and I had to be loyal to them. Advocaat wasn't happy with my decision to quit but he understood my reasons.

Apart from the odd penalty kick here and there, I wouldn't change a thing from my time proudly wearing the Oranje jersey! I had great times playing for my country and it was a genuine honour. I made many friends, played in some wonderful grounds and met some extraordinary people along the way. Playing in European Championships and World Cups are something else. The ultimate. Don't just take my word for it. Ask around and every player who has been lucky enough to be on that stage will tell you the same thing.

17

MY DREAM TEAM

When you've been lucky enough to play with as many talented footballers as I have then narrowing a list down to only eleven starters gives me a few headaches. I have decided to go for players I had a good knowledge of – on the field and in the dressing room. I take personality and ability into account and only guys I played with, at either club or national level. Yet, when I look down the list I've eventually chosen, I surprise myself that Marco van Basten, Ronald Koeman, Ruud Gullit and Frank Rijkaard are not in my team, because I only played a handful of games with these guys. Also, players like Dennis Bergkamp, Edgar Davids, Clarence Seedorf, Wim Jonk and Barry Ferguson are not in my team. I have tremendous respect for all of them but just couldn't fit them in.

I've been fortunate enough to play with so many top, top players that I could have selected three or four Dream Teams.

I've gone for a 4–4–2 formation and my team's coach is Dick Advocaat. I reckon my Dream Team would be a match for most.

My goalkeeper is **EDWIN VAN DER SAR**. It is a tough choice to select my No. 1. I've been fortunate enough to have played with some great goalkeepers such as Hans van Breukelen and Ronald Waterreus. But Edwin gets my vote for a number of reasons. He came through the national under-age teams with me and impressed me right from an early age. He was a commanding keeper and always coached his defenders through the ninety minutes. There was no way you would switch off with Edwin behind you because he never stopped shouting, handing out instructions and offering encouragement. A perfectionist and, if you didn't do your job, he would give you verbal abuse.

He was also good with both feet and loved joining in with the outfield players at training. Edwin is not your typical, daft goalkeeper. He is more calm, more measured than most of his opposite numbers. In club football, he won the European Cup with Ajax and then moved on to Juventus. It didn't go too well for him in Turin and they brought in Gigi Buffon. Edwin was transferred to Fulham and enjoyed a fine spell with the London club. Manchester United bought him in the summer of 2005 and I thought they were six years too late, as he was the perfect replacement for Peter Schmeichel when he retired from the game after United won the Champions League in 1999.

Edwin is a brave keeper, with good hands and good feet. He is now Holland's most capped player and deserves that honour.

BERRY VAN AARLE is my selection for the right-back position. Choosing a player for this position has probably been my most difficult call.

Michael Reiziger and Sergio Porrini were also in my thoughts but I've gone for van Aarle. I only played with him for a year at PSV but that was more than enough time to see why Marco van Basten reckoned Holland wouldn't have won the European Championships in 1988 had it not been for van Aarle.

In all top teams you have players categorised as the 'beer drinkers' and the 'champagne drinkers' – van Aarle is a beer drinker. He was like a terrier in his area of the field, never afraid to do the dirty work for the good of the side. He was aggressive, a total defender who just set out to make sure his opponent didn't get near the danger area.

He had a great career in the game and played a major part in the Euro 88 triumph and in PSV Eindhoven's European Cup success in the same year.

On the right side of central defence I couldn't ignore **JAAP STAM**. He signed for PSV from Willem II in 1995. He looks like a butcher but is a quiet, family man. Still, I wouldn't fancy my chances against him if I met him down a dark alley at 11 p.m.! Dick Advocaat signed him for PSV and quickly turned him into one of Europe's best central defenders. Jaap is strong and quick – for the full ninety minutes his opponent knows he is in a game. He has the same winning attitude in every training session.

He developed very quickly at PSV and smoothed out a couple of rough edges he had in his game. Strikers rarely got a sniff of goal when Jaap was around. His reputation quickly grew around Europe and many top teams wanted to sign him from PSV. Not long after the start of the 1997–98 season his future was the subject of constant speculation and PSV knew it was inevitable they were going to lose him.

Chelsea were managed by Ruud Gullit at that time and he wanted to take Jaap to Stamford Bridge. During my negotiations with Atletico Madrid they even asked me to tap him up for them. But they were all wasting their time. Manchester United were in pole position and he moved to Old Trafford for £12 million. He had a bad start under Sir Alex Ferguson and the English media questioned the amount of money United paid to get him. I think Alan Hansen was particularly critical of him.

But Jaap is a strong character and knew he would eliminate his mistakes and go on to become a top player for United. He did just that and helped them win the Champions League in 1999. Not long after that he was sold to Lazio and I think Sir Alex made a major mistake selling Jaap. I played with him many times for PSV and Holland and he is a wonderful defender. He knew his limitations, knew that when he got the ball he had to give it to a team-mate capable of creating something. Every team needs a Stam but not all are lucky enough to have one.

Partnering Jaap, on the left, there's really only one choice and it has to be **FRANK DE BOER**. I've known Frank since the age of seventeen. He was from the Amsterdam district and I was from the Haarlem district and we played against each other. We were also in the Holland under-17 team together and the Olympic team in our early days as young footballers.

Frank started off as a left-back. He was not the quickest, but good at one-on-one situations. He was great at reading a game. What he lacked in speed he made up for with his brain.

He was good in the air and always wanted the ball; he never hid. He always tried to create when he was in possession and could hit sixty-yard passes for fun. One swing of his left foot and the ball was zipping away in the opposite direction to set up an attack. He is a player who always looked for a solution with the ball and never resorted to just lumping it up the pitch. He hated losing possession and put himself under pressure trying to achieve this, but most of the time he came out on top and found his man with a pass.

On the pitch he was an out-and-out winner, a fierce competitor. He hated losing – even if it was to a five-year-old kid. He has passion and emotion on the pitch and will always tell you the truth to your face. Off the pitch, he is very quiet, relaxed and well mannered.

He was sometimes criticised for losing concentration, resulting in the opposition getting a chance, but he is one of the best in my opinion and would be the captain, playing on the left of the central defence.

Now, left-backs are quite hard to find. It seems to be a problem position for many clubs whether they're potential Champions League winners or fighting relegation in the second division. So I've gone for myself in that role. Yes, **ARTHUR NUMAN**. It's my dream team and I'm there because I'd love to play alongside these boys.

I started off as a left-winger but was moved to left-back. It's been beneficial to the guy in front of me that I used to play in his position. During my career for club and country I was lucky enough to have good players in front of me such as Marc Overmars, Bolo Zenden, Neil McCann and Peter Lovenkrands. They always said I gave them good service and that was nice to hear.

I was a better attacker than defender but always tried to give my opponent a hard game. I made it my business to ensure he was able to smell my breath from the first whistle, try to make him nervous.

Didier Agathe was a tough opponent when he was with Celtic. I called him 'The Roadrunner'. I knew I had to get close to him all the time because if he had a one-on-one opportunity to run at me then his pace made sure he would always win. Over the period, I coped quite well with Agathe. It was always my aim to come off the pitch knowing my opponent had a quiet game.

Other left-backs I admire and who are really world-class are Roberto Carlos and Paolo Maldini. The way Carlos gets up and down the pitch, you'd think he had two oxygen tanks strapped to his back – he has so much energy. Carlos is never injured and must have been a dream for a coach to have. Maldini was more calm, more of an organiser. He passed the ball well and has the respect of every footballer, which says it all.

I'd play four in midfield in a diamond shape. The sitting mid-fielder is **PHILLIP COCU**. Jan Wouters was in my thoughts because he is great in that role. One of the former directors at PSV described Jan as the 'cement between the bricks' and that is an accurate description.

Wim Jonk is another who could play that role. Wim was my room-mate for three years at PSV, after having a successful time at Ajax, and then came to Eindhoven after a difficult period at Inter. Wim went to Milan with Bergkamp and the Italians wanted them to re-create the magnificent partnership they had when they played at Ajax. Wim's main strength was his ability to make the killer-pass, the ball that would set up the chance for the striker.

Barry Ferguson also came into my thoughts. Barry is an excellent footballer and it was a pleasure to see him develop from a young man into a mature person and dedicated captain of Rangers.

But I went for Cocu because he is more of an all-round play-er, good at protecting the defence and also creating attacks and scoring goals. He has a lovely left foot and has played in left midfield and on the left wing. We first played together in the Holland under-21 team and he always impressed me. It was during his first spell at PSV that he really developed as a foot-baller. He was playing in the middle of the park and made things look easy.

It was no surprise Barcelona came in for him and he left in 1998 to go to the Nou Camp. He is now back at PSV and I was surprised he chose to return to the Philips Stadium. I'm positive Philip will go on to become a manager because he loves the game and is a deep thinker, a man who will be able to get his ideas across to a squad of players in an intelligent way.

GERALD VANENBURG is not one of the most well-known Dutch players in the eyes of the Scottish people but he is one of the most talented and underestimated players to come out of my country. He gets the nod to play on the right-hand side of midfield.

He should have been a big name in world football. Yet it was Johan Cruijff who played a part in why he never got more recognition.

Vanenburg came out with two videos during his career, on ball skills and tricks, and both sold well. He was small and tricky and made good impressions at Ajax and PSV and

217

with the Dutch national team. PSV adored him and even offered him a contract for life. But during an interview, Cruijff remarked that Vanenburg would never be a leader of men because he had a high-pitched voice. That stigma stuck with Gerald because most people hang on every word Cruijff says.

What difference does a high-pitched voice make? The only thing that matters is his football ability and Gerald was a fantastic player on the right-hand side of the pitch. He scored and set up goals. He always excited me and he was wonderful with PSV. Whether it was in training or in a game, Gerald would always produce something extraordinary.

Most of the big clubs around Europe tried to sign him but he never took them up. Italian clubs queued up to get him but he refused to go. I think he should have gone to Serie A but I'm glad he stuck around at PSV to give me the chance to play alongside him.

MARC OVERMARS gets the nod to play on the left-hand side of my midfield. There's plenty to say about Marc. A great player on the pitch and a mischievous character off it, it's appropriate that he's nicknamed 'The Devil'.

We were both young players when we first played together. I was delighted to see Marc's progress in the game. He was small and quick. He could cross the ball with both feet and was comfortable on either wing. However, just don't ask him to do any tricks with the ball – that was not his forte.

We had a great understanding when we played together for the national team. We just clicked and had an almost telepathic understanding. Whether the ball from me to him was a short pass or over the top, we knew exactly what the other was going to do.

His pace was his great weapon and he also scored goals by cutting inside defenders to give him an angle. During his time at Ajax and Arsenal he was unbelievable. His old boss at Ajax

Louis van Gaal paid 80 million guilders – about £25 million – to take him from the Gunners to Barca. I think the fee was paid over five years, at a time when the transfer market was totally outrageous. Marc had a good spell in Spain but it could have been better for him at the Nou Camp because he had a run of bad injuries and that hampered his progress.

I had a lot of time for him when we played together and I still do. We have always had a good relationship and I find him a funny guy. He could make me laugh very easily. And he used to do it in team meetings with the Dutch side. I used to go into these team meetings with my armpits and palms sweating with nerves, worried I might start to laugh and get caught by the manager. Wim Jonk and Jaap Stam were also involved and we all tried to make each other burst out laughing.

Pierre van Hooijdonk used to cough deliberately because he knew it would set me off. Overmars would be poking me in the back from the seat behind and it was hard for me not to laugh. I had to bend down and pretend to be tying my shoelaces. Thankfully, I was never caught out by the manager and it was always a relief when I got out of the room unscathed. If the public knew how some of us were behaving during preparation for important games they would probably have thought we were totally unprofessional!

In the midfield attacking role I've gone for **RONALD DE BOER**. Like his twin, Frank, I've known Ronald since we played against each other at district football. Back then, Ronald was a striker so he received more headlines than his brother.

However, he struggled to get into the Ajax first team and was still on the bench at twenty-one. Of course, there was no shame in that because Bergkamp and Steffen Petterson were ahead of him. So he moved to Twente Enschede to get a game. It was great to have him there alongside me, although he sometimes had to be encouraged to track back and I'd often find myself yelling at him to get back into position. The only downside to playing for Enschede was that Ronald still lived in Amsterdam and used to commute to the ground. Sometimes he would call me at midnight and ask if he could stay at my place instead of a hotel.

Twente was the perfect platform for Ronald to express his talent for two years and he was excellent for them. It was inevitable that Ajax came back to get him and he moved back to Amsterdam and helped them win the Champions League in 1995.

Ronald was great with the ball at his feet and his back to goal. He would turn his marker inside out, as the Rangers fans were lucky enough to see many, many times during his time at Ibrox. Michael Mols was also brilliant at doing that. Ronald had the ability to see a pass early and deliver it precisely. He was strong on the ball and loved to take on defenders. Overall, he was good at scoring and creating.

Again, like Frank, he is a total winner. Whether it's cards or dominoes, losing is not in his vocabulary. Occasionally, though, I'd find his winning mentality too much to cope with. At Rangers, Mols, Fernando Ricksen and Bert Konterman and I liked to play cards. But sometimes we would sneak away from Ronald at the hotel the night before a game and not tell him we were playing. The next thing, he would turn up at the relaxation area shouting and bawling at us for not inviting him to play. We just wanted a quiet, friendly game of cards but that was impossible when Ronald was around. To get his revenge for not being invited, he would walk around the table, look at our hand of cards, and say, 'You can't be happy with that' or, 'You should not have changed that card.' He was unbearable.

He was opinionated, too. He always spoke his mind and told players exactly what he thought of them. But he was only trying to be fair, constructive and honest – better than speaking behind their backs.

Even if Ronald had a bad game he would still rip into his team-mates. Some of the Rangers players were offended by his comments, but they shouldn't have been. He was only trying to help and encourage them.

Strikers are the ones that generally win games and I had so many to choose from. My first selection is **ROMÁRIO**. He was a brilliant player but the little Brazilian was also influential in PSV wanting to sign me.

I remember one of my first conversations with Romário just after I'd signed. With his trademark lisp, he told me, 'Listen, kid, we play 4–4–2 and you are the left-winger. When you get the ball, give it to me and I will score goals that will earn you money in bonuses. It's as simple as that.'

I was pissing myself laughing. No player had ever been as blunt and as confident as that with me. He was true to his word though and he did score vital goals for us.

He was small, had a strong upper body, low centre of gravity and was tremendously quick. He was also clever on the pitch – a great reader of the game – and could anticipate moves. You might not see him for twenty-five minutes in a game and then . . . bang, he'd score a goal! Romário was quite a loner and wasn't the most popular figure in the dressing room with some of his team-mates.

When I arrived in 1992 there were cliques in the PSV dressing room. Some players openly criticised Romário because they felt he didn't do his defensive duties. Yes, sometimes his attitude could have been better and I remember on a few occasions he would come in for training and just say, 'Romário is feeling tired today.' He'd be out on the training pitch but not contributing much. But it's not as though he turned up suffering with a hangover – I never once witnessed him drinking alcohol.

When he was in the mood, he was brilliant in training. A lot of our sessions were open to the public and the fans used to come just to see him. He often made a fool out of me with the ball at his feet and that was something you just had to accept. He was a world-class striker and it was my pleasure to play in the same team as him.

Partnering Romário would be his fellow Brazilian, **RONAL-DO**. He came to PSV in 1994 as a talented, but extremely nervous, seventeen-year-old from Brazil. PSV had a fine scouting network in South America and had been tipped off about this prodigious teenager. A lot of other top European teams were after Ronaldo, so it was quite a coup to get him to move to Holland. The world-famous company Philips were heavily involved with PSV and they played a part in tying up the deal.

The players were aware we had signed this boy and the talk in the dressing room was that if PSV had paid £3 million to get him then he must be some player – hopefully, similar to Romário.

So Ronaldo made his way from the Copacabana to Eindhoven and the first impression he made on all of us was his two front teeth. Wow, I'll never forget that smile of his.

On the training pitch he made an immediate impact and we knew this boy was going to be a sensation. He had a great first touch, was very quick and had excellent vision. Thinking about it now, he was back then what Wayne Rooney was a couple of years ago.

Of course, he took a little time to settle, both on and off the park. It was good for him that a few of the boys spoke Portuguese and could converse. A lot of the fans expected from him exactly what Romário had given us in previous years. That was a bit unfair on a teenage striker as Romário was much more experienced. To be fair to Ronaldo, he coped with it well.

At first he wasn't a superstar, he was a normal boy, friendly and he enjoyed a laugh. Eindhoven was a nice environment for him to be a part of. He lived just around the corner from me in an apartment he shared with his mother and girlfriend. The longer he was with PSV, the more he impressed me as a person and as a striker.

I remember he scored a hat-trick in a UEFA Cup tie in Germany against Bayer Leverkusen. One of his goals was a classic. He picked the ball up near the touchline, rolled it over one foot and then dribbled past three players, to make total fools of them. He then placed the ball past the goalkeeper with consummate ease. It was an incredible goal.

Ronaldo also had his faults, however. He could be lazy on the pitch and was not interested in doing any defensive duties. I and many of the players had a go at him, asked him to work harder, close down the opposition and track back more, but he rarely took any notice. But we knew his quality was scoring goals at the other end of the park.

I've followed his career closely and he was always going to become a world superstar. When he moved to Barcelona he used to come back to Eindhoven now and again for some privacy. He still had friends there and enjoyed just getting away from the Spanish spotlight. The last time I saw him was at the World Cup in 1998 – the toothy smile was still there and so was the incredible ability.

I was delighted for him when he broke Gerd Muller's record of top scorer at the World Cup finals. Truly, a world-class striker and he would have formed a prolific partnership with Romário.

I've been fortunate enough to work under Guus Hiddink, Louis van Gaal and Frank Rijkaard but I don't think it's a surprise I've gone for **DICK ADVOCAAT** as the coach of my dream team. I've known Dick since I was seventeen. He was in charge of the Holland under-18 squad when I was selected and he gave me my professional debut at club level for FC Haarlem.

I came on as a sub in my first game and played for twenty minutes. I didn't think I played too well and thought I'd blown my chance. But Dick stuck by me and gave me more chances, gradually introducing me to games, giving me more time on the pitch with each passing week. He always spoke to me before I went on and after the game finished. He would try to be positive to the young players, short and to the point.

Dick is professional and his knowledge of the game is immense. He's a deep thinker and everything he does is for a reason. He opened my eyes to the game of football. He was organised from top to bottom, his attention to detail was spot-on. He made sure he knew as much as possible about the opposition and would brief his own players on the individual battles they faced in the game. Strengths and weaknesses of the opponent, he had it all tucked away to pass on.

His tactics were good too, his preparation was meticulous and he had a strict code of discipline the players had to follow.

At Haarlem he liked to join in the training, especially the boxes where it was four against four. He was like a tiger, aggressive and fanatical. At PSV and Rangers he didn't join in as his fitness had gone by then! He preferred to stand on the sideline with his whistle and stopwatch and oversee the training.

I didn't really know a lot about Dick when he was a player. He wasn't a famous footballer in the Netherlands although he played in Holland and in America. In any photographs I've seen of him in his playing days, he always had his sleeves rolled up and his socks round his ankles. I think he was the Edgar Davids of the 1970s! Dick made his name from being a coach, working his way up from being the assistant to Rinus Michels at the national team to being a success as his own man.

It's no surprise he's had success throughout his career because he works so hard. From early morning until late at night, Dick is engrossed in football, trying to improve his players and do better for his employers. He is a top coach and I owe a lot to him from our days together at FC Haarlem, PSV Eindhoven, Glasgow Rangers and the Dutch national team.

We've had our ups and downs, good memories and bad. I'm not sure if I will ever become a first-team head coach, but if I decided to go down that road one day then the influence of Dick would be there in some ways. It would be foolish to ignore what I'd learned from him throughout my career.

18

. . . ALWAYS A RANGER

I'm often asked why I continued to stay in Scotland after I gave the game up in the summer of 2003. The answer is simple – my family and I love our life in Scotland and we're really settled and happy. Marjon, my two daughters and I enjoy living in Hamilton and love the warm and friendly welcome given to us by the Scottish people.

Holland and Scotland have many similarities and the culture of both countries isn't too different. They're both small countries, the climate's similar and the people are easy-going and hospitable. We've made friends in our eight years in Scotland and it would be a wrench for us to leave them behind. We may return to live in Holland within the next couple of years and will make that decision before Britt is due to start primary school in the summer of 2008. We don't want her to start her education somewhere and then uproot her to another country and a different schooling system.

We're in no hurry to leave Scotland, although a lot may depend on what happens with me if I become involved in football again. The biggest part of my life is ahead of me and I'm very open-minded about what happens in the future. I'd never say never about anything, but, to be honest, it wouldn't bother me if I was never involved in football again. I'd only take a job back in the game if it was right for me and after I discussed it with Marjon.

I'd never go back into football just for the sake of it. Since I retired three years ago, I've been offered a few jobs and rejected them all for different reasons. I was asked to go to Abu Dhabi, not long after I hung up my boots, to be director of football for one of the local teams. I asked for two or three days to think the offer over but we decided pretty quickly it just wasn't for us. Marjon wasn't in favour of it and neither was I. Britt was still a baby and moving to the Middle East just didn't feel right. We enjoy a normal social life, going out for dinner and drinks, and living in the desert would have made that difficult.

In the early part of 2006, PSV contacted me to ask if I'd be interested in becoming their head of youth – a post that involved overseeing their whole set-up from kids aged eight to eighteen. It would have been a seven-day-a-week commitment, making sure the coaching programme was being followed and taking in games to check on the progress of the youths.

Three people were on the shortlist for the job but I was probably the number-one candidate in the eyes of PSV. I was to replace a fine man, Joop Brand, who was retiring from the job. After thinking long and hard about it, I turned the offer down. I enjoy my freedom and like being my own man just now. However, it was nice to be remembered by my former club for such an important role. The former Vitesse Arnhem player and coach, Edward Sturing, was eventually appointed as Brand's replacement.

On a few occasions I've met David Murray since I retired and he's asked me to get involved with the youths at Rangers. But I've always resisted the temptation to accept his kind offers.

I was also tentatively asked if I'd be interested in becoming a football agent but, again, I politely declined the offer.

I don't really miss football, but what I do miss is the buzz of the big games like the Old Firm clashes and European nights. I always felt I played my best stuff in those high-pressured games and the more pumped up I was the better I played. I also miss the buzz, the feeling you get when you win games.

I may not miss playing, but one aspect of the game I do hanker for is the camaraderie of the dressing room. There's always great fun at the training ground and being divorced from that was difficult to come to terms with at first.

I used to pop in to Murray Park every now and again for a coffee and a chat with some of the players and the medical staff, to keep up to date with the gossip. I was always made to feel welcome, from the kitchen ladies and the chef through to the gaffer, Alex McLeish. But nowadays I'm reluctant to go back because it is a new regime and few players remain from my time as a Rangers player. I wouldn't interfere in Paul Le Guen's day-to-day running of the club, as my time is over now and I've taken a step back.

I can look back on some wonderful memories from my sixteen years in professional football and feel privileged to have been given such a fine life from it all. The game has made me and my family financially secure for the rest of our lives, but, make no mistake, I've had to work hard for those rewards. I sacrificed a lot in my early career to give myself a platform to reach the top. I wanted to do what was right for my career in my early decisions and knew the money would follow after that. I've also had the experience of playing for some fantastic clubs and winning prizes when I played for them. Nothing can take away those unforgettable memories.

Football also afforded me the chance to meet some world-famous dignitaries and celebrities. With Holland we went over to play South Africa in a friendly and were fortunate to meet Nelson Mandela. I was honoured to meet such a man, an inspiration to millions of people because he stood up for his beliefs and was ultimately sent to prison for daring to voice an opinion. All of the Dutch squad were excited to meet such a high-profile statesman and we all insisted on having our picture taken with him.

When the Dutch squad was based in Monaco for the 1998 World Cup finals, Prince Albert came to visit us and told us how honoured he was that we'd chosen his residence for our training and match preparation.

David Murray liked to surprise the Rangers players now and again, and none more so than on a cold, wet and windy night in Perth when we travelled to face St Johnstone. We were getting ready for the game and there was a knock on the dressing room door. Murray popped his head round and said he had brought someone special to meet us. The next thing Sean Connery appeared and walked into the dressing room.

Honestly, all of a sudden, the whole place went quiet and I could hardly move my jaws and most of the other boys were the same. It really was 007, James Bond. Wow. He said to us, in that unmistakable voice of his, 'Hello, gentlemen. The besht of luck tonight.' He walked round the dressing room and shook hands with all of us and I was thrilled to meet such a famous actor. People put footballers up on a pedestal but this guy is a 100 per cent genuine star. We're ordinary people lucky enough to make a career out of an enjoyable pastime. He's James Bond, a movie legend and worldwide superstar, not to mention the sexiest man alive in the eyes of millions of women.

Even in that short period I met him, Connery struck me as having a presence about him – an air of authority, a real confidence. Murray also loved the moment he brought Connery in to meet us. The Rangers owner relished the buzz of the dressing room, he liked to feel the pressure his players felt in the final minutes leading up to kick-off. He would always be up for a bit of banter, good-natured fun and liked to take the mickey out of the players in a nice way.

It's things like that I'd never have tasted had I not been a footballer. So the game has been good to me. But I don't miss it. I'd had enough of football and that's part of the reason I decided to retire. I could have played on for a few more years and still made very good money, but it didn't seem like the right thing to do.

I've enjoyed the few years I've had off since I retired and been to watch games as a supporter. No pressure on me, just sitting in the stand with a burger and coke watching games such as Barcelona v Real Madrid, Lazio v Roma, Fenerbahce v Galatasaray and AC Milan v Barcelona in the Champions League. It's been fun.

I like being in a stadium for a game but can't bring myself to sit down and watch a live ninety minutes on the television. I get bored and prefer to watch a highlights package. I suppose I've really taken the blinkers off and realised there's much more to life than a ball and a pair of boots.

It's nice to have time to spend with the family and suit myself. During my stay in Scotland, we got plenty of visitors over to see us and they loved Glasgow. Before I moved there, most friends I knew would go to Rome, London or Barcelona for a city break, but they came over to see me and the family and they fell in love with Scotland. It's only a seventy-five-minute direct flight from Amsterdam to Glasgow.

The shops are top notch and the city is buzzing. Glasgow's restaurants are excellent and I always recommend O Sole Mio for Italian food as Tony looks after his diners. Toppolino's also has nice Italian food and Andy and Christina are superb hosts at the Amber Regent for Cantonese. And there's not many better Indian restaurants than Mr Singh's where Satty and Bobby make everyone feel welcome.

Glasgow also has a fantastic nightlife and my brother Jeroen was over here every second weekend for the home games when I played. He would fly in on a Friday night and go home on the Sunday. I reckon he became more famous in the city centre than I did! So, during my eight years here I reckon I'm due a decent commission from the Scottish Tourist Board for promoting the country so well!

Scotland is a beautiful country and we've enjoyed exploring the stunning scenery up and down the country. As an indication of my feelings for my adopted homeland I wore a kilt live on Dutch television during the 2006 World Cup in Germany when I appeared as a pundit. People often ask me why I still live in Scotland and don't move somewhere with a much better climate and all-year sunshine. Well, the simple answer is, I like it, although I was sceptical about moving here originally.

Now, I enjoy getting up in the morning to go about my business. Sometimes I might have media work to perform and other days I will go to the Esporta gym in Hamilton for a workout. I like to keep myself fit, even if it's only a thirty-minute run. It's important I kept fit after I retired as it wouldn't have been healthy just to stop completely after my body was used to full-time training for sixteen or seventeen years. It's better to wind it down gradually and I also wanted to make sure I didn't put on fifteen kilos of weight within six months of hanging up my boots. Exercising is good for the body AND the mind because if I had nothing to do I would go crazy.

One of my hobbies is collecting various memorabilia from the 1950s and '60s. I like the vibe of that era – the big flashy Cadillacs with the shiny chrome wheel trims, the movies and the way people seemed to enjoy themselves. I'm lucky enough to have two original jukeboxes – both Wurlitzers – packed with great original 45s and 78s. I love the music from that era and enjoy listening to classic artists like Buddy Holly, The Platters, Roy Orbison, Elvis Presley and Frank Sinatra.

As well as the music, I have an original, antique Coca-Cola vending unit and a pinball machine. Other mementoes I collect, from 1900 onwards, are original hand-made advertising signs for products like Coke, Pepsi and cigarettes. My Dutch colleague Marc Overmars got me into collecting these signs and he also has a huge affection for that period.

I also do some charity work in Scotland and have climbed Ben Nevis to raise money for St Andrew's Hospice, a very worthwhile cause. The charity work has really opened my eyes to that side of life and the work that goes on behind the scenes by so many dedicated volunteers who help make the lives of others less fortunate as comfortable as possible. I'm happy to do my bit, to help raise awareness of an illness or disease and to raise the profile of a charity. Performing charity work gives me a real sense of worth and hope that my tiny contribution can make a difference somewhere along the line.

No matter what we do in the future and the country we eventually choose to settle in, I will always come back to Scotland, that is for sure. And I'll always have a special place in my heart for Glasgow Rangers. On the day I left Rangers, John Greig said something to me I'll never forget. It was short, but poignant.

He said to me, 'Arthur, don't be a stranger – be a Glasgow Ranger.'

I always will be.

ARTHUR NUMAN: STATISTICS

Club Career

Began career with Dutch amateur club SV Beverwijk

1987–1990	FC Haarlem
1990–1992	FC Twente
1992–1998	PSV Eindhoven
1998–2003	Rangers FC

Season	Appearances	Goals
FC HAARLEM		
1987–88	7	2
1988–89	32	0
1989–90	32	2
1990–91	20	1
FC TWENTE		
1990–91	20	4
1991–92	29	3
PSV EINDHOVEN		
1992–93	24	0
1993–94	34	10
1994–95	32	6
1995–96	27	3
1996–97	31	5
1997–98	31	3

RANGERS FC

1998–99	19	0
1999–00	43	3
2000–01	33	0
2001–02	45	2
2002–03	35	1
TOTAL	*494*	*45*

International Career with Holland

Caps 45
Won 28
Drawn 10
Lost 7
Yellow cards 3
Red cards 1

Date	*Result*
14.10.92	Holland 2 – Poland 2
16.12.92	Turkey 1 – Holland 3
19.01.94	Tunisia 2 – Holland 2
27.05.94	Holland 3 – Scotland 1
04.07.94	Holland 2 – Republic of Ireland 0
16.11.94	Holland 0 – Czech Republic 0
14.12.94	Holland 5 – Luxembourg 0
18.01.95	Holland 0 – France 1
26.04.95	Czech Republic 3 – Holland 1
07.06.95	Belarus 1 – Holland 0
06.09.95	Holland 1 – Belarus 0
11.10.95	Malta 0 – Holland 4
15.11.95	Holland 3 – Norway 0
29.05.96	Holland 2 – China 0
31.08.96	Holland 2 – Brazil 2
09.11.96	Holland 7 – Wales 1
14.12.96	Belgium 0 – Holland 3

26.02.97	France 2 – Holland 1
29.03.97	Holland 4 – San Marino 0
02.04.97	Turkey 1 – Holland 0
30.04.97	San Marino 0 – Holland 6
04.06.97	South Africa 0 – Holland 2
06.09.97	Holland 3 – Belgium 1
11.10.97	Holland 0 – Turkey 0
21.02.98	USA 0 – Holland 2
24.02.98	Mexico 2 – Holland 3
27.05.98	Holland 0 – Cameroon 0
01.06.98	Holland 5 – Paraguay 1
05.06.98	Holland 5 – Nigeria 1
13.06.98	Holland 0 – Belgium 0
20.06.98	Holland 5 – South Korea 0
25.06.98	Holland 2 – Mexico 2
29.06.98	Holland 2 – Yugoslavia 1
04.07.98	Holland 2 – Argentina 1
11.07.98	Holland 1 – Croatia 2
23.02.00	Holland 2 – Germany 1
29.03.00	Belgium 2 – Holland 2
26.04.00	Holland 0 – Scotland 0
21.06.00	Holland 3 – France 2
25.06.00	Holland 6 – Yugoslavia 1
01.09.01	Republic of Ireland 1 – Holland 0
05.09.01	Holland 5 – Estonia 0
06.10.01	Holland 4 – Andorra 0
27.03.02	Holland 1 – Spain 0
19.05.02	USA 0 – Holland 2